BACK TO REALITY!
LEEDS UNITED 2017-18

BACK TO REALITY!
LEEDS UNITED 2017-18

HEIDI HAIGH

HEIDI'S DEDICATION

This book is dedicated to the best team in the world who were responsible for making me the Leeds United supporter I am today.

Sprake, Reaney, Cooper, Bremner, Charlton, Hunter, Lorimer, Clarke, Jones, Giles, Gray and sub Madeley are the team I thought were Leeds United at their best, and I was privileged to have seen them play in person. Billy Bremner instilled in me the love and loyalty of supporting my team which I have done continuously for over 50 years. I will be forever grateful to Don Revie for giving me the best years of my life following my team! Seeing my Bremner Stone by Billy's statue will be a proud moment.

First Published in Great Britain in 2018 by DB Publishing,
an imprint of JMD Media Ltd

ISBN 978-1-78091-578-4

Printed and bound in the UK

FOREWORD

INSPIRATIONAL LEEDS UNITED FAN - MARTIN HYWOOD

I am doing a foreword with a difference as I want to promote what Martin has been doing to raise funds for Muscular Dystrophy with #Musclesmatter. As Martin is a sufferer of the disease, one of the challenges he completed was climbing a mountain. That mountain turned out to be Mount Snowdon on 1st July 2017 when a total of 38 friends, family and Leeds fans including myself accepted the challenge and joined him. Personally, I was undecided for a long time as to whether I would be fit enough to climb the mountain and hesitated to make a decision. What made me choose to do this in the end was the fact that if Martin could do this, then so could I!

The actual climb was a real challenge for Martin, who managed to get to near the half-way point before he needed assistance, and with the teams help, one way or another, we got to the summit. A fantastic achievement! For me I did better than I dared hope, but within an hour of reaching the summit I was struck with severe cramp in both legs and struggled to walk for a long time. But I realised that my discomfort was only for a short time whereas Martin struggles on a daily basis so I had nothing to complain about. It was a fantastic feeling to know that we got to the top and the children who climbed with us were outstanding.

Martin Hywood - Snowdon 1st July 2017

As this book is written as a fan for the fans, I have met thousands of fans along the way and credit to Martin for always going that extra mile. I am proud to have you as a friend! Marching on Together!

Martin Hywood - at the top of Snowdon!

Top of Snowdon

Martin Hywood - Snowdon 1st July 2017 - success!

TABLE OF CONTENTS

Prologue   **8**
Comments from fans   **10**

Chapter 1 – July 2017   **13**
Guiseley, Oxford United

Chapter 2 – August 2017   **24**
Bolton, Port Vale, Preston, Fulham, Sunderland (didn't attend Newport and Nottingham Forest)

Chapter 3 – September 2017   **47**
Burton Albion, Birmingham, Millwall, Burnley, Ipswich, Cardiff

Chapter 4 – October 2017   **79**
Sheffield Wednesday, Reading, Bristol City, Leicester City, Sheffield United, Derby

Chapter 5 – November 2017   **107**
Brentford, Middlesbrough, Wolves, Barnsley

Chapter 6 – December 2017   **133**
Aston Villa, Queens Park Rangers , Norwich, Hull, Burton Albion, Birmingham

Chapter 7 – January 2018   **172**
Nottingham Forest, Newport, Ipswich, Millwall, Hull City

Chapter 8 – February 2018   **201**
Cardiff, Sheffield United, Bristol City, Derby, Brentford

Chapter 9 – March 2018   **228**
Middlesbrough, Wolves, Reading, Sheffield Wednesday, Bolton

Chapter 10 – April 2018   **255**
Fulham, Sunderland, Preston, Aston Villa, Barnsley, Norwich

Chapter 11 - May 2018   **300**
Queens Park Rangers , Fixtures, League Table

Chapter 12   **313**
Looking forward – what happens next?

PROLOGUE

As the season came to a disappointing end for our team and our wonderful support once again, this book is the review of the season seen through the eyes of me the author, Heidi Haigh, written by a fan for the fans. I am a home and away season ticket holder whose popular blog *Follow Me and Leeds United* is shared with Leeds United fans all around the world. With fans clamouring to be in my photos at the games, having many photos in this book ensures those fans who can't get to games feel as if they are there too. Despite what went wrong on the pitch, one good thing has been the fantastic support and loyalty that our worldwide fan base has shown. I believe our support is second to none and this book shows what happens on our travels, with the photos showing the camaraderie amongst our fans. More and more fans want to see themselves in my blog and as always they only have to ask for a photo and I'll oblige. Just watch for my camera and also me wearing my trademark beret.

This season started off with high hopes after Andrea Radrizzani completed his 100% takeover from Cellino. Although he hadn't run a football club before, I was hoping that he would have the right people advising him who had Leeds at heart just like I did. Angus Kinnear came from West Ham and was appointed CEO and Victor Orta became Director of Football, coming from Middlesbrough. A lot of fans didn't like this model as they thought that Orta had left Middlesbrough under a cloud due to fall outs. As usual I was all for giving people a chance and decided to wait and see what transpired on the pitch.

Despite the previous season faltering at the last hurdle, I was looking forward to some stability as I thought this was going to be the first season in a long time that we were heading in the right direction. Unfortunately, as is often the story with Leeds United, we lost our manager Monk, who left to manage Middlesbrough instead. Also, Taylor had gone to Burnley along with Wood and Bartley had returned to Swansea after his loan period had ended. This meant turmoil again before another new manager, Thomas Christiansen, was appointed. Many fans were troubled by the fact that Christiansen had managed a team from Cyprus and hadn't any experience of the Championship, but I was looking on the bright side.

As our season kicked off, the bright side was indeed looking bright. Some of the football we played was sublime and gave us the best start for a long, long time. Sadly, once we lost our unbeaten run at Millwall we never recovered. The tactics we had been using (i.e. playing out from the back) were changed as we threw the towel in, dropped Wiedwald and in my opinion ended up with no one really knowing what we were playing at!

After a terrible defeat away at Newport in the FA Cup, I was disgusted that once again this great tradition of games, plus the fans who travelled there, were shown no respect by our club and manager. Making so many changes to the team was always going to impact on the game and although we took the lead when Berardi scored his first goal for us, we lost the game. Winning breeds winning in my eyes, and the club would have reaped the benefits of a good run in the FA Cup in my opinion.

As the season continued, having only one win in 10 meant that once again we were without a manager when Christiansen was sacked. Although I was starting to worry about things, I was still on the fence. Without having a crystal ball so I could see into the future, I will never know for sure whether sacking him was the right decision. What I couldn't understand though was bringing in Heckingbottom from Barnsley who hadn't won one in 16; it didn't make sense to me. Despite him being another one who said he hated Leeds, he was given a chance by the majority of the fans despite the misgivings of appointing him in the first place. Sadly things never improved on the pitch, but the highlight was the youngsters coming through with Bailey Peacock-Farrell being given his chance in goal and young Tom Pearce and Paudie O'Connor getting their chances. I've long been a believer that we should build our team around the youngsters with some old heads in between, as we did with Billy Bremner and the rest of the squad. That's why it upset me greatly when we lost the spine of our youngsters with the transfers of Byram, Taylor, Cook and Mowatt. Whilst Cook is having a great season and now playing for England, I feel the group of them needed each other to prosper together on the pitch.

Enjoy the read with the best fans in the world on the road following their team. The loyalty shown is second to none!

Heidi Haigh – A fanatical Leeds United supporter of over 50 years

Author of the following books:

Follow Me and Leeds United

Once a Leeds fan, Always a Leeds fan

Co-author with Andrew Dalton of The Good, The Bad and The Ugly of Leeds United, Leeds United in the 1980s

The Sleeping Giant Awakens, Leeds United 2016-17

Back to Reality, Leeds United 2017-18

Website: www.followmeandleedsunited.co.uk

Twitter: Follow Me And LUFC

Facebook: Follow Me and Leeds United

COMMENTS FROM FANS

Phillip Bracha   Great read Heidi as usual thankyou from Cyprus I missed watching it as I took a friend to the airport Just my luck 🕶️.

Anne Booth   Always great to read with the right amount of bias x

Adam Clarke   MOT Heidi, another great read.

Tim Greene   Great stuff keep it up for the season; will be keeping an eye out for your blog MOT.

Dave Baggaley   Great to read as usual, cheers Heidi.

Bobby Joyce   Reaney and Bremner guarding the posts - that brings back memories - good start by the lads.

Eddie Perry   Spot on about guarding both posts; lots of goals conceded because of only guarding one post.

David Towns   Great read and a great start by the lads.

Richard Goldsmith   Great read. Seems like fans are treated worse now than the seventies. Decent pies, beer, toilets when you visit the Pirelli. Looking forward to your write up on that game. QPR 9/12/17.

Paul Williams   Another great report of a fan's view of the day thanks again QPR 9/12/17.

Linda Smith   I almost felt like I was there Heidi hope you have a lovely Christmas and you get to sing jingle bells at Burton love Linda. Hull City 23/12/17.

Ilsf Andy   Thank you Heidi love you always make me feel as if I'd gone to the game after reading your blog. Burton 26.12.17.

Mark Philip Makey   That was a superb read! Happy Christmas #Gibraltarwhite Burton 26.12.17.

Dave Williams   Really admire your spirit to keep providing these superb write ups despite our shambolic performances Heidi, keep up the great work #mot Hull City 30/1/18.

Julian Thomson   Fantastic read as always RIP Eric & Jimmy. I fear that for the football next season I will be following the team from your reports... can't justify the expense anymore, certainly after the recent performances absolutely no joy for me in saying that as I approach 50 this Year .. MoT.

Eugene Kelly   Thank you Heidi reading your reports every week makes me feel like I am sitting beside you at the game. You tell it as you see and hear it. I think it's time someone had a word with AR about unveiling a huge poster of YOU on one of the stadiums stands looking down on King Billy's statue Bristol City H 18.2.18.

Lynsey Elizabeth Great read as always Heidi. Love your write ups of the matches. Not been able to get to away matches this season so I love reading these and looking at the photos. Hopefully I can get back to away days next season. Derby 21/2/18.

Trevor Champ Lovely write up Heidi. Nearly made me feel that I'd been at the game. Derby 21/2/18.

James Mawson Wonderful, thanks so much for the time and effort you take to make these great reports.

Christine Culley Enjoyed reading it from sunny Spain. Good to see you live with Dean. Keep up the good work Heidi. MOT!

Peter Warrington Pity the Leeds team did not share the passion of the fans. Lovely blog.

Derek Mulligan Well done once again Heidi Haigh, I have to admire your dedication to our great club through good times (easy) and bad (not so easy), one more game and we can put this shocker of a season behind us.

Dave Luke Nice write up Heidi. This club deserves so much better than what we've seen from this squad of players since Boxing Day. I think it will take another two seasons to sort this mess out if it's done properly though there has got to be a massive change on the recruitment of quality players. The table doesn't lie.

John Mcphillips Good report as always, been a long season a few ups and many downs as the song MOT says.

Dave Baggaley Thanks Heidi, another great read as it has been all season, MOT.

Arnie Pirie Thanks for the seasons writing and reading it helps so much getting a first-hand report in the depths of Kazakhstan MOT ON N ON ex Meanwood Whites. I still have the white rose badge you and Carole made for us all in 1974.

Mandy Hall Thank you Heidi, I've really enjoyed reading your blogs all season. MOT.

Andrew Kaye Thanks Heidi for your blogs as I can't go to games at the moment due to health problems MOT.

Sniffer Clarke Thanks Heidi for your very enjoyable match summaries throughout the season. Look forward to more in 2018/19. MOT.

Jan Perry I really enjoy your blog and photos Heidi, it's like playing where's Wally. Have managed to spot myself and my hubby a couple of times and so has my big Leeds fan sister who lives in France. Hoping for better things next season and if you could just capture C19 about 9 rows behind the Leeds dugout you will make two pensioners very happy lol. MOT always.

Heidi's response to Karl; Your comments are greatly appreciated. Being told that I am able to converse with people from all walks of life from people at the top to your normal match going fans is a skill and this is one skill that I have got, it really brings a lump to my throat. Thanks Karl!

CHAPTER 1 - JULY 2017

GUISELEY (A) – 8th JULY 2017

For some fans the close season has been a long one, but for me personally it has flown by. So much seems to have happened in a little while which has impacted on our start. Radrizzani has now completed his full takeover of Leeds and because of this we now own Elland Road once again, something I couldn't be happier about. Owning our home again means so much to me and others and gives me hope for the future. With a managerial change having taken place due to Monk's resignation, we now have Thomas Christiansen in charge. I wasn't happy with the way Monk hung Charlie Taylor out to dry for the last game of the previous season; seemingly to divert attention away from the fact that we missed out on the play-offs. You don't tell someone who has continually played with an injury that once we were out of the promotion race he wouldn't be used so he could let his injury heal. To then be thrown under the bus, or the Leeds fans to be exact, is something I can't forgive him for, so to be honest I'm glad he's gone. The Sutton debacle plus throwing the towel in makes me feel he won't be missed. The one thing I will give him credit for is getting the fans and the team interacting again. That alone made things more enjoyable last season and is something that has been missing for a long time. This is a must for the future too.

I drove to Guiseley on a lovely warm day singing along to the radio and feeling upbeat for the new season. I'm trying not to be too positive just so I don't put a jinx on the team! Seriously though, my thoughts before we had a change of manager were, and still are, that we have to forget the play-offs and go for automatic promotion as nothing else will do. Whether that materialises or not for now is a long way away, but it gives us something to aim for. I felt the league last year was one where anyone could beat anyone on their day, and if you go out with the right mentality then you never know. I still think that winning breeds winning, but we will see.

As I reached the ground I met my friend Sue and Adam from the Fullerton Park Branch of the Leeds United Supporters' Club before I went to the cricket club. I met up with Mick, Alex and the South Kirkby LUSC. It was good to see lots of familiar faces again, always Leeds, always loyal is the motto from the Supporters' Club. Just before I headed into the ground I went to the ladies, where a woman immediately started telling me about the Leeds fans she'd travelled in with on the bus, who had been very noisy. She proceeded to tell me about them drinking in the pub down the road where they had also been standing on tables, although one unlucky lad had fallen off! A big thank you to Lynsey and her daughter Katie for buying my book *Follow Me and Leeds United,* and I'll look forward to feedback once they've read it on their holiday.

I hung my flag by the tunnel as there were no advertising hoardings there. There were only a few flags today: Fullerton Park had one and there was another one hung up next to theirs. The Swedish flag came out when Dallas scored after 17 seconds. Welcome back to season 2017-18.

The team today was made up of everyone in the squad and we played a different team in each half. They were Green, Ayling, Bellusci, Jansson, Denton, O'Kane, Phillips, Dallas, Roofe, Hernandez and Antonsson in the first half and Wiedwald, McKay, Diagouraga, Cooper, Berardi, Vieira, Bridcutt, Gomes, Sacko, Doukara and Erwin in the second. Shaughnessy came on for Cooper five minutes from the end. The game was a sell out so, with the capacity being 4,000, both the Leeds fans and Guiseley fans intermingled with no issues, which were good to see. A great turn out of Leeds fans for our first pre-season game. Leeds won 5-1, with Dallas (2), Antonsson and Irwin (2) scoring for Leeds.

I hadn't brought my glasses into the ground so couldn't see so well at the far end, but Dallas, in front of me, got off to a great start with two early goals, both from similar angles. To be fair they were cracking goals too! Before we knew it, we had conceded a goal, but we managed a further goal after good work from Hernandez in the penalty area, which gave Antonsson the chance to put the ball into the net. Jansson had his angry head on when he clashed with a Guiseley player and both had to be spoken to by the ref. To be honest, Jansson didn't look too happy as the team walked off the pitch at half time. The last two to depart from it were Bellusci and Silvestri. The former came in for some stick (but it was quite tame compared to some I've seen) and he reacted to it. My opinion is that he is a disruptive influence and bad egg in the dressing room. On the pitch I would say he cannot be trusted and I would much rather he left and started anew somewhere else. I realise I don't have a say in this so will have to see if he stays or goes. I also think there will be a parting of the ways of some of the other players today, especially as we have a glut of midfielders. With Charlie Taylor having departed and the team being light in some other areas, it will be interesting to see who is brought in next week.

As plans are still in place for us to record all the old Leeds songs, which I am looking forward to, at half time I was going to go into the club to meet my 'singing' team, but unfortunately due to health and safety reasons it was full to capacity so I couldn't. Talking about old songs, we won't be singing a certain song from the past about man u that some fans were singing on their way to the ground today. In the past is where it should stay, we are better than that!

As I started walking around the ground to the other side for the second half, I wondered if I would see the large dog that was in the stand last year. I certainly did, so I took its picture once again. I also bumped into a few more people I knew along the way so I had a chat with them before I found Sue and the others. I sat next to a Leeds fan I didn't know, but it turned out that I did know him after all. Then when Erwin scored another goal for Leeds I heard barking all of a sudden, and I realised that Nikki was there with her guide dog Rita - she always barks when Leeds score a goal! It was nice to see them both too.

One thing I noticed about the game that was different to last season was that we were trying harder. It wasn't just a pre-season knockabout as it had been in the past, but we were actually scoring goals too. Whether that is something that Christiansen has instilled in them or Guiseley weren't as good as last year I don't know, but it was a positive show from Leeds. Just before the end of the game I went to get my banner as it had fallen down at one end, and I stayed by the players' tunnel as we ended up scoring a fifth goal, another from Erwin! Whatever happens from now on, the fact we started off with a 5-1 was good to see.

I waited with the others for the team to come out, and whilst some came out of the tunnel more came out of the side entrance. As I got my photo taken with Christiansen, another fan standing next to me, Paul, said to him that there were legends on the pitch and legends off it and I was one of the legends off it so Christiansen should get to know me, which I thought was a lovely thing to say. Thanks Paul that was appreciated, and hopefully Christiansen will see my photos now.

The next game I will be able to attend is the Oxford home one, so I'll have to remember to get my tickets ordered. I want to bring my granddaughters to that one hopefully. I was supposed to be bringing them to Guiseley but didn't tell their mum, who had organised a birthday party for my eldest Hannah, oops! When I got to the ground I handed their tickets in at the turnstile, just in case anyone turned up without any as they were sold out. Sadly for me, I can't go to Austria for the pre-season tour, as much as I'd love to be there. I will be there in heart and soul, but with my youngest daughter Emily getting married on the 21st July, at least I have something to look forward to here.

As I renewed my season ticket without completing the form, I forgot about the home auto cup scheme so I need to sort that. It makes it so much easier not having to worry about organising any tickets and having them come automatically. Bolton away is our first league game in the Championship, so we will get a big allocation for this one and I am looking forward to the new season. See you soon – LUFC – Marching on Together!

OXFORD UNITED (H) – 29th JULY 2017

It was good to be going back to Elland Road today, even though it was just a friendly against Oxford and not the start of the Championship games. The close season has flown by for me because of so many things going on: I saw my youngest daughter Emily get married last week on a perfect day from start to finish, and I couldn't have been prouder. My three granddaughters came with me to the game today as planned, but when I ordered the tickets online I didn't choose them myself, so we were near to the front in N2. Because Leeds had decided to make the kids under 16 tickets free as long as they were with a fee-paying adult, it meant that I had to pick up vouchers for ours. It was a great gesture but it did put pressure on staff today.

I'd not taken the time it would take for queuing into consideration, so we didn't arrive at Elland Road until 1.30pm. I had a quick chat with my friend Sue as we met at the traffic lights heading to the club shop. The queue was already as far back as Billy's statue. I left the kids in the queue with a woman watching them as I ran to the West Stand ticket office to hand some forms in, and the lady behind the counter quickly sorted them out, but when I got back to the shop the kids had only moved a short way so this wasn't going to be a quick get it done thing, so I debated

whether to come again after the game. A steward had told me that although we had to collect the vouchers from the club shop it didn't need to be today, but I decided to stay and we eventually got out at around 2.30pm but headed to the Peacock for a quick stop. I'd just missed Sue so we only stayed there for 10 minutes before heading in. One plus from the wait in the queue was a thank you from a lad whom I'd given permission to use some of my photos. I've no issue with anyone using my photos as long as they give me credit for them.

When we found our seats, I thought the view wasn't too bad, but I moved further over to the corner after the game kicked off as there was no way I could hold on to three kids at the same time if they had to stand on their seats. It worked out fine though and there were quite a few familiar faces around me to help.

The team were: Felix Wiedwald, Luke Ayling, Matthew Pennington (loanee from Everton), Liam Cooper, Gaetano Berardi, Eunan O'Kane, Kalvin Phillips, Pablo Hernandez, Kemar Roofe, Ezgjan Alioski and Chris Wood. Subs were: Stuart Dallas (for Alioski 63), Samuel Saiz (for Hernandez 63), Hadi Sacko (for Roofe 63), Vurnon Anita (for Ayling 78), Liam Bridcutt (for Phillips 78), Mateusz Klich (for O'Kane 78) and Caleb Ekuban (for Wood 78). Subs not used were: Robert Green, Bailey Peacock-Farrell, Tyler Denton, Madger Gomes, Pontus Jansson, Marcus Antonsson, and Souleymane Doukara. Attendance was 13,295 including 314 Oxford fans. Today also saw the return of Pep Clotet, who was now manager at Oxford. This was also the first game at Elland Road with Christiansen as manager (sorry I'm a traditionalist and don't like to refer to him as a coach). Leeds won the game 2-0, with goals from Roofe (36) and Dallas (83).

It's going to take me a while to remember who's who and I'll look forward to seeing the squad numbers so I can work out who is playing where. As it was, in the first half only Wiedwald, Pennington and Alioski were new faces, so it wasn't too bad to work them out. It was quite challenging to focus on the football and watch the three girls, with the youngest being only three years old. It reminded me of the times in my younger days that I used to bring my nephew Mark and niece Sonya. In those days of standing in the Kop, they used to stand in the Police Boxes that ran along the back. It seems such a long time ago now.

We attacked the empty South Stand in the first half (the only stands open were the Kop and the East Stand for this game). Despite a bad back pass in the first few minutes, Leeds had most of the game but Oxford did do some attacking. A couple of corners on the trot saw Wiedwald launch himself into mid-air to punch the ball away. Although we played the ball out of defence comfortably, at times it seemed a little too close for comfort, with Oxford players very close to the play. Alioski was playing on the right-hand side for a while but swapped with Roofe, who ended up scoring before half time with a well taken goal. He side stepped Oxford players in the penalty area before hitting a low shot in to the right of the goalie (looking from the Kop).

(At half time the kids enjoyed going down to the front of the Kop and it was nice to be introduced to Steve, who enjoys reading my blogs. Thank you for the feedback it is appreciated.)

The second half saw Leeds attack towards the Kop, and Berardi nearly got himself on the score sheet with a long range shot that their goalie managed to hang on to and prevent a goal. This wasn't the first time I'd seen our players taking a long range shot at goal and this is something that has been missing many times, when we have tried to walk the ball into the net instead. The first subs were made and Leeds started to attack more, with Sacko seeing plenty of the ball and running down the wing in front of the East Stand. Dallas continued where he left off at Guiseley with another spectacular goal from a similar angle to the two he scored there. Long may these continue please! As Leeds ran out 2-0 winners on the day, it had been nice to get back to watching the football. My granddaughters were upset that Pontus didn't play but as he is banned for the first two games of the season I imagine that is the reason why. Christiansen should now have an idea of who the team will be for the first game of the season at Bolton. Alioski looked lively and seemed very fast, and Saiz looks as if he can put himself about too. Hopefully when I sit back in my season ticket place for future games I will see more of who plays where.

At the end of the game I nearly didn't recognise big John, who travelled with the Kippax years ago, and it was nice to have a chat, although I lost the two elder granddaughters who carried on to Billy's statue, oops! I had to run after the little one as she carried on too! My fault for chatting too much as usual lol!

Next week sees the season start for real. After all the issues many of our fans had in getting tickets for this game because there is no loyalty system, I'm glad that I don't have to worry. The reason I got an away season ticket in the first place was because I couldn't get a ticket for Rotherham the other year. Also, being able to log on to a computer when tickets go on sale is getting harder and harder, so I sympathise with those who haven't missed a game for years and didn't get one. I think there should have been a small allocation for loyalty, before the rest were put on open sale. Having heard today that many fans missed the first 40 minutes of the game because of queues trying to get tickets refunded, it shows to me that there are improvements to be made for the future. I would certainly love to meet Radrizzani to have a chat about things in general. It will be interesting to see how the meetings with the fan groups go and I look forward to seeing the outcomes in due course.

For those going to Bolton, I look forward to seeing you there and singing 'United are back' once again! – LUFC – Marching on Together!

CHAPTER 2 - AUGUST 2017

BOLTON WANDERERS (A) – 6th AUGUST 2017

Today the football was back for Leeds United, kicking off at 4.30pm due to Sky. I was very upbeat even though we have had a takeover complete, Elland Road bought back, a manager change and new players coming into the squad, as well as some outgoings. What I see at the moment is hope. Hope that we are on the right track for automatic promotion this year as I'm still convinced we should forget about the play-offs. If we do end up in them, then so be it, time will tell of course but either way I'm hopeful for a good start today. It won't be easy as Bolton have just been promoted into the division and despite all their financial issues I'm sure they will put up a fight on the pitch.

I was travelling with the Fullerton Park branch of the Leeds United Supporters' Club as usual and our pub stop today was in Bury, where we have stopped many times over the years. It was great to see so many familiar faces and there were plenty of hugs around. (I want to give a shout out and well done to my friend Marie who has just been given a Yorkshire Hero award along with others for their food kitchen.) It was also great to see our overseas support here again, with fans from Norway, Denmark, Ireland and also long-distance ones from the south coast and Swansea. A big thank you to those fans who took the time to tell me that they are looking forward to seeing my blog tonight it is greatly appreciated. Sky know what they are doing when they target Leeds for televised games, as they know with our worldwide fan base that their viewing figures will be huge. Leeds sold out the whole 4,832 allocation of tickets in 15 minutes, and they could have sold many more despite it being shown live on TV.

Due to heavy traffic we didn't get to the ground until 20 minutes before kick-off, but on the plus side the coach parked outside the turnstiles, so despite the rain we got in to the ground quickly. It was nice to hear a steward say I was special as I went past too. I managed to hang my banner at the top of the stand next to Bournemouth Whites before I went down to my seat. But, oh dear I think Bolton have some holes in their roof; there were big drips coming down onto the

fans in front of me and then a large deluge appeared too. The last thing you want when you are supposed to be under cover is to get wet, so I'm to tweet some photos to Bolton, although as they still have financial issues it may be down their priority list at the moment.

The team were: Wiedwald, Ayling, Berardi, Cooper, Pennington, Roofe, Wood, Phillips, Hernandez, Alioski and O'Kane. Subs were: Anita for Berardi (dislocated shoulder), Shaughnessy (Pennington ankle injury) and Sacko for Alioski. Attendance was 19,857 including 4,832 Leeds fans. Leeds won 3-2 with goals from Phillips (7, 42) and Wood (30).

I had no idea who the team was going to be today but realised once they came out that it was the same one as the Oxford game. It was nice to see that Christiansen had kept a large proportion of the team who played together last season for continuity, which gives us a chance to build on it. We certainly got off to a great start; I zoomed my camera in on the far end as we won a corner, and it took me by surprise when we scored from that corner as Hernandez passed it across the penalty area and Phillips scored a cracker to put us into the lead. On the half hour mark, we were two up as another corner saw the ball come to Alioski, who headed it back to Wood to head into the net! Wow scoring goals and in the lead so soon? Then things took a turn for the worse as Bolton attacked our goal and Berardi went down under pressure. I immediately saw him signal to the bench as he held his shoulder and knew straight away that he had dislocated it. Play was held up for several minutes whilst he was treated and then had to be stretchered off the pitch. That was so sad to see as Berardi puts everything into playing; he went off to the fans singing 'Ain't nobody like Berardi, makes me happy, makes me feel this way.'

BBC Radio Leeds Preview
Billy's Bar 1st August 2017

Anita came on as sub and straight away Bolton won a corner. Anita immediately positioned himself at the right-hand post as we looked down onto the pitch in front of us. Unfortunately Bolton scored at the other post which was a shame, but I felt losing Berardi and having to sub him meant that we hadn't had time to readjust. I think it is important that we have people on both posts as we did in the Revie days with Bremner and Reaney, as they stopped a tremendous amount of goals being scored against us by doing that. With the Bolton fans celebrating, they started chanting that we weren't singing anymore. Well what can I say but a big thank you to Leeds United for shutting them up, as Wood and Phillips combined for the latter to score his second goal of the game. That couldn't have come at a better time - just before half time - to give us a two-goal cushion again. It was a good feeling to know that we had actually scored three goals away from home, but also that the players were backing each other up and fighting for the ball.

At half time it was good to get a personal thank you for helping one of our fans get off for an alleged offence after the Derby game last season. I had put them in touch with the Football Supporters Federation and they had put them in touch with the right contact to help get them acquitted after the incident, as they hadn't done anything wrong. Some of my photos helped to prove their innocence too so I am glad to help out as I hate injustice.

The second half saw Leeds come under pressure more as the heavens opened. We were trying to work out from the defence to go forward, as they did in the Oxford game. Sometimes the passes looked too close for comfort, but we were able to pass the ball around our players very well which was good to see. Unfortunately, I feel the conditions together with Pennington being tackled meant he had to go off with an ankle injury, although I thought it was more of a precaution. Things changed very quickly for us once he was subbed, as the ref almost immediately pointed to the spot to give Bolton a penalty. After duly scoring from the spot, the last 20-odd minutes of the game saw my familiar stomach churning appear. I certainly hoped we could see the game out and get the points as we didn't deserve to lose. Once again it looks like we had a referee carry on from last season as he didn't have a clue. The amount of times he didn't give us anything was beyond a joke. After another bad foul by Bolton he looked as if he was finally going to book one of their players but couldn't get the card out of his pocket! I went to collect my banner as four minutes of added injury time was put up, but during this period a Bolton player went off on a stretcher and I feared that we would end up playing another seven minutes as in the first half. Luckily for us we didn't play for much longer, managed to hold out, and get the three points, making this a good start to the season.

Wednesday sees the visit of Port Vale for the League Cup tie, which I am bringing two of my granddaughters to. It will be interesting to see what team is played but I am looking forward to progressing in the cup before our first home league game against Preston on Saturday. See you then – LUFC – Marching on Together!

PORT VALE (H), CARABAO CUP FIRST ROUND – 9th AUGUST 2017

I set off from home with my daughter Dani and two granddaughters Hannah and Laura, but we didn't get very far. As we hit the main road we were turned around by the police as it was cordoned off due to a road traffic accident. As we passed Shibden Park I was glad that we hadn't gone Brighouse way due to the diversion, as the M62 was down to one lane there due to a broken-down vehicle. Luckily, we got to Elland Road without any further issues, and as we got out of the car a black cat went past us and then Dani saw two magpies, so maybe things were looking up for us tonight!

I went to Billy's Bar to take photos of the new timeline. It looks great but, sorry to be picky, Salonika is missing from the timeline in 1973 and there is no mention of the League title in 1974. There is a space under the 1973 FA Cup final for this to go and I will ensure I pass this information on to the club. I was in Salonika for the European Cup-Winners' Cup final where we were robbed by a bribed referee, which was proven and he was banned for life after the game. Why the cup was never awarded to us because of this I will never know! This was my first trip abroad to see Leeds United and it is something I will always cherish despite the result.

As I was taking the photos I was approached by someone who enjoys reading my blogs, which is always good to hear so thank you.

I went to the Peacock to join the others before going into the ground. As we left I heard someone shout me: it was Tony from the West Midlands, who I haven't seen for a while, but he went everywhere to see Leeds with us as one time. It was good to have a quick catch up and he doesn't look to have aged either. I remember him having his car painted in Leeds United colours which he parked outside the Wolverhampton supporters' club bar. Unfortunately, that wasn't a good idea as he ended up with loads of problems, but I'll have to get an update from him for next time as I can't remember the specifics about what happened.

We got to the turnstiles but had to queue, so by the time we got inside the teams were already out on the pitch ready to start. The team were: Wiedwald, Anita (making his home league debut), Borthwick-Jackson making his debut (here on a year-long loan from man u), Ayling, Shaughnessy (making his home league debut), Vieira, Klich (making his home league debut), Saiz (making his home league debut), Ekuban (making his debut), Dallas and Sacko. Subs were Alioski (making his home league debut), Bridcutt and Gomes (making his home league debut). Hopefully I've got all that right lol! Subs were: Alioski for Sacko (58), Bridcutt for Klich (58) and Gomes for Ayling (70). Attendance was 15,431 including 801 Port Vale fans. Final score 4-1 to Leeds with a Saiz hat trick and Ekuban scoring the goals. Goal timings were: Saiz (13, 60, 62) and Ekuban (83), Tonge (37), an ex-Leeds player, scored the Port Vale goal. Their manager was Michael Brown and Danny Pugh, who were also ex-Leeds players.

With all the new names in the team it was hard to work out who was who for a while. I had to zoom in with the camera to see the names on the back of the shirts as I didn't have any idea of

FA CUP
VS ARSENAL
CLARKE

FA CUP FINAL

1973 REACH THE FA CUP FINAL

1972 **WIN THE FA CUP**
FOR THE FIRST TIME THANKS
TO ALAN CLARKE'S GOAL

1971 **WIN THE FAIRS CUP**

FAIRS CUP
VS JUVENTUS (3-3 ON AGGREGATE)
FIRST LEG (2-2)
SECOND LEG (1-1) CLARKE

the numbers to work out who was who. I know I shared a post with all the player numbers on, but I didn't actually take much notice of it. I remember things more by seeing for myself, but I just couldn't work out who Bridcutt was when he came on as sub as he looked completely different. I think it was because he has a beard now.

The team started off on the attack, which brought a save out of their goalie. There was some counter attacking from Port Vale before Leeds took the lead in the 14th minute. When Dallas crossed the ball, trying to emulate his recent goals, the ball bounced back off the post and fell to Saiz who hammered the ball into the net for a great goal! Leeds had the majority of the play and it was good to see us attacking and shooting at the goal. Unfortunately, just before half time Port Vale equalised and it was Tonge who got their goal.

At the start of the second half we attacked the Kop end and it wasn't long before Christiansen made a double substitution on 58 minutes, with Alioski replacing Sacko and Bridcutt replacing Klich. Immediately we went on the attack and within two minutes had gone back into the lead, with Saiz getting a second goal. And even better, two minutes later Saiz completed his hat trick with a further goal sending the Leeds fans into raptures. We hadn't finished there and Ekuban got a fourth goal to put the tie out of reach for Port Vale. It meant we were straight through to the next round and wouldn't have to rely on a penalty shoot-out. Some of the passing between Alioski and Saiz was out of this world, which was too much for one Port Vale player as he reacted to the mickey taking and was promptly sent off. Seeing the East Stand give a standing ovation to Saiz showed the impact he made on the pitch today. I had already said I liked the look of Alioski and on tonight's showing I wasn't wrong!

We were all buzzing at the end of the game. I said the passing was sublime (where that word came from in my brain I've no idea) and was joined by Jo, who was having a lift home with us, who said the same word had been used by her! We have played some fantastic football tonight; we have shown speed, skill, taken shots at goal on and off target and shown us all what we have been missing as fans for a long time. Monk has done us all a favour by leaving us for Boro as I feel we are in for some exciting times with Thomas Christiansen as our manager. It has been a long time coming and although I know there is a long way to go, I am looking forward to the future as a Leeds fan. I couldn't stop being giddy but it was a lovely feeling to be coming out of Elland Road like this.

I want to say a big thank you to Roy who purchased my jointly authored book with Andrew Dalton, *The Good, The Bad and The Ugly of Leeds United*, Leeds United in the 1980s. Having already bought my other two books *Follow Me and Leeds United* and *Once a Leeds fan, always a Leeds fan* it is a great endorsement that he has bought them all. I can't ask for better feedback than that and it is greatly appreciated! Also thanks to the fans who took the time to say they enjoy my blogs and look forward to reading them, it's great feedback too.

Saturday sees us host Preston at Elland Road and I am looking forward to seeing all the new art work around the ground, including the 'Side before Self' poster across the East Stand. Billy Bremner, who epitomised what being Leeds is all about, still is and always will be my hero and the quote is so apt. Tonight's win will see us being very close to selling out against Preston I'm sure. This is what being Leeds is all about and the future is looking bright! See you on Saturday – LUFC – Marching on Together!

PRESTON NORTH END (H) – 12th AUGUST 2017

I was due to meet someone at Elland Road around 2pm who was buying my second two books, but due to traffic and other things we didn't get there until 2.30pm. Sorry Richard I will get there earlier on Tuesday! Fans were still streaming down to the ground and my granddaughter Hannah and I didn't go to the Peacock as I knew there would be queues - my daughter Dani had said that the queues to get into the Peacock were right back to the road earlier. I took photos of the new banners outside the ground and love the 'Side before Self' quote. They certainly look good that's for sure. As we headed into the ground I'd forgotten to get a programme, but as Hannah was supposed to be in it we headed back to get one. At that moment Para Dave came up to me to say that Steve, a lad from Halifax who'd died recently, was also in it. Hannah was in the programme because she had recently had 12 inches of her hair cut off for the Little Princess Trust to help make wigs for children with cancer and had also raised over £1,000 in the process for Candlelighters. Well done Hannah I'm very proud of you. When I had my bag checked going into the ground I was surprised to see a hand scanner being used. I wondered what they were looking for as I thought of flares or drugs, but then realised it was to prevent sinister items being taken into the ground.

The team were: Wiedwald, Ayling, Cooper, Jansson (back after suspension), Borthwick-Jackson, Hernandez, Wood, Roofe, O'Kane, Phillips and Alioski. Subs were: Vieira for Phillips 61, Saiz for Roofe 61 and Dallas for Borthwick-Jackson 82. Attendance was 32,880 including 671 Preston fans. Score was 0-0. Vieira was booked.

As I got into the ground I said I wasn't used to the big crowds and wasn't sure if I liked it (tongue in cheek). Then I admitted I loved it, especially when there is a great atmosphere. It was buzzing and when we sang 'Marching on Together' it was great to hear a sizeable section of fans in the Kop singing the na, na, na, na, na, na instead of clapping. It is something I have always sung and as I'm a traditionalist I loved to hear it again! It was also good to see the minute's applause take place in memory of all the Leeds fans who have died over the year. This was very humbling as usual.

As the game kicked off it didn't take long for me to realise that Preston were up for it and it wasn't going to be an easy game. They were a lot harder opposition than our last two games that's for sure, but they also had a new manager in place after Simon Grayson took up the manager's job at Sunderland

recently. We did manage to get plenty of possession though, and as Alioski went forward towards the South Stand jinking past their players, his final shot was wide. Wiedwald was playing the sweeper role but at times we got a little too close for comfort. I don't like going back to the goalie too much as I feel it puts us under pressure. This became apparent when we were near the half way line when the ball was played back to Wiedwald and we were nearly caught out. One shot from Preston looked close, and at one point I thought it was heading in, but luckily it went over the crossbar meaning it was 0-0 at the break.

The second half carried on with Preston frustrating us more and more and some fans in the crowd were getting restless. I didn't realise that when Preston attacked the South Stand they had got the ball into the net as I thought it hit the crossbar and bounced back into Wiedwald's arms! I read afterwards that it had been disallowed for offside but I'd missed that bit. Some fans behind us were getting the songs going which was great, but I couldn't believe how slow the half was going. Not long after this, at about the half-hour mark, Preston had their number four sent off for a second bookable offence and I thought this was our chance to get something out of the game. Christiansen made a double substitution, bringing on Vieira and Saiz in place of Phillips and Roofe. We managed to keep a lot of possession, but I noticed we were trying to walk the ball into the net. After previously shooting from afar, this was actually a disappointment and it meant that chances of having a shot on target were rare until late in the game. When we did put pressure on them, we found that the Preston goalie made some great saves to deny us. One thing Preston were guilty of was the continuous timewasting, including plenty of times from their goalie. Unfortunately for us the ref didn't pull them up for any of it, which meant that this happened for most of the second half. This also carried on into the five minutes of injury time when I was very disappointed to see the ref let Preston waste at least a couple of these minutes without adding any time on. The plus points were that it wasn't a defeat and a point is better than none, but Preston came to do a job and succeeded in frustrating us. They could easily have stolen the points in the last minute when their attack ended with the ball hitting the crossbar. As it was we had to settle for a goalless draw and it wasn't to be, which was a shame for all those fans who have travelled long distances to be there. The birthday present of three points that my friend Carole and I were hoping for hadn't materialised sadly.

After the game Hannah and I went to see if there were any more of the large photos up outside the ground, and she asked if she could go and see the players. We ended up staying there for another hour and a half, but when I saw how excited she was at getting a photo with Pontus, and the others and getting autographs it made me realise I'm doing something right. There were plenty of others, both children and adults, waiting patiently for the same. We were disappointed to learn that we had missed Saiz and also heard that some of the other players had gone out of the ground a different way. For those players who did that it's a shame, because the fans had waited a long time for them to come out. A little bit of interaction can go a long way to getting idol status so please take note of that!

SIDE
BEFORE
SELF
EVERY
TIME

18+ T&CS APPLY

I hadn't realised we were playing Fulham this Tuesday for some reason. I will also have to apologise in advance to those who look forward to reading my blogs, but I will be unable to report on both the Nottingham Forest game and Newport game. An opportunity has arisen for me that I have to take, but I will be back reporting as usual after the international break. Next week also sees us visit Sunderland for an evening kick-off, when we meet up with Simon Grayson once again. It was a tough game for us today and an introduction to the Championship for Christiansen but fingers crossed we will come out fighting in the next two games. See you Tuesday – LUFC – Marching on Together!

FULHAM (H) – 15th AUGUST 2017

We went to Castleford Outlet before to the game and when my granddaughters met a young lad in the playground with a Leeds shirt on called Oliver they thought I should know him! As we were expecting a big crowd again, I knew it would be busy so I thought I'd avoid the motorway and come back Stourton way. Unfortunately it took longer than I thought as I somehow got lost and ended up on my way to Wakefield. I wouldn't mind but I've gone that way before so who knows where I went wrong? I had arranged to meet Richard tonight to give him my books as I didn't get to Elland Road early enough on Saturday and didn't want to get there late today. Luckily my granddaughter Hannah and I arrived at 6.20pm in plenty of time. We headed to the Peacock first, where Hannah had a good conversation with Chris Beeton and collected some LUSC fixture lists. As I sat at the table where Keith was, I had my back to the fans passing behind me, but I had to turn around loads as that many fans went past saying hello to me. Just after seven Richard rang to say they were nearly here so I told him we'd go to Billy's statue to meet him and his son. After a quick chat outside the Peacock with my friend Sue and her husband Paul, we waited at Billy's statue. A big thank you to Richard for buying both my books, your support is greatly appreciated. Just as I was getting ready to take a photo of Richard someone came up behind us to ask if I was selling my books, to which I replied yes. Another fan, Paul, told me he'd commented on a post of mine on social media about my friend Carole - as Keith reminded me later, our first game of the season in 1972 was away at Chelsea when we lost 4-0; Carole fell down the steps, broke her ankle and went to hospital in the same ambulance as David Harvey our goalie, who got injured during the game. Paul was on the Wallace Arnold coach that Carole was on, and they ended up going to the hospital to wait for Carole to be sorted and pick her up! She'll never forget that game that's for sure. Another lad came up to ask when my third book was out and I said it already was. The last time I saw him it was in the process of coming out so I've arranged to meet him in a few weeks to get it.

It was nice seeing lots of fans that we knew on our way into the ground. Hannah went straight up to our seats whilst I waited on the steps, but then I saw Lucas the Kop Cat, and knowing Hannah loves getting photos with him I shouted her down and went to get some more. I had a quick chat with Vaughan from Halifax and got some more photos. The lad with him said he'd ended up on one of my photos recently too!

The team were: Wiedwald, Jansson, Shaughnessy, Ayling (Captain), Anita, Hernandez, Phillips, Alioski, Saiz, Wood and O'Kane. Subs were: Roofe for Alioski on 63 minutes and Dallas for Saiz on 82 minutes. Booked were: Anita and Phillips. The score was 0-0 and the attendance was 28,918 including 576 Fulham fans.

Comments from some fans when they heard the team were that they were mystified to say the least about the selection, whereas I thought it was a case of waiting to see how they would perform. It took at least 20 minutes for Leeds to settle into the game, with numerous misplaced passes, and as Fulham saw plenty of the ball they kept attacking us. There was some restlessness on the terraces by some fans too, but it was more low key. During this period Fulham came close with a couple of shots before one bounced back off the bottom of the post to deny them the lead. More shots were peppered at the Leeds goal but were off target. Once we woke up, we started getting stuck into tackles, with Phillips and O'Kane beginning to gel. Wood got the ball into the net just before half time when he received the ball in the penalty area in lots of space. Unfortunately the ref blew for offside but BBC Radio Leeds said later that the goal should have stood as he was onside. If the goal had stood then I think we would be looking at a completely different outcome as we would have scored more.

The second half saw Leeds come out with renewed vigour, and Alioski and Saiz showed some of their touches from last week as we attacked towards the Kop. With the crowd getting behind Leeds, the Fulham goalie sent two kicks straight out of play to cheers from us. We had a couple of near chances which I thought would be buried in the goal, only to see it go wide. With us attacking more, Fulham were looking to catch us out by counter attacking, and when they were through on goal with only our goalie to beat, Shaughnessy came out of the blue with a fantastic tackle at the last minute. Well timed isn't the word! Fulham also ended up with just Wiedwald in front of them, and he pulled off a great save to deny them the chance of going a goal up. Things started to quieten down on the terraces as a few nerves were showing amongst the Leeds support. I wanted us to up the singing and become the twelfth man as we had been doing until Roofe came on for Alioski. I felt Fulham would crack with the fans in full voice, but the sting was taken out of the tail with the substitution in my opinion. We should have won the game in the final minutes when Dallas put a great cross across the box and I thought Wood would put it away. Sadly the ball wasn't put into the net as Wood missed it by inches.

After last Saturday's 0-0 draw I felt very frustrated, but I didn't tonight because at least we had chances and had been attacking. We are still unbeaten at the moment and our win has come away from home so it looks like we are going to have to beat Sunderland on Saturday! With Simon Grayson now managing them and the game being live on Sky again with another 5.30pm kick-off, I am hoping the pressure will be off a bit. We are stopping at Green Hammerton on our way to Sunderland along with the Welsh Whites so I'm looking forward to it. See you on Saturday – LUFC – Marching on Together!

SUNDERLAND (A) – 19th AUGUST 2017

Chris who?????? Hearing that Chris Wood had refused to play as he was going to be transferred to Burnley came as a big shock. He is irrelevant now!

I'd given Gaz and his daughter Ella a lift into Leeds for us to catch the Fullerton Park coach today. It was nice to see that the timeline outside Billy's Bar had been updated with our 1974 League Champions win, although our European Cup-Winners' Cup final in Salonika in 1973 was still missing. I tweeted the club after the Preston game to say these needed adding. We left Billy's Bar at 12.30pm and headed for our pub stop in Green Hammerton at the club there. The Welsh contingent were already there when we arrived, and I went to talk to Brian Bevan and a couple of others. Brian had brought one of my books last time we were there on the way to Newcastle, and it was nice to hear that he enjoyed reading it, so a big thank you to him for the feedback. We had a nice chilled out time and I enjoyed my pie and peas, which reminded me of the old Supporters' Club building on Fullerton Park where we always used to go during my early days of following Leeds. Pie and peas were always served in the social side if I remember correctly.

We had a group photo prior to leaving the club at 3.15pm, and it seemed like no time at all that we arrived in Sunderland, at around 5pm, in readiness for the kick-off and live Sky game. As we got off the coach it was a bit windy, but we were soon climbing the stairs to the top of the stand where luckily it was sheltered. As the front two rows of the stand were not to be used by our fans I was able to put my banner up with lots of others. I love it when they can all be displayed together, showing where lots of our fans come from. I didn't feel safe standing up at the front of the stand though so was glad to go and find my seat a little further back in the top part. Although it was a good view, I thought it was a bit too high up and you are far away from the play. Looking at the Sunderland fans turnout, which seemed pretty poor, I reckoned they could have given Leeds fans the whole stand and I'm sure we would have sold them all, especially when the allocation was sold out in minutes once again.

The team today were: Wiedwald, Ayling, Cooper, Jansson, Anita, Alioski, Saiz, O'Kane, Hernandez, Phillips and Ekuban. Subs were: Roofe for Hernandez (25 went off injured), Dallas for Ekuban (62 went off injured) and Klich for Saiz (81). Wiedwald was booked and Leeds won 2-0 with goals by Saiz (21) and Dallas (76). Attendance at the Stadium of Light was 31,237, including approximately 3,000 Leeds fans, although I would never have guessed there were that many fans at the game overall because of all the spaces on the terraces below!

It didn't take long for us to see that the team were up for it today. There was some brilliant footwork going on, especially from Saiz and Alioski, and lots of quick passing amongst the team. Phillips was getting stuck in too and this was replicated by other members of the team. The fans were in good voice too, which was good to hear, and they sang for the whole game. By comparison, the Sunderland fans were as quiet as church mice. Today's game saw us up against Simon Grayson,

who was now the manager of the opposition, but with the Leeds fans chanting his name hopefully it tugged at his heart strings. Leeds were attacking towards the Leeds fans in the first half, and time and time again Alioski, with some pace, was bearing down the wing with acres of space. Each team member was fighting for the ball and backing the other players up and this looked so good. Leeds launched another attack and Alioski passed the ball for Saiz to hit the ball past their goalie to put us into the lead. Great celebrations from the Leeds fans and the noise became even louder! Just after we scored Hernandez went off injured and Roofe came on. It took me a while to realise who had replaced him though. The first half belonged to Leeds and we were all over Sunderland, and although they had a couple of chances they never looked like scoring. It was good to go into the break in the lead.

I went downstairs, and on the steps some young lads stopped me to ask for a photo. They love reading my blogs and it makes me feel really happy and that I am doing something right. I had a chat with Gary Edwards at half time before heading back into the stand. The second half started where the first half left off, and Alioski was getting some great runs down the right-hand side. It was good to see the pace we now have, and the players playing as a team - and long may it continue. Things became more difficult when Grayson made a double substitution and it wasn't so easy to run rings around Sunderland. After settling back into the game we had another attack when Ekuban and Roofe won the ball. Somehow at the end of this Ekuban ended up in the back of the goal injured. Eventually he got half way across the pitch before going down again and after treatment was more or less carried off the pitch. It was such a shame as he looked in a lot of pain and he was just getting on top of his game, I thought. Vieira, who was warming up at the side of the pitch, had renditions of his song sung to him. Ohhh Ronaldo Vieira, ohhh he's only a teenager,

ohhh he never gives the ball away 1, 2, 3, 4, and it was nice to see him return the appreciation to the fans above him. Dallas came on to replace Ekuban and, after another great attack by Leeds, Saiz crossed the ball for Dallas to head the ball into the net and send the Leeds fans into raptures once more. As the Sunderland fans streamed to the exits the Leeds fans chanted 'is there a fire drill' at them. The gallows humour from our fans once again took over when we sang 'Leeds, Leeds are falling apart again'. As they attacked us at that time I had an anxious moment thinking they would get a goal back. They repeated a move from the first half where they put the ball across the box, but none of their players could connect with it thankfully.

I am chuffed to bits for the team today as they played some great football with precision passes, were able to fight for the ball, plus they scored two great goals to give us the three points. The win put us into fifth place and, as I've said many times, still aspiring for that automatic promotion place. The attitude and commitment shone out today and there was a great togetherness from both the fans and the team, especially at the end of the game. I still think no other fans can touch us for our loyalty, and through all the ups and downs we've had, fingers crossed, our future is looking bright. The atmosphere was brilliant today too and I love being part of it.

After the game I went down to get my banner so I was stood at the front when the team came to clap us. A very happy buzzing Leeds support came out of the stadium as we headed to the coaches, then all of a sudden we were hit by a gale force wind and I had to hold on to my beret. It must be the design of the ground that had created a wind tunnel there because it came out of the blue.

On our journey home, just as we dropped our Green Hammerton fans off, we heard that there was someone locked in the toilet on the coach. We had to get a screwdriver from the club, and eventually the driver was able to release him. As he had been in there for at least 10 minutes he was quite shaken up - I'm glad it wasn't me who'd been locked in! As we got to Leeds I got off the coach and ran to my car. As I was putting my bags in the car I suddenly realised that I hadn't travelled alone this morning, I'd better wait for Gaz and Ella! They'd thought they were going to have to get a taxi instead, but I told them no way they'd have had to ring me. Unfortunately, my memory is shot half of the time as I'm doing that many things at once so I forget these things very easily. I just need reminding and honestly I don't mind lol!

Tuesday sees the Newport EFL game at Elland Road and then the away game at Nottingham Forest, but unfortunately I won't be at either game, although I hope to get the stream for Tuesday and find a pub to watch the latter. On the way to Sunderland today I said that we would be winning our away games and drawing at home in the league, which has obviously happened so far. Once we've learnt how to overcome teams that come to frustrate us at home, I reckon we will be a force to be reckoned with. Here's hoping! See you all at the Burton game – LUFC – Marching on Together!

CHAPTER 3 – SEPTEMBER 2017

BURTON ALBION (H) – 9th SEPTEMBER 2017

Having missed the last two games to Newport and Forest because of an opportunity I just couldn't refuse, it was good to be back at Elland Road after the international break. I managed at long last to go to Florida and Disneyworld on holiday with my family and swim with the dolphins, which was something I have wanted to do for the last 14 years. The only drawback to this was Hurricane Irma. With some of the group still over there it has been very worrying to hear that they would have to ride out the storm because there were no places on the planes. It has been such a relief to hear they have now got on the last flight out of Orlando before the airport shuts in a few hours, and the sooner they are on their way the better. I have seen on WACCOE that there are some of our fans still out there with their families, so please stay safe and my fingers are crossed that you escape the worst of the storm.

On my way, my first visit was to the tunnel at the bottom of Lowfields to see the mural that has been painted, which was paid for by Leeds United Supporters' Trust funds. Although I didn't vote for this design, it looks great and is a fitting tribute to Wilko and the team. After taking photos of it, and then of the new fan bar outside the North East corner, I headed to the club shop then Billy's Bar to meet Peter Wilkinson, who had come over from South Africa and is a member of the

Johannesburg Supporters' Club. After having a chat to Steph and William I said I was going to look for Peter, but he was already right in front of me as he'd spotted me. Lots of people were going past and saying hello to me. It was nice to be told that I'd been missed and also that because I hadn't written my blog they were glad I was back! There were some Irish fans there from East Antrim and Louth who I was introduced to before I had a chat with Susan. She has just got a puppy and knowing my love for the great Leeds United number four, she named him Bremner! That's so nice.

The Peacock was my next port of call and I was asked to take some photos by some of the regulars, including Terje from Norway, and then I had a good chat with some more. One asked me what we would do today and I said that I expected us to turn up as a team, not like in the past where the break affected the play big style. It was pointed out that Christiansen had also said that he broke that duck in Cyprus. I just felt that things would be completely different under this regime as they want to win. On my way out I saw the lad from Germany who supports Carl Zeiss Jena and said hello. The team name always brings back fond memories for me as that is the only home game my dad attended with me as he came from Zeitz (near Leipzig) in East Germany. I can always remember passing the ground on the way to see some of my dad's family when it was under the Russian rule. Again, today has already shown the breadth of the great Leeds United worldwide support including a shout out to our fans travelling from Cornwall and down south, as ever our true loyal support for what was going to be a big crowd of over 30,000.

The team today were: Wiedwald, Anita, Cooper, Jansson, Ayling, Phillips, O'Kane, Hernandez, Saiz, Roofe and Lasogga making his debut. Subs were: Dallas for Anita (45), Klich for O'Kane (56) and Grot for Lasogga (62). Subs not used were: Lonergan, Shaughnessy, Cibicki and Alioski. Attendance was 33,404 including 372 Burton fans. Leeds won 5-0 with goals from Lasogga (20) and (59), Phillips (35), Hernandez (pen) (44) and Roofe (54).

There was a great buzz about the ground as kick-off approached, and I was expecting a good atmosphere and good football. The first thing Burton did was turn us around so that we attacked the Kop in the first half. My first thoughts were that it wouldn't make a difference as playing towards the South Stand when it is full of Leeds fans too means that we don't get inconvenienced anymore. We had two attacks in the first few minutes, where we were unlucky not to take an early lead, denied by an off-the-line clearance and their goalie. It didn't take long for Lasogga to score on his debut and put us into the lead. When Phillips hit a shot from the edge of the box to give us a second, this immediately gave us some breathing space. The scoring wasn't over either, and Saiz linked well together with Lasogga, which meant the latter hit the post before having a further shot tipped over the bar. We didn't have long to wait until we were awarded a penalty, which Hernandez took to put us 3-0 up at the break. Even though someone had told me that that was Eddie Gray's score prediction earlier, I don't think even he expected that result by half time!

The second half saw Leeds continue where they left off as Burton remained well and truly under the cosh. Roofe was the next one to score before Lasogga scored his second of the game with a header. The bit that really impressed me was Wiedwald using the sweeper keeper role to our advantage, then the pace of the attack, which resulted in the ball nestling in the back of the Burton goal before you knew it. 5-0 and it was game over. Well almost, as Burton had a rare attack, but as the final shot ballooned over the bar there was nothing at all to worry about. One thing I will say about Lasogga is look what happens when someone believes in you and gives you some TLC!

This was what us Leeds fans had been waiting years for, seeing the team playing as a team, having a manager that could bring out the best in his players and an owner who recognised the side before self and the loyalty of a great support. With a near sell-out crowd today, what I will say is that United are back! We are finally looking at a club moving forward in the right way, and this is something I feel very positive about. This is the start of the journey of the sleeping giant, who has awakened to become a big force in football once again. Because of this, my blog from last season has been put together for a book called *The Sleeping Giant Awakens, Leeds United 2016-17*, which should be out for Christmas! Despite it being early doors, the fact that we have gone eight games unbeaten and want to win games goes a long way to giving us a great start to the season. Believe me, I think there are some good times on the way for our long-suffering fans. If you can get to Elland Road to be part of it, go to away games, watch the game on TV, listen on the radio or read my blog; we can all share our passion for this club, and, as always, I think our fans are second to none! Leeds, Leeds are falling apart again rang out from the terraces with our gallows humour and I love it! It was great seeing the South Stand sing East Stand, East Stand give us a song, who did just that and the Kop joined in. There are special times coming back to Leeds, and even though we may have ups and downs along the way, we should take each game as it comes and enjoy it. Let others worry about having to play us once again, but they can let us have the three points every time please!

Tuesday sees our second home game in a week against Birmingham, and after going second in the table today after our 5-0 win it would be great to see us carry this on. Instead of playing a one-dimensional game that never changes, we have been playing some fantastic football with players who want to play for the shirt. Giving their all, the same as the fans, is all we ask and long may it continue! See you Tuesday – LUFC – Marching on Together!

BIRMINGHAM CITY (H) – 12TH SEPTEMBER 2017

I always go on about our fantastic worldwide fan base, but it's true. I always wear my colours whenever I'm not working and did so when we travelled to Florida last month. Having stayed at the Great Western, Altrincham, the night before, a minibus was coming to pick us up to take us to the airport. Lo and behold when the driver saw me he shouted out that it was fantastic to see another Leeds fan in that place across the Pennines. I said, apart from two in our group, the other eight of us were all Leeds fans! He was a mate of John Sheridan, and he used to travel everywhere when he played for us as he got free tickets. To my delight and the dismay of my son-in-law Steve, he then proceeded to play 'Marching on Together' all the way to the airport, so we had a sing song! Loved it, couldn't have had a better start to our holiday! Meeting Leeds fans didn't end there either as just as we were boarding the plane someone shouted me who knew me from the message boards to say a mutual friend was out in Florida at the same time. We acknowledged each other with the Leeds salute. Then, on the way back from Orlando airport there were a couple of kids with their Leeds shirts on, and again we used the Leeds salute to acknowledge each other. There were other Leeds fans out there at the same time as us, as I saw the Leeds shirts from a distance, and it just shows the camaraderie amongst our fans.

As this was a night game, it really shows how the appetite has been whetted as we gathered another crowd over 30,000 for the second time in a few days. The marketing of the ticket bundle price shows that the fans will come if given the right encouragement - plus the goods on the pitch are looking great!

My other half came to the game today along with Ken, who hasn't been to a game since an Arsenal home game in 1999. Captain, my hubby, had commented on the fact that we could go top of the league tonight and that it normally goes wrong when we're in this situation, but I told him not this time it won't, as things are different. Ken travelled everywhere with the Halifax branch and then when I started running the Selby branch of the Leeds United Supporters' Club, he used to travel with me from Halifax and come on my coach. I made sure I got a picture of him with Don Revie. As I got to the statue, Paul from down south said I must be Heidi and that he enjoys reading my blog, so of course I took his photo.

In the ground I decided to go down to the front to see if I could get some better photos of the team coming out, as it had just started to rain. I was standing at the bottom of the steps waiting for the team to come out as it was just before kick-off. A steward walked down from the top of the steps to tell me to stand at the side out of the way and not to block people coming down the steps. Okay…. but what a jobsworth as not one person came down the steps anyway so a bit of common sense wouldn't have gone amiss! A lad then came to say I was standing in his seat, but once I explained I would only be a few minutes taking photos he was happy to leave me there. Whilst standing at the front another fan said he reads my blog and I was happy to take photos of him with his boys.

The team today were: Wiedwald, Ayling, Cooper, Jansson, Anita, Phillips, O'Kane, Saiz, Alioski, Lasogga and Hernandez. Subs were: Berardi for Cooper (69), Roofe for Alioski (60) and Dallas for Hernandez (80). Leeds won 2-0 with goals from Saiz (17) and Dallas (90 + 2). Attendance was 31,507 including 614 Birmingham fans.

As the game kicked off it didn't take long to see that Birmingham would be a lot tougher opposition than Burton had been. There were some bits of good play but our passing wasn't as precise as it had been in recent games, with many going astray. One thing that did stand out for me though was the passes we were spraying across the field that did reach our players, which were fantastic to see. At times I felt very confident that things would go our way as we were cool, calm and collected. At other times, with our sweeper keeper, things got a little too close for comfort. One good thing though was that the team were fighting to get the ball back if they lost it and many times managed to do just that. The backing up of each other and never giving up does makes a difference. At one time, just as a few fans were starting to get restless, the Leeds fans started singing which drowned this out luckily. We were very unlucky not to go ahead when Hernandez's shot was cleared off the line. It didn't take us long after that to take the lead though, as Lasogga hit a powerful shot that brought a great save from the keeper, only for Saiz to get there first to put the ball into the net. Spirits were high after that until just before the break when it went very quiet. I reckon most of the singers had gone to the bar! We nearly conceded right on half time when Wiedwald was beaten, only for Ayling to fling himself across the goal and clear the ball away for a corner. That was a close shave but a great save to protect our lead.

In the second half we carried on in the same way we left off in the first half, and although we had a fighting spirit and a couple of chances I felt sure that we would sub someone shortly. Alioski hadn't made the same impact tonight and was subbed but had been tightly marked as Birmingham didn't make it easy for us. I didn't realise it was Stockdale in their goal until after the game, but he pulled off a few great saves to stop us going further into the lead. As it was it was Birmingham who nearly equalised, but I'd seen the linesman put his flag up for offside so wasn't unduly worried as the ball hit the net in front of the South Stand. The conditions weren't great, with heavy rain throughout the game, and it was still backs to the wall as Birmingham never gave up. Just before the end of the game some Leeds fans started singing 'Leeds are falling apart again' and I thought shhhh as I started getting a bit anxious that they would get an equaliser, but my next thoughts were that our fans needed to up the atmosphere and make us the 12th man and intimidate Birmingham. In the eighties that's exactly what we did with both the Gelderd End and the South Stand. The Leeds fans then did up the ante and in injury time were rewarded with a second goal when Dallas scored from the edge of the box. That was it, game over, as the ecstatic fans went into raptures singing about being top of the league. The final minutes were absolutely fantastic and it was a wonderful feeling to know we had topped the league. Despite it being early days and despite it not meaning anything other than pride at this moment, it was something to cherish as it's been a long,

long time since that has happened. Still unbeaten and scoring goals from players all over the park means we are not relying on one player. As it is, no one really knows which team will start the game, which isn't a bad thing in my opinion as it will make it harder for the opposition to prepare. Birmingham did put up a good fight and will be unhappy about the final score, but at the end of the day so be it! They were a lot harder opposition that's for sure, but we had to dig our heels in and fight for the three points. The team spirit along with them embracing the fan base is good to see. I really feel we are going places once again and for the majority of the time I am confident that we can build on this great start to the season. The little doubts only last a minute or so and give me chance to banish them to the back of my mind.

The only sour point on the night was reaching my car and finding out that the van next to me had been broken into and all the tools pinched. I felt so much for the lad as that is his livelihood. These things have been happening for a while, so it surprises me that the helicopter isn't used more to overlook the area around the ground.

Saturday sees an early start for Millwall but at least I can sleep on the coach. We just need to carry on and get as many points as we can and let the other teams worry about us. Burnley away in the cup follows on Tuesday before Ipswich at home and Cardiff. Lots of games in a short space of time but at least we can look forward to some great football once again, which I love. See you there – LUFC – Marching on Together!

MILLWALL (A) – 16TH SEPTEMBER 2017

It was pitch black when I woke up 20 minutes before my alarm was due to go off so instead of going back to sleep I got up - I had visions of me missing my alarm if I hadn't. Getting up at the unearthly hour of 5.10am could only mean one thing, an LUFC away day and Millwall here we come! Just as I was getting ready to leave the house this absolute beast of a spider ran at me so found itself under my foot squashed before I had time to think. Horrible thing, I don't want that running about my house!

After an uneventful journey to Leeds I headed to McDonalds and found Chris and Phil from the Griffin branch going in at the same time. There were quite a few Leeds fans in there too and I had a chat with Andrew Dalton who co-authored my third book *The Good, The Bad and The Ugly of Leeds United* with me. We all started reminiscing about previous visits to Millwall. When we first returned there a few years ago the journey out of the ground on the coach was like getting out of the Alamo. We ran a gauntlet of their fans outside all the pubs who were attacking the coaches as they went by, one aiming a kick at the minibus in front of us. I gave a big sigh of relief once we got away from there unscathed, but the Griffin branch had the outer layer of a window on their coach put out. My first visit to the Den in the eighties meant I travelled with the Kippax branch, as their coach came from Selby near where I lived. Seeing their fans on street corners make gestures of cutting throats shows that some things never change as they have still been seen doing this in recent visits too.

The disadvantage of having a large coach today meant there wasn't a toilet on it, but for long journeys that is something that some of us can't do without! After a stop in Greenwich, where we were served drinks in plastic glasses due to football being on, we headed for the police escort. Even though we were bang on time to meet it, we were going the opposite way and unable to turn around so we missed the convoy of three coaches. We got to the layby where a couple of police were waiting for us and they said to please ensure that no one on the coaches used the gardens of the nearby houses as a toilet. Well it was okay for the lads to use the bushes just up the road but no good for us female fans. Eventually, by the time we got our escort in, we arrived just before kick-off and by then I was desperate to get into the ground, and I wasn't the only one. Also, by being late it meant that we didn't have a reception committee of Millwall fans outside their pubs. It was only the ones in the vicinity of the ground, but for once I didn't feel intimidated.

After starting to queue I was pointed in the direction of the middle queue for the females to be searched by the female steward. We also had a couple of lads in our queue who were happy to be frisked by her too! It was nice to bump into Collar and 18 so I had a quick chat with them. A big thank you once again to those fans who took the time to say they love my blog! The praise does give me a warm glow as it makes me feel it is worthwhile doing this, despite it taking a few hours to complete after a game.

As we headed up the stairs to the ground they were playing a song over the tannoy so I started singing na na na na na na na, na na na na Mick Jones, Jonesy, Jonesy, Jonesy. Some young lads in front of me were killing themselves laughing, and Coke from Wellingborough turned around to say hello too. I'd brought my banner with me and was going to hang it over the front of the stand where another banner was, but I decided against it as the space left was too small, plus I didn't like the steep drop to the stand below.

Leeds had sold out all the tickets for today once again, plus the game was being beamed back to Elland Road which had also sold out. The team today were: Wiedwald, Ayling, Jansson,

Shaughnessy, Anita, O'Kane, Hernandez, Saiz, Alioski, Phillips and Lasogga. Subs were: Dallas for Hernandez (45), Roofe for Alioski (45) and Grot for Saiz (72). Leeds lost 1-0 (73) (first defeat of the season). Attendance was 16,447 including approximately, 2,000 Leeds fans.

It didn't take long to realise that it wasn't going to be an easy game today as we were under the cosh from the word go. It is always a bad ground to visit; I think we have only had one win in nine games there. Millwall also took the lead, or so they thought, very early on only to have it chalked off for offside. Having looked at a replay later on I think Morison (our ex-player) will feel aggrieved it didn't stand, but I was glad he didn't score against us. Wiedwald had got down for the ball, but as he spilled it Morison had hammered the rebound home. Looking at the replay there was another one of our players playing him onside. Wiedwald made up for his error by making many fantastic saves as Millwall continued their onslaught. My view of it being a difficult place to come didn't change as the game progressed; we were struggling to get any fluency going to attack. Jansson was being kept busy in defence alongside Shaughnessy because Millwall were getting through our midfield quite easily, which meant constant pressure on them. We were not playing to our own strengths and ended up using the long ball to ease the pressure. When we did play it on the floor we were able to progress up the field better, although I can't remember us having any real chances to score despite a couple of corners. I just wanted us to get to half time on level terms as I knew Christiansen would make some changes. I thought it was a game that needed battlers, and I don't think Hernandez is that type of player. I also didn't think Anita was doing very well, and neither was Alioski. Personally, I would have brought Vieira on for Hernandez and Berardi for Anita. I thought this would give more support to Alioski. Thankfully we managed to go into the break at 0-0.

After the half time break I come back up into the stand and a lad shouted to me that his mate was a fan of my blog, so they got their photos taken - surprise, surprise. Then our head steward said, 'who did I think I was, David Bailey?' I replied that I had to do it didn't I?

At the start of the second half Hernandez and Alioski came off for Dallas and Roofe, and, whilst I understood that Christiansen was looking for a speedy attack, unfortunately it didn't give us the steel in the middle of the park that was required. Millwall carried on where they left off and continued on the attack. After hitting the post, they eventually took the lead about 17 minutes from the end of normal time. The ball ran into the box at the far end from us and their player slotted it home. At the time I thought because they had scored they may take their foot off the pedal, so we could still get a draw, which would have been a good result in the circumstances. Unfortunately 10 minutes from the end Jansson went down injured and we played the last minutes without him as he went off straight down the tunnel. Some fans said it looked like his hamstring, but I'm hoping it was just a precaution. We seem to be having no end of injuries so far this season sadly. It also meant that because we had used all of our subs (Grot had come on to replace Saiz) we had to play the final 10 minutes plus four minutes' injury time with 10 men. At times we started playing with the ball at our feet but continued to try and walk the ball in, so we ended up with our first defeat of the season. Just as their fans were celebrating, all the Leeds fans started chanting 'we are top of the league still', so at least it made me feel a little better. I knew the defeat would come at some time, but we were out battled and out fought today so it will be a learning curve. We won't win every game that's for sure but we will have to pick ourselves up for a better performance than today to get something out of the next game. Millwall deserved their win to be honest.

While at the game, I'd been asked to take a small video clip for Monday evening's *Made in Leeds* for a phone in. Well technology and I obviously don't go very well together lol. I was laughed at because I wasn't actually recording on my phone, and after a few attempts I realised it was because there was no memory left. I tried to do something with my camera without success, but thanks to my friends I've got something now as hopefully they recorded me instead. I had a good laugh at myself too so will need to look at it first to see if it's any good.

We got a police escort away from the ground but ended up in central London, eerily on Westminster Bridge, which had been the scene of a recent terrorist attack. To be honest I was glad to get away from there, but there were still plenty of tourists around. A good thing I saw is that there are now barriers to prevent vehicles from running people down along both sides of the bridge. By going this way though it also seemed to add time onto our journey. Luckily, I went to sleep and woke up just before our stop at Watford Gap. Now to the fella who made comments about my anatomy, I thought I'd travelled back in time to the seventies! In the end I just laughed and walked away shaking my head. Some things never change!

Tuesday sees us head to Burnley for our league cup tie. I had an argument (if you can call it that) with a lad on Twitter who said we should put all our reserves out and get beat 6-0 so we can get knocked out of the cup. Sorry but I don't agree as winning breeds winning and we saw what happened after the Sutton debacle last season didn't we? It is also the entry route to Europe, so it would be good for us to win something for once. The lad said getting promotion was the be all and end all, but you don't put all your eggs in one basket and then fail at everything. You have to aspire to do well, and, although I realise there will be some changes to the team, we have to go all out to win the game. I am a traditionalist, having been brought up with the masters of the game: Don Revie, Billy Bremner and the rest of the team. I know I am privileged to have been there to see the greatest ever team play, and Billy was worth his weight in gold as he always gave 110% every game. That is what I want to see from our team today, fighting to win and going all out to give us a good cup run. We may not win it but we have to try! I'm getting a lift in with Jo on Tuesday so hopefully will get to the cricket club early enough to park so may see some of you in there. See you there – LUFC – Marching on Together!

BURNLEY (A), CARABAO CUP THIRD ROUND – 19TH SEPTEMBER 2017

I was looking forward to the short journey to Burnley today as I was getting a lift with Jo and Carmel. After we parked up we headed straight to the cricket club and enjoyed sitting on the balcony enjoying the sunshine. There were quite a few people we knew in there so I took a few photos. When I heard someone shout my name, I automatically turned around as Pete took my photo instead of the other way round.

I kept losing the other two as I kept stopping to chat to other fans. A Burnley fan was just telling another fan about Ray Hankin and I said I remember him and I've still got a photo I had taken with him at Menwith Hill. As we walked away from the club we found a police horse following us and we kept expecting it to charge at us. We were glad when they moved to the side as Carmel said we should get a selfie!!

A few coaches had just arrived when we got to the turnstiles, but there wasn't too much of a queue as we had our bags searched. I was asked about my banner and I told the girl what it was, but she hesitated so I said it was my blanket. I then went to get my ticket out but thought I was looking for my keys for some reason. Somehow, I don't think they'd have got me through the turnstiles.

Once through we found Phil Cresswell and lots of our stewards there. After a chat with some of them I heard a man say that on our website the tickets said 16-22 and Burnley were saying they were to 21 only and wouldn't let the lad in. Our steward went to have a word so hopefully it got

sorted, then I also heard someone say they couldn't bring it in, so I assumed they meant their flags. As we were near the entrance a fella told me that the first thing he looks for after a game is my blog. That was lovely to hear and I really appreciate the feedback. Just then Terry Yorath came in, who I think was on the same coach as the fella, and joined in our conversation. We stood chatting for a while and one of the guys from Harrogate asked me to take a photo of him and his daughter, who was over from Australia, so I obliged as usual. We decided to go and see where our seats were first, then try and put my banner up near the front. A Burnley steward told me that I couldn't hang the banner behind the disabled area without their permission, but that I should have a word with the head steward and he'd be able to tell me where to hang it. As it was, there was a segregated piece at the end of the seats next to the no man's land, so I was able to lay it on there with the help of a steward. I had a chat to a few of our stewards, including Mouse, and found out that some of the G4 stewards were Leeds fans but work for them too as they pay more. Just before kick-off we went to our seats.

The team today was Lonergan playing his first game since returning to Leeds, Ayling, Berardi, Shaughnessy, Borthwick-Jackson, Vieira, Klich, Roofe, Dallas, Cibicki and Grot. Subs used were Sacko for Borthwick-Jackson (60), Hernandez for Pawel Cibicki making his debut (79), Lasogga for Grot 85 and Alioski for Roofe (104). The score after extra time was 2-2 - scorers were Sacko 80 and a Hernandez penalty 90 + 4. Leeds won 5-3 on penalties - scorers Lasogga, Hernandez, Klich, Alioski and Dallas. Attendance was 11,799 with 2,194 Leeds fans.

Lots of Leeds fans gave Charlie Taylor and Chris Wood abuse due to their recent moves to Burnley. I didn't join in but still state that the way Monk hung Charlie out to dry at Wigan was a disgrace. He had played continually whilst injured as there was still a chance we could get to the play-offs. The agreement was that once we were out of the race he would be allowed to rest so he could get fit for next season. He had not been involved in any of the build up to the game and as far as he was concerned his season had ended. Monk could have played anyone that day, and in my mind the only reason he tried to call him back was to save his own skin and put the heat onto Charlie instead. What Charlie should have done is defended himself and put the truth out there rather than an untruth that was allowed to fester into a real hatred and won't be forgotten, sadly. He did put plenty of good crosses in for Burnley though but ended up on the losing side.

At the match, lots of people said hello to me and it was good to see lots of familiar faces, despite issues regarding loyal fans having a free for all in getting tickets and missing out. I'm not sure what is happening with the ticket allocations, but you must look after the fans who haven't missed a game for years as they are the ones who have supported Leeds through thick and thin. We have a fantastic worldwide fan base and we are spreading our love of Leeds and the players, which of course gets new fans on board. Please don't forget our core support Leeds, they don't deserve that! As well as selling out our allocation tonight, the game was beamed back to Elland Road as well.

The play was a lot more even today than it had been on Saturday, where we were under the cosh for the whole game. We may not have had a shot on goal until the 60-something minute tonight, but despite all the changes in the team there is still some continuity in the way we play. Burnley, for all their possession, had plenty of shots but they were off target. Borthwick-Jackson seemed to be having a mare of a game though and Grot, despite his size, was underwhelming. Game time is something they both need to improve, but I'm not sure if they can play in the under 23s. In the past you'd play for the reserves but as it's all changed now; I'm not sure how it works. The one thing I will say is that Christiansen and I seem to agree on who to sub though!

At half time someone said it was a nightmare trying to get through the fans downstairs, so I went to the furthest entrance and luckily it was fine getting down to the toilets. That familiar horrible smell of a flare soon stunk the place out though. Talking of smells, the beer in Burnley can't be up to much as the smell coming from someone in the vicinity of my seat in the stand was absolutely rank!

When Christiansen made his first sub, bringing on Sacko for Borthwick-Jackson, I couldn't believe it. Jo, Carmel and I only had a conversation in the car coming over saying that Sacko seemed to have disappeared off the face of the earth. Carmel had had a conversation with him in Austria telling him he had to pass the ball; well he certainly looked to have come back firing on all cylinders. He was fast and put in a really good low hard cross, which upped the pace of the game. Lonergan was called on to make some saves and did well to keep Burnley out. Our second sub of Hernandez became the game changer; he sent a fantastic long cross with his first touch for Sacko to run onto, who then put the ball into the net in front of the Leeds hordes and they exploded in rapture. It was hard to get any photos because of everyone celebrating wildly and standing on the seats in front of me, so I stood on the back of my seat too. I admit I may have got carried away, well who wouldn't, when all of a sudden I felt a push in my back. When it happened again I turned round to see an angry woman behind me saying she couldn't see. I said, 'sorry' and she said, 'well get down then' in an aggressive manner as I looked at her! There was no need for the aggression at all, she could have just asked nicely - it doesn't take much to show some manners. This is what happens at football games and we are all supporting the same side, so a word of advice, please drop the aggression as it wasn't needed.

As the end of the game neared I decided I'd better go down to the front of the stand to retrieve my banner, or at least be near it if the game did end after 90 minutes. But the game carried on and suddenly the Burnley fans cheered as the ref awarded them a penalty at the far end. I've no idea what for as I couldn't see but heard it was for a shirt pull. Chris Wood went to take it and I was hoping he'd miss it, but unfortunately for us he scored. Damn, as this meant we had extra time looming. Six minutes of injury time, but the drama hadn't finished there though as Leeds attacked towards us. A blatant shirt pull right in front of me saw the Leeds fans cheering as we were awarded a penalty too. I was desperate for Hernandez to score, which he certainly did, sending the celebrating Leeds

fans delirious. I checked my watch and could have sworn the ref played more than the six minutes of injury time, which unfortunately resulted in Burnley equalising once again from a free kick. It used to be 45 minutes each way and that's it but now they have injury time on top!

I decided to stay down at the front of the stand behind the goal for extra time. I couldn't believe how cold I felt standing there though after being so warm earlier. There again, having seen three degrees when I set off for work this week it shows the nights are drawing in. With the first half of extra time being even stevens, it looked like a penalty shoot-out would decide the game. A couple of our stewards stood next to me and we were astounded to see Alioski getting ready to come on. We'd made all our subs, or so we thought, as we counted and recounted who had come on previously. When Alioski did come on we hoped we hadn't done a Stuttgart when they played an ineligible player, but then decided the rules must have changed for the cup, which turned out to be the case. It was a worry at first though as none of us had any idea this was the rule. I went to get my banner at the half-time break and some Leeds fans helped me undo the ties. One shouted to a policeman in the no man's land to undo the tie nearest to him, which he did. To say the Burnley fans were at the other side of the wall near to where I was stood, it was good to see there was no abuse flung at me. I found out later that there were some Leeds fans amongst them so that probably explains it.

The second half of extra time carried on with more of the same, and Burnley came close but not close enough thank goodness, and Lonergan was determined to keep them out. Before we knew it the tie was at an end and to be decided by penalty kicks. There was a discussion at the side and Carol, who was standing behind me, said there is no way the penalties will be taken at our end and it will already be decided. Well she wasn't wrong as they headed to the other end. Leeds took the first penalty with Lasogga scoring, before Burnley took the next one. Another change to how penalties were taken happened next, as Burnley went to take the next one, then Leeds took the next two, with Hernandez first then Klich. Burnley took the next two, scoring one, but then… there was a man with his camera focused on the Leeds fans but when the second player took his penalty he turned around. He must have sub consciously known that Lonergan was going to save it! The next two penalties were in our favour as first Alioski scored and then Dallas put the winner away to send us through to the next round. Fantastic scenes for the celebrating Leeds hordes as we'd put a premiership team out of the cup!

The Leeds team came towards us clapping after they'd had their own celebration. I loved the look on Ayling's face as he was smiling and looking at us all with such adoration. He and Berardi, who'd ended up bleeding from a cut eye after another crack, led the team by example, and it is nice to see how everyone comes together as one. A few shirts were flung into the crowd but not near me unfortunately!

The buzz and singing from everyone going out after the game was brilliant and a great atmosphere. The Burnley fans had emptied the ground very quickly and didn't hang around. We got back to the car in extra quick time and were soon on our way home to Halifax. We saw the cars in front of us pulling out but couldn't see why. When we got level we saw it was a sheep trotting along the pavement having its own adventure!

We will know shortly who we will be playing in the next round, and unless it's a team we haven't played before so I can get a new ground in, I would want a home tie against one of the bigger clubs!

Back to league action on Saturday with the home game against Ipswich, we are looking at another near sell out. Whatever happens, the feel good factor is certainly back at Elland Road and long may it continue. Kristine is coming over from Norway for this game and I will be meeting her for a catch up. See you then – LUFC – Marching on Together!

IPSWICH TOWN (H) – 23RD SEPTEMBER 2017

Waking up to the sun shining made it feel like a good day for football. As Leeds United have another sell out home crowd today, it is going to be buzzing around Elland Road, and I can't wait. Talking of not being able to wait, when I picked up my granddaughter Hannah last night, I hadn't even gone inside her house when she put her things straight in the car and said we were off. Admittedly only to my house first, but ready for the game today lol! She was soooo excited to be coming to Elland Road and had also brought her spare Leeds shirt to be signed by the players. Oh dear, that means I'm not going to be going straight home after but heading for the players' entrance! A new generation of Leeds fans getting a good start in life being brought up the right way though.

After the defeat at Millwall last week, things looked up with our midweek cup game at Burnley, where we won on penalties. I was resigned to the defeat but ecstatic with the win - the different emotions of being a Leeds United fan, but I wouldn't change supporting them for the world as they have been part of my life for over 50 years. I would just like to say that I hope the two Leeds fans who got beaten up outside the Den at Millwall have recovered from their injuries. Sadly, by taking a wrong turn they ended up getting beaten up by their fans, who were baying for blood just for being in the wrong place. This is the one thing that I do not want to end up being the norm again, it's better left in the past.

I've had some proud moments this week: I appeared on the phone link to the new *Made in Leeds* phone in on Monday evening, where Josh Warrington commented on and agreed with what I said - thanks Josh. When I asked tongue in cheek whether my promotion for season tickets interview on LUTV at the end of May helped with season ticket sales, I was told it certainly did and I should ask for commission next time! And my comment about getting a rollicking off my hubby for getting a £19 phone bill for ringing the Leeds United ticket office was picked up. This ended up with the announcement yesterday that the phone number was changing to 0371 334 1992 instead of 0871 so no more ripping off the fans. Excellent things happening at the club and shows they are listening to fans.

I was supposed to be meeting Kristine from Norway, but unfortunately due to an illness in her family she hasn't made it to the game today and my good wishes go to her and a speedy recovery to her family member. I did meet some other Norwegians in the Peacock though, along with a West

Coast White from the USA. With it being a full house this normally means lots of our overseas fans attending, including our Irish fans as we followed a car from Ireland off the M621. We went into the ground in good time today and for once there were no queues. It was possible many were still in the fans' zone and as we passed it 'Marching on Together' was blaring out over the speakers.

We had a catch up with Susan, Debbie and James before Hannah went to our seats and I stayed lower down the Kop ready to take my photos. I then saw Trampas lower down so went down to have a chat and a catch up. I stayed there initially as the team came out as it was closer for the photos.

The team today were: Wiedwald, Ayling, Anita, Cooper (back from injury), Shaughnessy, O'Kane, Phillips, Saiz, Alioski, Lasogga and Hernandez. Subs were: Berardi for Anita (60), Dallas for Hernandez (76) and Grot for Lasogga (86). Leeds won 3-2 with goals from Lasogga (13), Philips (32) and a Bialkowski own goal (67). Ipswich scorers were McGoldrick (30) and Garner (71). Attendance was 34,002 including 693 Ipswich fans.

Leeds started off brightly, attacking the South Stand, as the Leeds fans were in full voice. We put pressure on Ipswich, and within 13 minutes we were ahead. Shaughnessy put a great through ball to Lasogga and I was poised to take that perfect photo, only for fans to jump up in front of me as he put the ball into the net! Still that was a good start to the game. We didn't really build on this as Ipswich were still in the game and the majority of it was end to end. When Ipswich won a free kick to the left of the goal it was a small push on their player, who went down like a sack of spuds! It was a soft free kick to give away, which then resulted in an equaliser when their player had a free header to put the ball into the left-hand corner. That was a disappointment but no sooner had the Ipswich fans started celebrating then Phillips ran onto the ball in their penalty area, got the ball round the keeper and put it into the net to restore our lead. That was a welcome goal within a minute, to keep us in front on the day. We had a great chance to go further into the lead when Saiz got the ball in space at the edge of the box and I expected him to blast it into the net, but he took too long so the chance went. I wondered where Anita had been when Ipswich scored, but he certainly prevented them getting a second equaliser just before the break when he was on the near post to head the ball off the line. Phew!

The second half saw Leeds head into it with the one-goal cushion, and we didn't have it all our way. With our defence doing some great passing to each other and also using our sweeper keeper, at times this got too close for comfort. Wiedwald went haring down the left-hand side and got to the ball first with one Ipswich attack. Rather than blast the ball out for a throw in, he played a skilful pass around their player and to one of our players. We weren't so lucky at other times as Ipswich came very close and won the ball to put us under pressure. We were still coming out of defence and putting in some great crosses, which Saiz and Alioski were running onto, although it was a shame we didn't have a go with a first-time ball a couple of times. By taking too long we looked as if we were trying to walk the ball into the net, giving Ipswich time to get back and stop us. That first-time shot would have caught them unawares. All was not lost though, and when

Hernandez sent a corner over from the left-hand side the ball ended up in the net courtesy of an own goal. I couldn't see what happened but with the Leeds fans singing 'it's your keeper's fault' I assumed he dropped the ball and it went over the line. Unfortunately, today saw the scoreboard out of action so I'd no idea how long was left. If we thought having a 3-1 lead meant it was game over, we were sadly wrong. Ipswich attacked the far goal and, although Wiedwald saved the first shot, the ball went straight to an Ipswich player who put it into the net and clawed back a second goal. As it was, there was approximately 20 minutes to play plus injury time as Ipswich put up a fight to get an equaliser. Leeds kept breaking away with some great moves, although the finishes didn't match as we took one pass too many before shooting.

We managed to hold on and keep our place at the top of the league, and at the end of the day all that counts is that we got a win and another three points. I thought we did enough to win the game though, and it was the complete opposite of the Millwall game where we were under the cosh for 90 minutes. One thing I like about Christiansen is that he always goes onto the pitch at the end of the game to thank everyone but then leaves and lets the team receive the plaudits.

In the ladies at the end of the game there were some women who had no idea how the queuing works. There are two doors and we always queue half and half with each queue using the cubicles on one side and two in the middle. Now this has worked every game for years and years, but somehow when we get a lot of new people attending we get some irate women for whom common sense goes out of the window. What I don't expect to see is a female thinking it is alright to barge into another Leeds fan and assault her (my daughter) to prove some point as she didn't think our queue should take precedence. It was also someone old enough to know better. This is out of order and as with the women who thought it was okay to push me in the back twice at Burnley, this is not what being Leeds is all about! No one is perfect but a little give and take and knowing how things work can go a long way, there is no need to react aggressively.

Hannah and I headed for the players' entrance and I was surprised that the barriers weren't already up, although it didn't take long before they were. I saw the Irish lads wearing their hats with badges on so I got their photos. It was nice seeing the Galway and Portsmouth Whites and a big thank you for my chocolates and badge. I'd already caught sight of their hats in the West Stand and taken a photo. When Lasogga came out it was good to hear that his wife had given birth to a little girl yesterday, and I asked him in German if it was a girl or a boy. Congratulations to them both. There were a few fans there as well as Hannah waiting to see Saiz, and it was nice to see them all so happy once he'd signed autographs and had some photos taken. A funny thing happened just before Saiz got there, as Eunan O'Kane was just coming to where we were. One girl was getting really excited to see Eunan, and as she went to get a selfie I heard another women laugh and say it was his wife. I wasn't quick enough to get a photo though! As we were leaving I didn't see Pontus pass us, but Hannah saw him. Fans shouted to him, but he didn't hang around and ran up the steps to the Fullerton Park area. Hopefully his injury isn't too bad then!

Some fans don't seem to have been happy with the performance today, but I'm happy we got the three points. When I think of all the times in recent years that we have had a full house and found the team didn't turn up at all, I think we have come on leaps and bounds. I'm proud of how far we have come, and yes there will be ups and downs along the way, but we have to just 'Keep Fighting!' I'll take each game as it comes and we have another couple of big ones with Cardiff and Sheffield Wednesday to contend with. Time will tell how we do, but I'm going for a good couple of games going our way.

Next weekend sees the practice session of singing the old Leeds songs from the terraces. I'm just in the process of rearranging and updating the words ready for it and am looking forward to the run through. Prior to this is the LUST AGM so it is going to be a busy weekend. See you there – LUFC – Marching on Together!

CARDIFF CITY (A) – 26TH SEPTEMBER 2017

You know the feeling when you are trying to help another Leeds fan get in touch with someone you know without success? I tried to ring the number only for it to be unattainable, oh dear. Mmm, that had alarm bells ringing, especially when I realised all the texts I'd sent to the 'new' number hadn't had an answer! I thought I'd messed up when I put the new number into my phone in one of those moments when you do stupid things, but, as I found out later on in the evening, it wasn't my fault. After giving me the new phone number someone else had recommended, he ended up keeping his old number. Unfortunately I'd never been told this, but at least all's well that ends well, as I now have the correct number in my phone and the Leeds fan I tried to help was successful in getting sorted out!

It was going to be one of those games where I was relying on others, and my grateful thanks once again go to the people who know who they are.

The team today were: Wiedwald, Ayling, Jansson, Berardi, Cooper, Roofe, Dallas, Phillips, Hernandez, Alioski and Klich. Subs were: Pennington for Hernandez (45), Vieira for Klich (67) and Grot for Alioski (62). Attendance was 27,160 including approximately 2,674 Leeds fans. Leeds lost 3-1 with Roofe (67) scoring the Leeds goal, meaning we lost the top spot. Cooper was sent off just before half time for a second bookable offence.

It was good to get there in time for kick-off, so I managed to put my banner up before finding my seat. On our way into the ground it was nice to be treated with respect by the female stewards, who were looking for unacceptable slogans on any flags but they agreed Sue and I were respectable!! There were loads of Leeds fans still arriving after kick-off as we found our seats at the start of the game. I hadn't realised we were up against Warnock, our ex-manager, and Bamba, our ex-player, until the night. For the first twenty minutes or so Leeds saw plenty of the ball and things were quiet even on the pitch. The ref up to that time hadn't been too bad, but then it was as if someone whispered in his ear and he gave us absolutely nothing, which meant Cardiff went from strength to strength. Their first goal came from a mistake by us though. Jansson got the ball and instead of turning and going forward he passed the ball back to Wiedwald, who passed it straight back to Jansson. He then passed the ball out to the wing to Klich, who had the ball covered until he slipped and Cardiff took full advantage. With their fast counter attack, they had the ball in the net on the half hour point, giving them the lead.

We were struggling to contain Cardiff, making it look like our team selection was wrong. The ref surpassed himself when he gave a free kick to Cardiff but didn't send their player off the pitch after treatment. He was more interested in giving our players a ticking off, and even though they pointed out that their player needed to go off, he totally ignored them. Someone mentioned later on that as he booked our player a new rule meant he could stay on the pitch, not something I had heard of. Hopefully someone else will confirm whether this is the case but it wouldn't surprise me as 'rules' seem to get broken many times. A couple of times the reaction of their fans made the linesman flag for a free kick. After a short while Cardiff attacked us again, leaving us at sixes and sevens as their player put a hard shot past Wiedwald from the edge of the box. To cap it all just before half time we found ourselves down to 10 men as Cooper tackled their player on the far side and was sent off for a second bookable offence. That knocked the stuffing out of us. Just before half time we thought they'd got a third goal when the ball hit the back of the net, but it was disallowed for offside. Going in at half time two goals down wasn't good though.

During the break it was nice to catch up with Caerwyn, one of our fans from South Wales, and Simon, who'd come up from Cornwall for the game. I received lots of nice comments about my blog from fans and thank you to everyone who took the time to speak to me about it. I want to say a big thank you to Dylan and his son Lucas for their support in buying one of my books. Enjoy the read and I look forward to receiving feedback in due course. I also received feedback from my second book, *Once a Leeds fan, always a Leeds fan,* which was read by another of our fans and he'd really enjoyed it. As usual all comments are appreciated.

Immediately at the start of the second half Pennington was brought on in place of Hernandez to shore up our defence, with Cooper getting sent off. Before long though we were three goals down and it was game over.

Leeds didn't give up though and we started to play better with 10 men than 11. As the Cardiff fans celebrated with top of the league chants, because they had been in third place in the top of table clash (it's been a long time since we could say that), the Leeds fans came into their own showing their loyalty and support for getting behind the team. A constant rendition of 'we all love Leeds' over and over again kept going up a notch, and eventually the Cardiff fans sat down and you couldn't hear them at all. As play stopped after a foul, a rendition of 'Marching on Together' rang out in full voice from the Leeds fans who then carried on where they left off with 'we all love Leeds' until the end of the game. In between all of this, Roofe scored a goal to pull one back for us and although we thought there would be a revival and aspiration for a draw, sadly it wasn't to be.

It was a disappointing result tonight; there is no getting away from it, and I thought Christiansen may have learnt from the Millwall game. I appreciate he wants to play football but the team selection didn't work in that respect. We were bullied out of the game and again in my opinion Vieira should have been on from the start to add that bit of steel into the midfield. I haven't been impressed with Grot so far and after he came on as sub I am still not impressed with him. That said, they should be proud of the support they got from the Leeds fans today, and it was good to see Christiansen join the players in clapping us at the end of the game.

It will be a late homecoming for lots of fans and especially harder for those of us who are back at work the next morning. It will not be as far for all our Welsh fans and those who don't live too far away though. Luckily I was able to sleep both going and coming back, but I know that plenty of black coffee will be required to keep me going.

Saturday sees the Trust AGM before the singing practice of all the old Leeds songs with a group of Leeds fans. If you know of any singers that should be involved there may be space for them, but I will make no promises and they'd need to contact me ASAP if interested.

Sheffield Wednesday away on Sunday beckons, so we have to bounce back. Christiansen will have to reflect on what hasn't worked away from home for us. It's been a breath of fresh air enjoying the season so far, so the result is a bit of a downer, but there will be another good following of Leeds fans at Hillsborough so we need to turn it around - and fast. The international break is around the corner once again, which causes further disruption at the wrong time and is one thing we could do without! Forever and ever, we'll follow our team; we're Leeds United we rule supreme. See you there – LUFC – Marching on Together!

CHAPTER 4 – OCTOBER 2017

SHEFFIELD WEDNESDAY (A) – 1ST OCTOBER 2017

Yesterday saw us with some free time as the game is tomorrow, so I went to the Leeds United Supporters' Trust meeting first and then headed to join other fans for our singing practice. Unfortunately because of the latter I had to leave the AGM before Allan Clarke spoke, which was a shame. Allan is still as passionate about Leeds United as us fans, and it is great to listen to him as I did the last time at an LFU meeting. Our singing practice went really well with a group of Leeds fans and hopefully our recording of all the old Leeds songs and some of the later ones from the terraces will be finished soon.

An early kick-off beckoned for the rearranged game due to Sky, and Leeds had sold out their allocation of approximately 4,600 in minutes again. Unfortunately some of our loyal fans were left wanting for tickets due to the influx of fans clamouring for them. Billy's bar was open for bacon sarnies before we set off for the game. When our coach arrived for the police escort, we pulled up behind a Tetley's coach. All of a sudden both coaches started moving and then a group of fans ran alongside us both chasing the other coach! It did look funny, but at least they were lucky they weren't being left behind as they were only moving us further up the road. Our police escort was very good, especially when all the traffic was stopped for us and we drove on the wrong side of the road past everyone. When we arrived at the ground I was surprised to find we were dropped off

outside the turnstiles and our coaches were going to be there when we came out. That was good though, as normally we have quite a walk, which is an issue for some of us. Here, they were usually pretty good to our disabled fans though, who were normally taken on a coach to and from the ground.

The first thing I noticed was a fence had been put up between the home turnstiles and ours outside the Leppings Lane entrance. Having seen a video recently of the Sheffield Utd fans and Wednesday fans posturing at each other, I reckoned that was why - to separate the two sets of fans. As soon as I got in I went to the front of the stand to hang my banner up, and what I can say other than a steward was really helpful and friendly, which was good to see.

The team today were: Wiedwald, Ayling, Jansson, Pennington, Berardi, Phillips, O'Kane, Alioski, Saiz,

Lasogga and Roofe. Subs were: Sacko for Alioski (62), Hernandez for Roofe (62) and Dallas for Jansson (71) who went off injured with a shoulder injury. Leeds lost the game 3-0 and attendance was 27,972 including 4,600 Leeds fans.

Everyone was in high spirits even though we'd had a couple of hard away games at Millwall and Cardiff. The Sheffield Wednesday message boards had been in melt down due to playing us, as they hadn't had such a good start to the season. I couldn't tell you where they were in the table or how they'd played or anything, as I don't take any notice of the opposition, apart from knowing Tom Lees still played for them! The one thing I found I couldn't tweet on this week, because of my paranoia that when I say we'll win we lose, was LUFC's tweet which said that the last time we'd played them there we'd won 2-0. Maybe I had a premonition! A big thank you to Nigel from the White Rose LUSC for his support in buying my book and enjoy the read! I was glad to catch up with Cayne and his dad Lee as it was Cayne's first away game today.

In the first 20 minutes of the game it was all Leeds, and we really should have put the game to bed in that time. We had a couple of clear chances and my thoughts were that we had to take our chances when they were there. Saiz had a great run and his cross saw Alioski head it into the side netting. It's a shame it wasn't on target as it deserved a goal. At that time, I felt that Wednesday were there for the taking as they didn't seem to have much confidence. I can't say what really changed the play, but all of a sudden Wednesday upped their game and scored. First Jansson then another of our players missed the ball as their player beat Wiedwald to score their first. That was just the tonic that Wednesday needed, and they became a different side to the one I'd seen in the opening minutes. I don't really think Leeds were in the game much after that, and we actually made them look good. The goal had given them confidence and belief and we were at sixes and sevens with our players clashing a couple of times as they went for the same ball. Passes were going short or astray and collectively were looking very poor. As the Wednesday fans chanted 'Leeds are falling apart again' and 'We all hate Leeds scum,' it was with great satisfaction that we saw them shut straight up and deflate when the Leeds fans, with their gallows humour again, sang the same back at them.

As they scored their second goal before half time, many Leeds fans were getting agitated. From my point of view, we were getting overrun in midfield once again, and it looked like lessons had not been learned from our last two away defeats. One suggestion I would like to make to Thomas Christiansen is that he learns from Don Revie. Don would always have one of his colleagues sitting in the stand with the fans. As they were higher up than the side of the pitch they were able to see from a different perspective why things were not working on the pitch and were able to make important changes. The fans around me could all see that we needed to bolster midfield because Wednesday were bypassing them and putting constant pressure on the back four and goalie. Also, we became our own worst enemies by constantly passing back to Wiedwald to enable him to play out from the back; we were putting more and more pressure on our defence. The best form of defence is attack, so by keeping possession going forward we would keep the ball away from the opposition. When one attack came in and they shot at Wiedwald in front of us he palmed the ball away when others around me were shouting he should have caught it. I just thought he maybe wanted to make sure he got the ball away. I really felt that we should have changed our shape in the first half but we didn't, continuing with the same formation, which meant that Wednesday carried on running rings around us.

At half time it was nice to catch up with Tim, who was one of my local Leeds fans I went around with in the seventies. We go back a long way as Leeds fans, and hearing that he'd had some bad news with his best friend's family, my heart goes out to them all. That's what Leeds fans do: support other Leeds fans when needed.

There were no changes at the start of the second half, so we carried on where we left off at half time - on the back foot. We were crying out for Christiansen to change things around, especially as he said he would have a few game plans. Don't get me wrong, I like him very much and what he is trying to achieve, but it seems that he has not learnt from the last two away defeats, even though he changed the personnel. Just before he made his two subs on 62 minutes, Leeds had won a corner on the left-hand side to us. When Alioski hit it so hard it went flying past the goal and out at the other side for a goal kick, everyone groaned. My initial thoughts were why did he hit it so hard, and then I realised a sub was coming on. I knew then that Alioski was going off, which proved to be the case. Was that a reaction from him, knowing he was being subbed?

We started off playing brighter and looked more up for the game and we started to put pressure on Wednesday. Shortly after the subs though, Jansson went down injured with his shoulder and ended up going off on a stretcher, which was all we needed. It was a case of s**t or bust then as Dallas was brought on. Unfortunately we never really got going after that, and to cap it all a bad pass from O'Kane when trying to play out from the back meant Wednesday got hold of the ball and scored a third. They hit the post and Wiedwald made two cracking saves before that, otherwise they'd have slaughtered us! It was a bad day at the office today and a very quiet fan base. After the support shown at Cardiff it was a little disappointing that we didn't sing as much, but there again there is only so much some fans can take. There were some boos from fans at the end, although that isn't something I did and I stayed until the bitter end despite fans from both sides disappearing to the exits. On reaching the crossroads to the turnstiles where the Wednesday fans were coming out, we had to walk in between them and the police to get across to our coaches. At least it was placid enough thank goodness. We now have no game next week due to another International break, although it looks like Jansson will miss out after being called up for Sweden because he was stretchered off during the game with a shoulder injury.

I feel that we were very poor collectively as a team today. I know many fans are blaming Wiedwald, saying that he isn't strong enough in his area. With the way we play out from the back, we need our midfield to take the strain and keep the ball more up front. We spend so much time going back towards him that we are constantly putting Wiedwald under pressure, so no wonder it looks bad from a fan's perspective. Personally, I do think we have to work from the back, but we also need to keep going forwards more rather than backwards so much. We also need to field a stronger midfield away from home and have a different formation. Again, I do feel Christiansen is trying to play attacking football, especially on the break, but that seems to be playing into the hands of the opposition. We cannot afford to keep on doing this and have to have a different way of freezing out the opposition, and if it means an extra man in the midfield, and I don't mean Roofe or Alioski on the wing, then so be it!

After the break we have Reading at home to look forward to, plus Bristol City away and Leicester in the next round of the Carabao Cup. Let's hope the rest does us good, and if Christiansen wants to send one of his coaches in to the away stand with us fans, he would definitely see a different game to what he sees pitch side. It may help him see what we see! See you then – LUFC – Marching on Together!

READING (H) – 14TH OCTOBER 2017

My new book *The Sleeping Giant Awakens, Leeds United Season 2016-17* is in the final stages. Having got the draft back for proofreading yesterday, I was doing this late into the night and this morning, which meant that the early start for Elland Road didn't happen. Falling asleep all the time didn't help though! Having only got the last part to finish before sending it back to my publisher means that the book will be at the printers shortly, so exciting times ahead once again, and more good news is that it will also be available in the club shop!

With my daughter Danielle and granddaughter Hannah, we ended up getting to Elland Road at 2.25pm, so we went straight into the ground, and getting there late though meant that I missed the build-up to the game.

Not getting to the Peacock meant I missed my friends Sue and Paul, plus Dylan Waugh, Martin Hywood and family, so sorry I didn't make it there. My first port of call was the Kop bar, as I'd arranged to meet a Leeds fan through Gaz, who wanted my book *Follow Me and Leeds United*. As it was, I recognised him straight away so I must have bumped into him on my travels, so thanks for the support Mal it is appreciated. I then spoke to some of the Kippax lads about the song recordings to see if any were singers before chatting to some of the Halifax lads. As I was going into the stand I spoke to a woman who enjoys reading my blogs. She told me she bought my first book and her Burnley fan husband had read it and said it was exactly how it was back then. Thanks for the compliment! Despite getting there late, there were still loads of fans who I knew saying hello.

Talking about the old songs, we are very close to getting our recording day sorted, so I'm looking forward to that, especially as our singing practice went really well recently. We will not remember every song and some cannot be included for obvious reasons, but if anyone wishes to contribute to any of the songs please get in touch to be added to the group. If we don't already have it on our list you will be accredited with any you tell us about. We have set up a Facebook page called 'Leeds United we'll support you evermore' for anyone who has anything to add.

The team today were: Lonergan, Ayling, Berardi, Cooper, Jansson, O'Kane, Phillips, Hernandez, Roofe, Lasogga and Saiz. Subs were: Sacko for Roofe (68), Grot for Lasogga (77) and Dallas for Berardi (89). Leeds lost 1-0 with ex-loanee Barrow scoring for Reading. Attendance was 33,900 including 434 Reading fans.

I was listening to BBC Radio Leeds on the way into the game, and on hearing that Wiedwald had been dropped for the game I was disappointed. My reasons being that he had become a scapegoat for our latest defeat at Sheffield Wednesday. It was a collective team defeat and for the first goal I still maintain the two defenders in front of him should have cleared the ball before it got to him. He made two great saves to stop Wednesday getting more goals, which seems to have by-passed many. We were trying to play a certain way, but the players in front of him had

started passing back so much that we found ourselves under more and more pressure. Now fans are entitled to their opinion and I may be in the minority, but I would have maintained status quo today and kept him in goal. After proofreading my latest book, the parallels from last season at this time are frankly uncanny.

I have nothing against Lonergan and he did okay today, making one really great save in the second half, but our playing out from the back was very poor, again collectively. We also resorted to the long ball with goal kicks that went straight to their players at the other end, where Reading started an attack once again. I didn't pinpoint anything specific today as I did when I saw our midfield getting overrun in the defeats of late, but we didn't look very good at all in the first half. Hearing boos from the crowd near us after 10 minutes was a little too early in my opinion because getting behind the team could have improved their play. I know we were still making the same mistakes further up the field, which was hard for some fans to take, but personally I was watching closely as to how we would play without having the sweeper keeper to play out from the back. Saiz was the only one who really stood out for me though.

The sell-out crowd once again were expecting a better performance, but even though we've got off to such a good start this season and done better than we dared hope it isn't going to be a quick fix. It will take time and we have to be patient. I realise patience is thin with many fans, which is their choice, but to turn things around on the pitch will take longer than the first few weeks of the season. This is a long-term project, and whilst the club are looking at the play-offs I still maintain we need to aspire for automatic promotion this year. Playing for the shirt is a must, but I know this will not happen overnight. In the first half I can't really remember us putting their goalie under any pressure, and the crowd were pretty quiet, which was not surprising really. The ref as usual started booking our players very quickly, and eventually when he gave us a free kick the crowd showed their sarcasm by cheering loudly. He surpassed himself when Reading got a free kick for offside and it was taken in our half - what on earth was going on?

At half time I was downstairs with Carole, Ashley, Margaret and Keith behind the betting area when a Leeds fan asked for a £10 bet on Lasogga to score! We had a laugh with him but said he'd lose his money, but I'd be happy to take it!

I noticed more in the second half that O'Kane was playing very deep and had been involved in a lot of the play in the first half, picking up balls across the back four I think. This meant that Phillips was playing in the midfield with Hernandez and Roofe with Saiz further forward. I don't feel this had the desired effect as Phillips needed more support alongside him to make the midfield work. The second half carried on with more of the same, but things did brighten up a little when Sacko was brought on, especially as he kept getting lots of space down the wing as we started attacking in the last 20 minutes. And things got slightly better still with Grot coming on, as the other players upped their game, but this wasn't because of Grot. I don't know how it happened as we had been on the attack, but all of a sudden Reading went forwards toward the South Stand, where Barrow put the ball into the net to put them into the lead. We should have got a point out of the game in the final minutes when Saiz was brought down in the area and the ref pointed to the spot. As I wondered who our penalty taker would be, I saw Hernandez had hold of the ball. I watched as O'Kane hovered as if to say he should be taking the penalty, but then he walked away. I blame the lad who stands behind us in the Kop for the penalty miss! As Hernandez went to take it, he told us where he was going to put the ball and he was going to miss. I said it was his fault the goalie saved it, but it was a very soft penalty to be frank, with not a lot of power behind it. I suppose I felt resigned to things not going our way by the end of the game, and on the whole it was a very poor performance. We didn't put enough pressure on their goal, and whilst we did get some shots in they were way off target. It was good to see the scoreboard back in action today, but I don't like the fact that it doesn't show the score.

It is back to the drawing board for Christiansen. Whilst we need the spine of the team and stability within the club, we have got to be able to change things around, which unfortunately hasn't been good of late. Whilst other fans are already writing games off, I will always take each game as it comes. Bristol away next week with a Friday game against Sheffield United the following week and the Carabao Cup game at Leicester in between will all be a test as to whether we can change things. Our best form of defence is attack and it is what got us through the first few games when we remained unbeaten. Resorting to type by passing back to the goalie and playing deep, along with other clubs sussing us out, has impacted on us greatly. Some Leeds fans from Dublin

were in high spirits at Billy's statue after the game as we waited for my sister and her grandson to turn up. It was also nice to see Terje from Norway there too.

I just want to mention that last week I was doing some website training with Simon O'Rourke and his skills and knowledge are absolutely fantastic, which were a great benefit to me. As he'd had to rearrange the venue at the last minute, we headed to the White Rose so we had WIFI access before heading to the Peacock. As usual I had my Leeds shirt on when I saw someone walk past us who I recognised. With that, he came back to ask if it was me and tell me that he reads my blog all the time. I knew Peter's face straight away and it's nice when fans come for a chat.

The other good news last week was that Elland Road is now an Asset of Community Value and well done to the Leeds United Supporters' Trust for achieving this. After Radrizzani bought Elland Road back, this news and the plans for the Matthew Murray site and bringing the training facilities back to Leeds from Thorpe Arch, it is good to see all the things going on in the background. Let's hope it won't be long for the team to get back to winning ways and give us hope for the future. See you at Bristol – LUFC – Marching on Together!

BRISTOL CITY (A) – 21ST OCTOBER 2017

I can't believe how quick my new book *The Sleeping Giant Awakens, Leeds United 2016-17* has appeared on Amazon, and it will be in the Leeds shop at the end of the month! Great stuff! As usual I will be getting a quota to sell and will autograph copies for those who want them through me. I always carry one copy of each of my books with me to games so if anyone wants to meet up please let me know.

As I was getting cash out of the machine last night, I heard a voice behind me saying someone is trying to attract your attention. There was no way I was taking my eyes off my card and money as I feared a scam, so stuffed my money into my bag quickly. As I turned around to leave, the voice behind me said again that someone in the car next to me was trying to catch my attention. I did turn around this time and there was a young lad shouting Leeds, Leeds, Leeds to me, then his dad appeared out of the shop shouting Leeds to me too – oops, sorry lads! As usual, though, Leeds fans are everywhere.

We weren't leaving Leeds until 8am so it was a normal wake up call at 6.30am before getting to Leeds for the coach. The weather was fine but we would be heading into storm Brian in Bristol, so I wasn't looking forward to the damp and cold. I'd forgotten Sue wouldn't be travelling with me today so had a seat to myself. Before I left home I'd tweeted and put on Facebook 'come on Leeds, three points today'. I also tweeted Leeds to say they could do it and to believe. With so many fans writing us off already with a defeat, I had my bolshie head on, and no we wouldn't get beaten; we would have our backs to the wall, we would battle and must believe. As Elvis Presley came on the radio singing I just can't help believing, I wondered if that was a good omen for today, and I would know by 5pm.

We stopped off in Gloucester and I was one of the first off the coach into the pub. What I will say is don't ever ask me to get any drinks in, because half of the coach got served before me as somehow I always end up invisible at the bar! Apparently, they were six staff down, who'd all phoned in ill, and reinforcements had not yet arrived. The girl who eventually served me had noticed the people who I knew needed to be served in front of me, which was right, but I still don't know how everyone else from our coach got in front of me though. Instead of queuing again I used the Wetherspoon app and couldn't believe it when they apologised for the delay! I got my food within 10 minutes so no delay - and I told them so.

A group of us had a good chat in the pub about the team and what we reckoned would happen today and I also had a catch up with Mick Hewitt. We have 18th November pencilled in for our song recording, and I'm looking forward to it immensely. The practice went really well and it will be good to finalise our ambitions of getting the CD/DVD done in good time. I was on a Facebook thread the other week on one of the Leeds groups, but for the life of me cannot remember which one. The thread was about our old sings and I was going to get in touch with a couple on there to see if there were any songs I'd forgotten to include. If anyone can remember being part of this please let me know as I'd be happy to speak further on this.

We arrived at the ground 20 minutes before kick-off and ended up getting off the coach a few at a time as we were stuck in traffic. As I got through the security lines, I was looking for entrance 38 so ended up at the far end of the terrace. After asking our steward where the entrance was it

turned out that it was the area inside the ground, not the turnstile entrance number – doh! As I queued up, it was getting closer and closer to kick-off, and I suddenly saw some of our fans going mad who'd already got into the ground. It turned out that the turnstile was broken and in the end fans were climbing over it. I wasn't looking forward to climbing over it, but luckily the one at the other side was letting fans through so I went through there. If I'd have gone in the first turnstile I'd come to when arriving at the ground I'd have been at the right place, but instead I had to walk right back to the other end. When I got into the stand I saw that all the Leeds flags had been placed at the front instead of the back, so I put mine up and decided to stay there just to the right of the goal as there were spaces.

The team today were: Lonergan, Ayling, Berardi, Cooper, Vieira, Phillips, O'Kane, Lasogga, Alioski, Saiz and Pennington. Subs were: Sacko for Alioski (81), Anita for Saiz (83) and Grot for Lasogga (90). Leeds won 3-0 with two goals for Saiz (4, 14) and one from Lasogga (67). Attendance was 24,435 including 3,717 Leeds fans, giving Bristol their highest attendance of the season. Dallas had pulled out of the squad after his mother died and condolences are sent to Stuart Dallas and his family at this sad time.

The swirling wind and fine rain started more or less as soon as we kicked off, so it was going to be a battle against the weather too, but I thought that would work in our favour as it would be a backs-to-the-wall game. Within five minutes Leeds were in the lead with a long-range shot from Saiz that flew into the net with a deflection at the far side of the ground. The celebrating

Leeds fans were in good voice and the early goal did everyone the world of good. It wasn't much later before Saiz scored a second, sending everyone wild. 'Leeds, Leeds are falling apart again' had the Leeds fans showing their gallows humour once more. Bristol never gave up though and were seeing plenty of the ball. They were a threat, but Leeds dealt with it. Having Vieira back in midfield alongside Phillips and O'Kane was what I thought we needed to shore it up, and it certainly worked. Their first shot on goal was fumbled by Lonergan but he stood tall after that. I felt quite calm for the majority of the game, but as it got near half time I just wanted to ensure Bristol didn't score, as I felt it was vital they didn't get back into the game. We saw fantastic support from the Leeds fans, although when we scored the dreaded smoke bombs appeared on the pitch - a blue and a yellow one. After the second goal one was thrown and ended up underneath my flag, and I was glad when their steward got it away from there.

At half time I said to some young kids that I would take their photo. Bless them, they said hang on a minute and all took their jackets off to show their Leeds shirts. I'm proud of you lads, especially as you were doing the Leeds salute. Obviously you've been brought up correctly! I tried finding Sue without success and went downstairs to try and find the toilets. As I headed towards the middle of the stand I thought there was no way I was getting through there as the singing hordes of Leeds fans were going mad. As I came back up into the concourse I could smell the smoke, and just as I reached the door, someone let off a massive 'bomb'. Sorry but whoever let that off in the middle of a crowd of fans really needs their head testing. My nervous disposition meant the word 's**t' came out of my mouth as I jumped out of my skin. I wasn't the only one, as I went down the stairs I saw a man with his crying child.

The second half saw Leeds come out and attack our end. The Leeds fans sang for the whole game and, despite the blustery conditions, the team continued where they left off. They played as a team and were backing each other up, even though at times we were chasing shadows as Bristol got past us. They never gave up, which is all that is asked of them, and kept fighting, which gave us a chance. When Phillips took a corner, the ball came to Lasogga in the box to head home for our third goal and send us all into raptures once again. They were absolute fantastic scenes on the terraces from the celebrating Leeds fans, with many who probably couldn't believe the score. I knew we could do it! I just wanted us to see the game out without giving them a goal. Around the 80-minute mark there was an altercation in the middle of the park nearer to the bench than us. I missed what happened and even after seeing videos of it afterwards, saw their player square up to Berardi, who stood his ground. Some said Berardi had nutted him, others said there was no contact, and I couldn't make my mind up about what happened as he was sent off. I thought their player was play acting and the next thing he got sent off too once he'd been treated for his 'injury'! There was lots of jostling by the tunnel and then I thought something had kicked off in there as someone went running down it. I felt better knowing they'd lost a man too because despite us having a three goal lead I didn't want Bristol to score. As I was getting my flag untied, a Bristol

Steward who had been having a good look at it earlier helped me so a big thank you to him for the assistance.

As it was, we saw the game out to get the win and the three points. Look what happens when they believe in themselves and the fans get behind them. Lots of happy fans were singing the Vieira song as we went out of the ground. I saw some young lads without shirts on as the police headed towards them, although I didn't see anything untoward happen. At least they carried on up the road with the rest of us. I was surprised that there wasn't a welcoming committee of Bristol fans, as there has been in the past, but there again the ground had emptied very quickly! It was raining very finely on the way back to the coach, and it was sad seeing our exhausted disabled fans making their way back. With the weather being so bad, waiting at the end of the road wasn't a good idea. We were soaked by the time we got back to the coach and I was glad I'd brought some hot water with me for a drink. I took my wet jacket off and I had left my big jacket on the coach so was able to keep warm for most of the journey. By the time we reached Tamworth services, along with the Harrogate and Keighley whites, I was glad to get a Costa to warm me up.

The bad weather started to kick in as we reached Sheffield, and despite the weight of the coach it felt a little too precarious for me going over the viaduct. I was glad to get over it quickly and in one piece. Apart from having to negotiate a flood near hell fire cross roads, I got home safely and was back in good time. My daughter Dani then showed me the videos of the team having to make two attempts to land at Leeds Bradford airport after flying to the game. I'm glad they arrived safely and it was funny watching them, but I'd blame whoever decided they would fly! There again it is probably because of the Josh Warrington fight tonight and maybe there are more people than just Berardi heading to watch him. Good luck Josh.

We have a busy week with the visit to Leicester in the next round of the Carabao Cup and the Sheffield United home game next Friday. As I've said before, let's just play to our strengths and enjoy ourselves and let the other teams worry about us. Hitting them before they have woken up was brilliant! See you then – LUFC – Marching on Together!

LEICESTER CITY (A), CARABAO CUP – 24TH OCTOBER 2017

It was a late set-off today but it ended up being even later as the coach we were travelling on had broken down earlier in the day, so we had to wait for it to get back on the road to take us to the game. Despite this and the traffic being quite heavy, we arrived at the ground just before kick-off. A policeman said hello as soon as I got off the coach, and the steward who searched me was very pleasant too. When I said I was carrying my books, she said, 'would I be reading them during the game?' I said, 'no I'm an author with my fourth Leeds book coming out', and she said she would look out for them.

After a quick trip to the ladies, my first sight was the back of a fella in one of the cubicles - at least shut the door please! Then another fella came out of another cubicle. I said, 'for crying out loud use your own loos.' Saying that, I double checked on my way out that I had indeed gone into the ladies just to make sure I wasn't in the wrong, having made that mistake at Donny once. I went into the opening in front of the ladies' sign instead of behind it, and as I got further in I thought something didn't look right. A steward came chasing after me and escorted me out, but luckily for me I didn't see any embarrassing scenes!

Although we were going to Leicester's new ground, the King Power Stadium, I had always liked going to Filbert Street as we always took loads of fans. One memory I have was walking to a pub that some other Leeds fans couldn't get in to, and the bouncers just stood aside to let us in. I got a great cheer from some of the Halifax lads when I got in. Big Brian from Halifax (number 13), aka Uncle Buck to my kids and granddaughters and Godfather to my youngest daughter Emily, died a couple of years ago, but he's never far from our thoughts, RIP. Another memory I have is of a few of us girls queuing up to get into the boy's entrance and the police chucking lads younger than us out of the queue. They told the coppers we were older than them, but they weren't believed as we were allowed to stay where we were and got in.

The team today saw some major changes and included Wiedwald, Anita, Jansson, Shaughnessy, Roofe, Hernandez, Phillips, Grot, Borthwick-Jackson, Cibicki and Klich. Subs were: Ayling for Borthwick-Jackson 45, Sacko for Cibicki 65 and Vieira for Phillips 72. Leeds lost 3-1 with Hernandez scoring for Leeds (26). Attendance was a sellout crowd for Leicester of 31,516 including 3,300 Leeds fans.

As the game kicked off it was good to see us settle into it pretty well. The Leeds fans were in good voice and put the Leicester fans to shame as they needed to have a drum to try and get their singing going. They were poor overall but did start singing once they were winning later in the game. You only sing when you're winning comes to mind. We'd had a couple of attacks and didn't look overwhelmed by the Premiership side. Phillips had put two fantastic crosses in from in front of the Leeds fans over to the opposite side of the pitch, only for Roofe to fail to get on the end of the ball. The lad in front of me said he should have cut inside and not let the ball bounce. All of a sudden Leeds had an attack, and as some were shouting for the ball to be passed at the edge of the box I thought have a go. With that the ball sailed into the net courtesy of Hernandez to put us into the lead, 1-0.

As Leicester tried to get back into the game, we were playing further up the field but then allowing them to break through the middle and put us under pressure. We weren't being outplayed at all, but Leicester got an equaliser not long after we had scored and before half time. The ball was cleared by Wiedwald but only to the edge of the penalty area and ended with one of their players putting a shot past him to score. It was a big disappointment that we couldn't hold on to the lead. Despite this, the Leeds fans kept singing lots of songs, including some of the older ones that will be recorded next month.

At half time, as I went downstairs, there were two policemen standing at the top of the stairs and I had a laugh with one of them. It shows how bad my eyesight is as I thought it looked like he was carrying a drill (it was actually a video camera, well at least I think that's what it was). I had a conversation with one of our fans and have agreed to meet him on Friday in the Peacock to autograph my book which he bought. Thanks for the support. As I got down onto the concourse smoke was rising to the left of me, along with the familiar smell of the smoke bombs. At least none were thrown onto the pitch this time and no big bombs (which were like massive fireworks) were set off thank goodness. On the way back up I was talking with the policeman and another Leeds fan on the stairs. The former thought we might sneak it as he thought we had been playing well, and that was from someone who comes from Leicester.

The second half saw Leeds bring on Ayling at the start in place of Borthwick Jackson, who took a knock earlier. We were playing well in parts but were still passing back to Wiedwald too many times though, which is what puts us under pressure. After one attack Anita was shielding the ball and Wiedwald raced out to get it. We were lucky to get away with the decision as he carried the ball out of the penalty area, but the ref and the linesman didn't react. Sacko was given the ball down the side in front of us a couple of times but, even with all the acres of space along the line, he either went inside and lost it or passed it back. He needs to get the confidence to take the ball to the bye line in the space he has and cross it from there. Near the end of the game, I suddenly realised Jansson was playing, and for some reason I'd forgotten he was on the pitch. We certainly didn't disgrace ourselves as Leicester eventually came out 3-1 winners. Although it was disappointing, I am proud to support Leeds United. Seeing the Leeds fans sing even louder and continue to show their support is phenomenal. We show other fans how to support their team with non-stop singing and they definitely miss playing us and can't wait for us to come back. It will be interesting to see what their next home gate is after a sell-out crowd, as I bet, like Cardiff, it will be way down on tonight. 'You're only here to watch the Leeds' comes to mind. Seriously though, we are one of the biggest draws around and I'm proud to support my team.

At the end of the game I took my flag and went downstairs. Some lads asked for their photos to be taken and some others ran across to join us and get in it. Unfortunately, one slipped on the floor, which was quite treacherous, but at least he was a good sport and had a laugh. I'd been walking gingerly to ensure I didn't fall. Luckily for us the coaches were outside the turnstiles. When we got out a lad came out to ask if I'd had my camera out to film at the end, to which I said no. He said the stewards in the stand had been facing the Leeds fans and ignoring the Leicester fans behind them, and they had been throwing things at the Leeds fans. As there had been some retaliation, it was the Leeds fans getting into bother not them - my friend Sue said she couldn't get out of the stand and it was very scary for her so I'm glad I missed it. But it was nice to hear that my blog is the first thing the lad looks out for after a game and has a look through my photos. Your comments are greatly appreciated and thank you. With a police escort away from the ground we were back on the motorway in no time at all, but it wasn't long before it went down to one lane. Obviously, they knew approximately 3,000 Leeds fans were heading that way. After a good run, it was nice to be home relatively early at just gone midnight.

Friday sees us return to league action with the visit of Sheffield United. As I'll have broken up from work for the October half term I aim to get there very early, so I can soak up the atmosphere. I'll have to pick up my friend's daughter and my granddaughter Laura on the way though. See you then - LUFC - Marching on Together!

SHEFFIELD UNITED (H) – 27TH OCTOBER 2017

I couldn't believe how quickly my new book *The Sleeping Giant Awakens 2016-17* has ended up being published as I'd only done the final proofreading the other week. Leeds United's Club Shop got their quota yesterday and I'd agreed to go in and sign them all for them. My own quota arrived today and I managed to sell one to a neighbour as soon as I walked out of the door! I dropped my daughter Emily and granddaughter Laura at the White Rose Centre whilst I signed all of my books that were in the shop ready for sale. I would like to say a big thank you for the hospitality shown to me in the shop and also for sorting out my tickets for me. In the middle of signing the books, it dawned on me that I had left my season tickets at home. As I was leaving the house my bum bag broke so I transferred everything to another bag, or so I thought. I didn't look in the pocket where the most important things were kept! It was nice to have plenty of fans come and speak to me in the shop and even buy my new book so a big thank you to them. I also got called a legend by one fan which was nice to hear. Before I forget I'd better give a shout out to Hungry Duck and Stutcha who I met in the Peacock and took their photos.

Today was called the Team Toby day: Toby Nye, aged four, is fighting Neuroblastoma and his family are trying to raise £200,000 for his treatment which isn't funded by the NHS. With all the staff at Elland Road donating their wages from today and fans raising money too, hopefully the family will get the amount they need. I decided as my books had arrived that I should donate one of them towards their fundraising, and a copy was handed to the family tonight by my daughter Michelle as every little helps. I was so glad to see that Toby, along with his brother Ollie, was able to lead the teams out for tonight's game. Everyone gave Toby a round of applause on four minutes which was good to see. Good luck with your fight little man.

The team today were: Lonergan, Anita, Ayling, Pennington, Cooper, Saiz, Alioski, Phillips, Lasogga, O'Kane and Vieira. Subs were: Jansson for Cooper (56), Hernandez for Alioski (70) and Grot for Anita (83). Attendance was 34,504 including 2,533 Sheffield Utd fans. Leeds lost 2-1 with Phillips scoring our goal (34).

The game kicked off and with more or less Sheffield's first attack they found themselves a goal up. As the ball came to the middle of the goal right in front of us, it came to Billy Sharp (ex-Leeds) on his own and there was no way he was missing that one. That wasn't a good start to the game for us and not a good start for my camera as it turned out the memory on the SD card was full! It looks like I'll have to do some rearranging of files and back some things up on both my computer and camera before we play Derby. For the next 20-odd minutes we found ourselves at sixes and sevens as Sheffield swarmed all over us and we didn't get much of a look in. With us passing back a lot, Lonergan was nearly caught out when he held on to the ball too long and nearly had it whipped off his toes. With the ref not booking their players for the fouls they were committing left, right and centre, it meant Sheffield continued doing it for a long time before they got their first booking. We eventually started to get an attack together when the ball came over to Phillips near the edge of the box; he struck the ball into the net to equalise on 34 minutes. We were lucky not to go behind again before half time as Lonergan made a fantastic double save to deny Sheffield United another goal. I did think that Sharp handled the ball twice with one attack though.

At the start of the second half, Leeds upped their performance as the fans really got behind their team. Saiz started causing Sheffield all sorts of problems and was fouled so many times. With another attack it looked like a goal all the way from Saiz, only for the ball to rebound off the upright. He set up Alioski with a great cross but his header was saved by their goalie. With one free kick we were trying something different in front of goal, with four of our players grouped together in the middle of the penalty area behind everyone else. As soon as the ball was about to be kicked, they all went back into an onside position. Unfortunately the free kick from Phillips went wide and didn't test their goalie. We had been putting pressure on the Sheffield defence for most of the second half, although not really testing their goalie. When Hernandez came on as a sub I was disappointed that Alioski was brought off. I feel that by subbing him all the time (well it seems that way) isn't a good idea, as happened with some of our younger players in the past, as he needs to play for the whole game to get the best out of him in the long run. We started to lose our shape again and within three minutes of bringing on our final sub Grot, Sheffield United took the lead once again. Whilst I thought we still had time to get something out of the game, it was disappointing to see the reaction of many fans. I was surprised to see that they just seemed to accept defeat and whilst many left the game, the rest were left in stunned silence. Whilst I appreciate it was a knockout blow, our fans normally get straight behind them and for some reason they didn't. Okay they were right, because we didn't do anything else that looked like we might sneak another equaliser. At this stage I would have taken a draw, especially when I heard their fans singing they were top of the league. That took me by surprise as I don't really take any notice of other teams exploits and wasn't aware that they were doing well as newcomers, having been promoted at the end of last season. One thing Leeds, can we please have the scores shown on the scoreboard for the whole game and not just when we score? It might make the players realise we are losing too!

Reading the message boards after I'd got home, there were lots of scathing comments from fans. Personally, though, I do accept that after our great start to the season things have taken a downward spiral. I realise that things are not going to happen overnight for us either. Once Sheffield United went into the lead for the first time, for some reason instead of playing to our strengths we resorted to passing back to Lonergan time and time again, who ended up hoofing the ball out of defence. When we started playing to our strengths the game changed. Whilst disappointed, I'm not downhearted as last season it took a while before things turned in the right direction, and I still have hope that things can work out for us in the long run. With Tuesday's home game against Derby coming up before our visit to Brentford next week, we really do need to win and get the three points. See you then – LUFC – Marching on Together!

DERBY COUNTY (H) – 31ST OCTOBER 2017

As we made our way to Elland Road, I wasn't looking forward to the cold, but there again I think it was colder in our house than outside! After a quick trip to the ticket office and club shop we headed to the Peacock. I was meeting Garry to personalise the two books he was aiming to buy in the club shop, but it turned out they had sold out of them. As it was, he caught me before leaving home so I was able to bring some copies with me. Thanks for the support Garry, it is appreciated. After chatting with some fans about the game and others about our song recording on 18th November, it was time to head into the ground in time for kick-off. It seemed quieter outside than at recent games, but as it was a different half term for many I still assumed we would have a decent crowd.

At the start of the game we had the Royal British Legion and the Yorkshire Regiment in, and as it was our nearest game to Armistice Day the last post was played on the bugle before a two minutes' silence. This was impeccably observed and as usual great respect was shown to the fallen soldiers in the World Wars and recent times.

The team today were: Lonergan, Ayling, Pennington, Jansson, Dallas, Roofe, Saiz, Alioski, Lasogga, Vieira and O'Kane. Subs were: Sacko for Roofe (76), Grot for Pennington (84) and Hernandez for Alioski (84). Leeds lost 2-1, with Lasogga scoring our goal (7). Attendance was 28,565 including 852 Derby fans.

Leeds started off strongly, attacking the South Stand, and it didn't take long before we took the lead. Saiz passed the ball across to Lasogga, who was in a good position at the right of the goal and scored in the seventh minute. The one thing I noticed was that we had limited our passing back to the goalie, which in itself stops the pressure on our defence. We made some fantastic moves, especially from Saiz once again, but couldn't build on our goal lead. We were playing well and kept Derby at bay for most of the half, although after a couple of attacks their number 17, I think it was, threw himself to the ground twice in blatant dives. Luckily nothing was given but the first dive was so blatant he should have been booked for it. I didn't realise until further into the game that Bradley Johnson and Scott Carson, both ex-Leeds players, were in the Derby team. We looked in control of the game and I wanted to ensure we went into half time still in the lead to give us a good chance in the second half. As it was, Lonergan was redundant for a lot of the first half, although once when he got the ball he slowed the game right down, waiting for everyone to get back into position. He should have immediately thrown the ball out to Alioski on the wing to set up a quick counter attack. Now that's one thing Wiedwald was good at, being able to turn our defence into attack by playing out from the back.

At the start of the second half Derby came out with renewed vigour and were already on the pitch waiting before Leeds came back out. We immediately started passing back at the start of the half and Jansson was nearly caught out a couple of times with short passes. For some reason we had reverted to type instead of carrying on playing to our strengths. We nearly got a second goal when Alioski had Carson tipping the ball out of the top corner, and we had a couple of good attacks before it looked like we had run out of steam. I wondered if we should change things after the hour mark and thought Roofe wasn't really in the game at that time. How I wished that sub had been made because all of a sudden from our attack, which broke down, their player was haring down the left-hand side towards the South Stand on his own. Roofe was still standing on the half-way line watching him when he realised he needed to chase him, but it was too late and before we knew it the ball was in the net. This also gave Derby the impetus to start attacking us, although we still looked as if we could contain them at that point. I can't remember at which point the crowd were doing a great WACCOE, but when everything went quiet you could feel the tension in the air. I still thought we could get something out of the game until the ref pointed to the spot at the far end after their player was fouled near the edge of the box. Many have said the foul was outside, but I cannot be sure as I haven't seen it. As their player sent Lonergan the wrong way to put Derby into the lead, you could see the game slipping away from us. We still had a couple of chances, but Grot and Lasogga went for the same ball, denying one chance. Lasogga missed a great chance to equalise

when his shot went above the crossbar rather than under it, sadly. I would definitely have taken a draw at that stage once again. It was a very disappointing end to the game and it feels like our fitness levels aren't good enough. As my hubby pointed out it reminded him of when Wilko started out and we could only play for 60 minutes, then 70 and eventually managed to play for 90 minutes.

As I listened to BBC Radio Leeds on the way home and the slating both the team and TC were getting from both the panel and fans texting in, I felt quite sad that expectations had gone from high to so low very quickly. I have a great coping mechanism for this: I can forget what happens on the pitch very quickly and just move on to the next game. I know I've said there will be plenty of swings and roundabouts and ups and downs along the way, but we have to be patient. What many seem to have forgotten is that we have had to start again this season with a new team and manager, and it is going to take time for things to go in the right direction. I realise with our great start to the season that it gave us all the hope that this time things were going to work out well for us, but reality has set in once again.

We head for Brentford on Saturday with a teatime kick-off for the live game on Sky. I always hope we can turn things around and in one sense we were unlucky to lose today, but at the end of the day it is results that count and we really need the three points to give us some hope back. Fingers crossed we can put up a good performance and do another Bristol City please. See you there – LUFC – Marching on Together!

CHAPTER 5 – NOVEMBER 2017

BRENTFORD (A) – 4TH NOVEMBER 2017

Good news with the fundraising for Toby Nye - £150,000 has been raised so only £50,000 to go. This should be achievable by Christmas with auctions and other events arranged. I also had an appearance on Radio Yorkshire on Thursday morning, and as usual I talked a lot. As I was told afterwards that is what they want!

With a late kick-off today of 5.30pm for the live Sky game, we still set off from Leeds at 8am. This gave us a decent run down to London, where we stayed in Staines until 4pm. Our original plans to go to Twickenham changed due to a big rugby game being played there today. We had a laugh whilst in the pub when one of our party got his phone out of his pocket as it was ringing, but when he got the phone out it was silent. I said I could still hear something, and then he took his own phone out of his pocket, which was the one ringing, and he had no idea whose phone the other one was. He had us in stitches. He'd only been in one other pub nearby, so he went back there to see if anyone had lost it. It only turned out to be the landlords, although he'd no idea how it had turned up in his pocket. He'd probably picked it up as he left thinking it was his, but at least all turned out well.

When we arrived at the ground we were dropped off at the end of the street and decided to go straight in as it was only 40 minutes to kick-off. After a quick search of the bags we went in and

Sue and I hung our banners across the back of the stand. I only realised later that some fans had hung theirs over the front of the stand. I then went back downstairs onto the terraces to take some photos before the game began and chat to a few fans. Due to the recent defeats it was vital we got at least a point today, although Griffin Park hadn't been a good hunting ground for us previously.

The team today were: Lonergan, Ayling, Berardi, Cooper, Jansson, O'Kane, Phillips, Vieira, Lasogga, Alioski and Saiz. Subs were: Hernandez for O'Kane (45), Roofe for Lasogga (45) and Grot for Alioski (80). Attendance was 11,068 including 1,647 Leeds fans. Leeds lost 3-1 with Alioski scoring for Leeds (67).

Leeds started off under the cosh from the start of the game and it was a very nervy few minutes. With Brentford's first attack Lonergan flapped at the ball as they won a corner. Brentford were making the most of playing in the tight knit ground, although the referee was falling for every little touch as their players kept hitting the deck. One time the linesman to our left had put his flag up to give us the throw in, only for the ref to overrule him. We had a couple of shots on target, which were easily saved by their goalie.

A comedy show happened next as the ball came over to Lonergan, who wasn't under pressure, only for him to drop the ball, giving their player an easy tap in of the ball to put Brentford into the lead. Damn, damn, damn - up against it once more. The first half played out with Brentford on top and us struggling to do anything else of note. It was made worse when Brentford were awarded a penalty as Jansson took their player out in the penalty area. I shouted that Lonergan could make amends and save it, but as it was he didn't need to, as their player skied the ball over the net. I was hoping that would be our get out of jail free card.

At half time my stomach was churning like mad with nerves as I stopped to have a word with Gary Edwards. As we were discussing the game so far a couple of men in front of him joined in. I didn't agree with their version of events, especially when discussing Lonergan flapping at the ball. Although he did make one great save in between, I didn't like the way we were passing back all the time getting put under pressure then hoofing the ball up front. I said he was still doing the same as Wiedwald had been doing under pressure, and they said Wiedwald was a coward and should never play for us again, but I disagreed. When they said they would have Silvestri back in his place, that did it for me and I left them to it saying never in a month of Sundays would I have him back! Opinions, opinions! Trying to get down the steps at half time was very difficult because of the number of fans, but eventually I got to the half way mark before going back into the stand for the second half.

Christiansen had made a double substitution at the start of the second half, bringing on Roofe for Lasogga, playing him in the middle and Hernandez for O'Kane. It didn't take long for us to start playing better and put some pressure on Brentford. We had suddenly upped our game and looked in better shape as we attacked towards the Leeds fans. It was the first time I had a good view of the goal in front of us from the seats as I was on row B, just to the right of the goal. When

110

the ball came over from the right their goalie did the same as Lonergan, missing the ball, which Alioski gratefully headed into the net to equalise. As Alioski headed to the Leeds fans to celebrate most of the others were heading back to the centre circle to get on with the game. As the game carried on I thought we could go one better and clinch all three points at that stage as we took the game by the scruff of the neck.

Unfortunately, as soon as Christiansen made his third sub, bringing Grot on for Alioski, it changed the game, as Roofe went back out to the wing instead of staying in the centre of the park. I have no idea why this sub was made as we were on the attack, and he should have kept things as they were. He probably thought Grot could be a game changer, but sadly for me I have seen nothing in his play that would make me think that. I feel he needs to play for the younger lads or go out on loan for game time as he hasn't done anything for me. With that, Brentford managed to get their noses back in front again with a free kick that sailed into the net from the edge of the box. Admittedly they'd had a couple of long-range shots that I was grateful had hit the woodwork, but we had come close too, with Vieira having his strike saved by their goalie. As I untied my banner in the last few moments I missed Brentford putting the game out of reach by scoring a third. We were well and truly beaten, whereas I felt pig sick and totally deflated.

As I did a fan video for Sportsline on Monday evening, all I could think of was we have been beaten both times I have done this, the first one at Millwall and then today's effort. I may have to refuse to do anymore if this carries on! As I was doing this, one lad said he was embarrassed to be Leeds so I said I never would be, but agreed it was a deflating situation. Lots of fans are pretty upset at the moment, with a few wanting to jack things in and many wanting Christiansen sacked. I don't know where we are going to go at this moment in time as I wanted us to persevere by keeping Christiansen. With Orta having made the signings, it is very much a different set up these days and I don't know how changing manager would make a difference in this case. Although we are now in 10th place, having been at the heady heights of top of the league in September, we have come down to earth with a bump. We did stand a chance with the half-time changes but then our change of suicidal tactics with the last sub cost us the game.

As we walked out of the ground, Del from the Thames Valley Whites was waiting for me to get my new book, and a big thank you for the support as usual. We got away from the ground very quickly and I was just dropping asleep when our driver beeped the horn as a Hungarian lorry encroached our lane on the motorway, waking me up with a jump. The same thing happened again later on the M1 with another lorry. We ended up going straight through to Leeds without stopping and managed to get through the roadworks before the lanes were shut and didn't get diverted. The journey passed very quickly as I slept most of the way back and was home right on midnight!

We have another international break next week, and the song recording will be on 18th November before Middlesbrough come to Elland Road on 19th November, with the return of Monk. As things stand, they have started to get a few wins under their belt just at the wrong time

for us. Time will tell what will happen in the meantime and whether Christiansen will still be here. I would like to think we can work through this as a team, but unfortunately I haven't got a crystal ball to say that things will turn out okay for us by persisting with him. See you at the Boro game LUFC - Marching on Together.

MIDDLESBROUGH (H) – 19TH NOVEMBER 2017

It's been such a busy week in the background. Monday evening saw me travel to Leeds to be in the Trust's Podcast, and it was nice to see someone tweeting about it from America. I also saw someone today who said they were the person who'd said it was a great listen, so thank you. Yesterday saw the unique recording of the old Leeds United songs from the terraces from the Shed days until the present, and I want to say a big thank you to everyone who turned up to take part. By the time I got to Elland Road to do that I was so emotional I thought I would cry. When I was on the motorway it mentioned an incident and the traffic slowed down and I thought I may be delayed, so it was such a relief to see that whatever had happened was on the other side of the motorway. After a quick meet up with some friends in the Peacock, Gary Edwards, Mick Hewitt and I headed to Radio Yorkshire for an interview to promote the recordings, which went very well. A very big thank you to Leeds United, especially Angus Kinnear and Laura Mitchell, for their help in letting us use the LUDO lounge for both the practice and the recording, which is greatly appreciated.

Today I set off early from home with my granddaughter Laura, and despite the frozen windscreen the sun was shining. Although it was quite cold, I knew it would warm up, but the conditions felt great for a football game. As we came around the roundabout at Elland Road, I saw two magpies out of the corner of my eye then spotted four in total. That's it, I said, we are definitely going to win now! The reason for the early start was because I had an interview to attend with Adam Pope and Katherine Hannah from BBC Radio Leeds regarding the song recording. I tried to look yesterday to see where the Lucas Radebe lounge was as I couldn't find it. I thought it was in the West Stand where the Director's entrance is now, which turned out to be the case. We headed down the West Stand side which was blocked off for Leeds fans and got through to where we needed to be with some help from a steward. It was nice to meet up with Adam and Katherine and have the interview, which went out at half time today. Hopefully I can get a copy for my website. Laura was chuffed to bits to get asked a question too, and we got some photos after I initially forgot! We also caught up with Noel Whelan too and some of our Danish fans before heading back around the ground via the Kop, bumping into Becky and Chris from the West Midlands and some of the Galway Whites. As usual, stopping for a chat and taking photos meant Laura wanted to know when we would get to McDonalds for her dinner. I wanted to call in the club shop first because I'd had a chat with Cath, our steward, outside the Director's entrance about her wanting my new book, and I told her I'd check if the shop had any as I thought they might have sold out. We called in there and I couldn't see them, so I will have to email and check the situation. As we were sitting in McDonalds, a man asked if I was Heidi and he told me that he enjoyed reading my blog, so I made sure I got a photo so he can see himself on it tonight. A family came looking for spaces and I said they could squeeze in next to us and they said thank you. There wasn't enough room for the whole family to sit down so I ensured they got our places when we got up to go. As I took a photo and told them I would put it on my blog tonight, the man asked my name, and he recognised my *Follow Me and Leeds United* user name. It turned out we both knew the same person and had been commenting on the same thread! It's a small world, and hopefully our friend Simon will soon be back with his family and that won't be a moment too soon!

I don't know what is happening with the bag search before the game, but they are well and truly going way over the top in my opinion. Why oh why have they started taking people's drinks off them when the same things can be bought at the other side of the turnstiles. Today I also saw two or three bottles of perfume that had been confiscated. Knowing how pricey these things can be, I really think this is getting out of hand!

After a quick trip to the Peacock, where I got chatting to a young Coventry White at the bar, we got into the ground early as I knew another large crowd was expected. Also there was going to be a mosaic held up in the East Stand and flags put in every seat in the Kop and South Stand. Sadly there was some bad feeling shown about it on social media. I know many people thought this shouldn't happen at Leeds but I felt this was different to drums and clappers, which we definitely don't need. We are a traditional and unique support but I thought the East Stand would do what they were asked to do. Personally, I wish it had said Marching on Together rather than just Together, and I also knew the kids plus some of the adults would enjoy waving the flags.

Personally I'm all up for taking scarves and banners in, especially if we can recreate the days when everyone held their scarves up aloft in the Kop singing 'You'll never walk alone'. The best one we ever did was against Manchester City in the FA Cup when Trevor Cherry popped up to score in the last few minutes as we were just resigning ourselves to a replay at Maine Road. The scenes that day were awesome and will always be remembered by me. It was also my one and only time of standing on the barrier after we'd scored - I kept falling off and got up four times in all. Now I realise why Collar, who always lead the singing on the Kop, was always held on by someone when he was stood on a barrier. I decided to take a video today rather than just photos when the team came out, to ensure I captured the whole atmosphere. Whatever anyone's misgiving were, the East Stand looked impressive, as did the flag waving. It wasn't just the visual aspect that was good, I felt it contributed to the atmosphere as a whole, especially as the team were up for the game from the word go.

The team today were: Lonergan, Ayling, Berardi, Cooper, Jansson, Phillips, Vieira, Hernandez, Roofe, Saiz and Alioski. Subs were: Ekuban (first game after his broken foot) for Roofe (79), O'Kane for Saiz (88) and Pennington for Alioski (90). Leeds won 2-1, with goals from Hernandez (24) and Alioski (54). Attendance was 33,771 including 2,535 Boro fans.

Just as I reached my seat, I realised that because I'd changed bags I'd forgotten something once again. In this case it was my football glasses, so I was glad it was a good sunny day as it would hopefully mean I wouldn't miss too much. I just can't read numbers on the backs of players or see their faces from a distance. As this was going to be the first time we came up against Monk on his return to Elland Road since defecting to Boro over the summer, it meant he would come in for some stick from the Leeds fans. I just wanted us to become the twelfth man today because in the past this is something that has proved its worth time after time. It meant teams were intimidated from the start and that's a bonus to start with.

As we kicked off, Leeds showed they were up for the game straight away today, and it was fairly even for the first 20 minutes. Although I wasn't unduly worried today for some reason, Lonergan made a great save in front of us that seemed to happen in slow motion. Boro appealed for a penalty and showed some bad habits in diving all over the place. The referee was particularly bad, giving loads of free kicks to Boro and leaving challenges on us unpunished, including one on Berardi when he 'somersaulted' a few times and then got up, and their player wasn't even spoken to. I thought if he'd stayed down the Boro player would have been sent off, but Berardi showed professionalism by getting up straight away. It wasn't long after this that we took the lead. We attacked and the ball came from Alioski on the right and ended up with Hernandez in space, who cracked the ball into the net. Brilliant, it was so good to get a goal and go into the lead. The team were in high spirits, fighting well and playing together, which was good to see. Although Boro had a few attacks we dealt with them well and went into the break still in the lead. There was a great deal of litter from the Mosaics all across the front of the East Stand due to the big children effect coming into play, with paper aeroplanes flying all over. These turned into paper balls at the start of the second half, which one of the stewards didn't find amusing.

The second half started with Leeds on the attack, and before long we scored a second beauty of a goal which came from sheer determination. Roofe battled to win the ball, eventually overcoming their player, and passed it to Hernandez on the West Stand side. He put a peach of a cross in for Alioski to finish it to put us two goals up, cue fantastic celebrations on the terraces. Saiz had a wonderful effort denied by the post as we started to play some really attractive football, especially coming out of defence and running at Boro, putting them under pressure. We could have put the game to bed when Cooper ended up beating the offside trap as the linesman kept his flag down and had an open goal, but his header went wide. That was such a shame but wasn't meant to be. Whilst Boro had a couple of chances I thought we coped very well defensively, although I wasn't aware Ayling had kicked one off the line!! The worst decision of the game was made when Boro were awarded a penalty on the say so of the linesman; as someone said it was an off-the-ball incident. After seeing the replay of this after, both the referee and linesman should suffer repercussions for the disgraceful decision that was made. Their player flung Ayling to the ground and he then grabbed the Boro player's leg and pulled him down. Seeing the replay and that the boot of their player was heading straight to Ayling's face, there is no wonder he grabbed hold of his leg to prevent a kicking! There were loads of angry fans in the South Stand who were going berserk and plenty of plastic flag poles found their way to the pitch side. Pontus tried calming some fans, but I don't think it worked, although I wasn't sure if they'd reacted badly to him. This gave Boro a chance to get back into the game as they scored the penalty, sending Lonergan the wrong way. The lad behind me told him to go to his left, which is where the ball ended up. He got it right this time! The timing of the goal meant there was still plenty of time until the end of the game.

A couple of times the fans in the South Stand kept the ball, and, although they came close a couple of times, we started counter attacking and putting in some fantastic crosses. Ekuban came on for Roofe, who had been leading the forward line today and had played better in his position of strength. Ekuban himself also showed some great pace and Alioski ended up on fire, with so many attacks coming down the left of the pitch, so it was a great shame to see Alioski substituted by Pennington on full time. He didn't want to come off the pitch though and looked gutted, and when my daughter Dani commented that he came off after Howson spoke to him it didn't register with me. With seven minutes of injury time facing us, we were showing our best form of defence is attack, and I thought maybe Pablo going off would have been better even though he played well too. As it was, despite the length of the injury time we managed to keep Boro out and claim the three points to see Leeds very happy all around. It was only as the players were thanking each other that I realised Jonny Howson was playing for Boro as I'd forgotten that he'd gone there.

As the players were going off the pitch, two men came onto the pitch, one in a feathered coat who I'd seen in the director's box at one of our recent games. They were running all over the pitch having a great time, and it turned out to be a couple of Italian comedians similar to Ant and Dec. At least there were plenty of flags at the end for the kids and plenty of fans going around collecting spares. My youngest granddaughter Alexis thought it was great when we got back to their house and she was given a flag. It was also lovely to have a great Sunday tea cooked by my daughter instead of me doing it, so a big thank you to her.

We have a mid week game at Wolves facing us, although I didn't realise they were top of the table, followed by the early kick-off game at Barnsley facing us next weekend. I take each game as they come and don't expect any easy games, but the win today will have done a great deal to raise the confidence and self-esteem of the team. The atmosphere was great today, with only a short spell after they scored that deflated the Leeds crowd. Keep going Leeds, as I've said many times there will be swings and roundabouts, ups and downs, but we will get there in the end. Stability is the key. See you at Wolves and Barnsley – LUFC – Marching on Together!

WOLVERHAMPTON WANDERERS (A) – 22ND NOVEMBER 2017

First of all, I would like to give a big apology for forgetting to mention Wayne Ogden in my blog on Sunday, who escorted me to Elland Road in his little yellow car. He recognised my beret as he passed my car and I recognised his registration plate so thank you lol!

Today was going to be a late set off to get there after work. As we were going straight to the ground too, it didn't feel like I was going to a football match, and later on Sue and I said we maybe should have gone to see the Christmas lights switch on instead. It's funny how memories from

the past can come flooding back. As we passed a big roundabout outside Derby, it brought back immediate memories of the mini bus I was driving when it was attacked by Newcastle fans. Luckily I saw them crossing the road ahead of us and as there was a gap in the traffic I put my foot down on the pedal to get past them. They saw the scarves hanging out of the windows, banged on the side of the van and nicked a scarf if I remember right. A bit further along the way to Wolverhampton I recognised another roundabout where my mini broke down on the way to Birmingham. After a push we got it going again and managed to get to the ground before my friend Sue, who had carried on in her car but got lost.

As traffic was heavy, we arrived at Wolves just before kick-off, and luckily the rain kept off whilst we walked down to the ground, although I had to keep hold of my beret so the wind didn't take off with it. I kept to the path at the top of the hill though, as I had visions of ending up on my backside in the mud. Luckily, although loads of our fans arrived at the ground together we got in relatively quickly. After a couple of photos and putting up my banner, I found my seat, which was right on the half way line and near the front and I had loads of fans around me that I knew.

The team today were the same as on Sunday: Lonergan, Ayling, Cooper, Berardi, Jansson, Vieira, Phillips, Saiz, Alioski, Roofe and Hernandez. Subs were: Ekuban for Roofe (68), O'Kane for Hernandez (68) and Dallas for Saiz (77). Leeds lost 4-1 with Alioski scoring the Leeds goal (48) and Wolves being awarded a penalty for their fourth goal. Vieira was sent off for a second bookable offence, although I will have to see it again to see what happened. Attendance was 28,914 including approximately 2,300 Leeds fans.

The game started off pretty even, but we were guilty of some very bad passing from many of our players which meant the ball was intercepted too often. We had an attack before Wolves started coming at us, and they were breaking us down very easily and had a lot of pace. When it looked like a long pass would go out for a throw in, a Wolves player ran so fast he kept it in and the resulting cross meant Lonergan had to make a great save. Wolves had shown what they could do though. Jansson passed the ball back to Lonergan, which had me screaming at him to not do that as it puts us under pressure, especially as he booted the ball up front and Wolves won it straight back. They attacked us once more but won a free kick outside the penalty area after a foul from Cooper. As soon as the ball left their player's foot it sailed above our wall, which had also left a big gap, into the left-hand side of Lonergan, and he had no chance of getting near the ball. It was very poor defending from my point of view. Wolves then took the game by the scruff of the neck with constant attacking. Although we had the same team as Sunday, we needed to change the formation to close them down in the middle as we were constantly caught out by their speed. I said we needed to do this before they got a second goal, which of course we didn't. With Hernandez out of position over the opposite side of the pitch, Berardi was left wide open with no support as they ran through to score a second goal. It was a good goal but something that we shouldn't have let them get despite all the mistakes in passing, as we had a chance to change the formation and stop this happening. For the rest of the first half they ran rings around us. The ref as usual started booking our players as Wolves were let off. I don't know when I saw their number 15 for the first time, but he was a giant of a player so it was no use hoofing balls up for Roofe to get as he didn't stand a chance against him. It reminded me of games in the past where when we had a tall centre forward - we would put balls along the ground - and when we had a small centre forward, such as Aidan Butterworth and David McNiven, we would always cross the ball high into the box!

A couple of fans took off to the pub as they'd seen enough. If beer had been served in the ground I reckon many others would have joined them creating great gaps on the terraces, but they'd have made a killing. As it was, no one booed the team off at half time, I suppose because they knew we were playing the league leaders at this moment in time. Sue thought we would get beaten today though as she'd had a feeling, whilst I thought a draw would be good and anything more than that a bonus. At times we had looked scared stiff of Wolves and that caused us to make constant mistakes.

At half time I met one of the lads who was at our song recording last weekend and had sung a couple I didn't know for me to record. I made a mess of this first time though as I don't think the video worked - argh! I also heard Kevin Sharp was on the pitch at half time, but when I got back up into the stand I couldn't get a good photo. Sue said she watched it on the screen, but silly me never even saw that!

At the start of the second half there were no changes on the pitch, so I said it was sh*t or bust basically and I hope Christiansen knew what he was doing. As we kicked off, straight away we were playing how we should with the ball on the floor and with more vigor; could it be a tale of two halves? When a lovely pass from Saiz set up Alioski, he beat their defender to volley the ball into the net and pull one back and I hoped we could get a second and at least get a draw. Playing like this, we started to get a grip on the game, only for things to take a turn for the worse again with the Vieira sending off. Another game with 10 men again and probably up against it once more. Even though we kept at it we were on the back foot again as Wolves scored a third to really put the game out of reach. The score line then ended up even worse when Lonergan and their player tangled as he tried to stop them scoring just to the right of his goal. That was it then, game over and a big defeat in the end.

It wasn't unexpected for many fans, but I was hoping we would have got at least a point out of it. The tactics in the first half really lost us the game because, by not closing them down, they were running through us with ease. On Sunday we had Vieira and Phillips playing alongside each other, making us stronger in midfield, whereas today one played more up front than the other. Back to the drawing board, and, although I shrug my shoulders and carry on to the next one, it is disappointing to see that for most of the game we weren't even in it.

At least Jack went home happy, having been given Ayling's shirt at the end of the game. As I went to leave the ground I realised I'd lost my little Toby Nye badge which gutted me, so I went back into the stand to look for it. Hopefully, I can get another and it is well worth the £1.50 I paid

for it as it goes towards his cancer funding. I certainly found out I'm not fit - I suppose I shouldn't have set off running, but as there were very few Leeds fans left in the ground at this point, I thought I'd better go quickly. All I ended up doing was puffing and panting all the way to the top of the hill - not good!

As I reached the road and glanced up to the right, I had visions of our earlier days of visiting Molineux and being in the South Bank when it was such an imposing stand. The game before we went to Paris for the European Cup final in 1975 was terrible for us Leeds fans as not many of us went to that game. My friends and I had travelled by train and went into a pub opposite the station first and then one next to the subway by the ground. We saw Sally, a Leeds fan from London, get wrapped around a lamp post and her scarf pinched as she was kicked and punched. All of this is written in my book *Follow Me and Leeds United*. Leeds fans were waiting for the gates to open when Wolves' fans came up behind us and attacked us. Although the lads put up a fight, we were seriously outnumbered and in the end Sue and I ran with the others and I tripped over a wall in the process. There were continuous running battles after that and it was awful. Some things you never forget.

I thought we may get back on time with no detours this week, as normally travelling back from away games most of the motorways end up shut at some point. Well I was wrong, just as we wanted to pull onto the motorway a police car blocked our way due to an accident and we ended up on the toll road. At least we had a short service stop then as I could feel a headache coming on, so a welcome Costa coffee beckoned.

Saturday sees another early kick-off and we'll have to go straight to the game. I do prefer the stop on the way to a game though or at least having a bacon sarnie in Billy's bar before we leave. At least with getting back early (although no doubt we will travel all around South Yorkshire before ending back at the same place an hour later) I might go Christmas shopping. I hope it is us singing 'you should have gone Christmas shopping' to the Barnsley fans and not the other way around. As it's coming up to my favourite time of the year though I might as well make the most of it!

We'll see what our visit to Barnsley brings this time. Last season we got an early goal then lost, so it isn't an easy ground to go to; in fact, we've had some absolute shockers there. Hearing Nikki and her dog Rita haven't got a ticket for QPR is sad as they go everywhere and are part of our loyal support. I realise fans want to see us play but loyal fans should always be looked after. These are the people who stay with the team through thick and thin and are not fickle or supporters who only come when times are good. If Leeds can't help get Nikki tickets, I wonder if QPR can. Let me know if anyone has any ideas? See you on Saturday LUFC - Marching on Together.

BARNSLEY (A) – 25TH NOVEMBER 2017

Yesterday evening as usual I'd changed into my Leeds shirt to go to an event, any excuse to wear my colours. As soon as I walked in I heard my name shouted by a fan and then saw the Leeds salute, which I reciprocated. Later we had a chat, and he told me he wasn't going to Barnsley (he's a home season ticket holder) but his son was. After the event I decided to go to Asda at Bradley on my way home. I'd only been there five minutes when I heard someone shouting my name out loud and I saw another Leeds fan who works where I do! Leeds fans everywhere.

Waking up to a cold morning, I was glad that there was only a spattering of snow in Halifax. I put two jumpers on underneath my Leeds shirt and it was only when I got to Elland Road I realised that, although I'd brought my big jacket, I hadn't brought my tracky top. Oh dear, my memory gets worse! I went into the club shop and I want to say how great it is in there now with all the different memorabilia. The stock levels are also on the up by the look of it as more and more things are put on show. I am really grateful having the support of the club

now, who are selling all my books in there. For those who have recently bought them or are buying them shortly from there or anywhere else, if they do not have an autograph in and you want one, then please ask. I will always sign them whenever you want as I am grateful for the support. It was nice to get feedback from Dawn later on at the game who had just bought *The Sleeping Giant Awakens*. She bought it last Saturday and had read it by Monday as she couldn't put it down, which is good to hear. There were some incidents that I had mentioned in this and she was glad that I'd put them in, and also having their photos in there was great for them to see.

Before the coach came I nipped across to McDonalds for a hot drink, and whilst in the queue some lads started talking to me and asked who we were playing. I ended up talking to a lad who was a Sheffield Wednesday fan and he said don't tell my mates but I've got a soft spot for Leeds, as I'm living in the city and working in passionate fans' houses! As I say, I talk to anyone and everyone about Leeds!

It was good to see that the police had got the coach escorts sorted better today. We came off at an earlier junction instead of having to go past Barnsley to the next exit and turn around and come back to it on the other side of the motorway. I thought it sounded like they were doing something similar with any coaches coming from the south. It was a lot better though that's for sure. We arrived at the ground a good hour before kick-off, which I thought was 12.15pm due to the televising of the game by Sky, but it turned out to be 12.30pm. Loads of fans were going up to the Centre at the top of the hill where there was a drinking area for the Leeds fans, but Sue and I decided to go straight into the ground instead as there was no chance of getting served there. As it was cold, we thought it would be easier and better to get a cup of tea inside, which it was. I had a quick word with Phil Cresswell first as I've got to autograph my book for him at some point. He's already read a good bit of it and said he likes the way it is set out including all the collages. I wanted to include as many photos as possible because I take so many and I'm really pleased how they have turned out in addition to the individual photos. He also asked if I was going to do a book every year now. As it is based on my blog it is very likely that will happen.

There were already queues inside but I didn't have long to wait to get a pie and a cup of tea. After chatting with Dawn I took a couple of photos of the Bournemouth Whites and Dublin Whites. I'd already been to put my banner up behind the goal where the first couple of rows were netted off. It was freezing in the stand as there was no sun, but I hoped it would warm up a bit. After a chat with a few fans I ended up in my seat towards the left-hand side of the stand. At least I was just to the right of the tunnel going downstairs, as last season I was right above it and didn't feel safe at all. What is really nice is to get good things said about you and I really appreciate it. Being told that to converse with people from all walks of life, from people at the top to your normal match-going fans, is a skill and this is one skill that I have got, it really brings a lump to my throat. Thanks Karl!

The team today were: Wiedwald back in goal, Berardi, Ayling, Jansson, Cooper, O'Kane, Phillips, Hernandez, Saiz, Alioski and Ekuban. Subs were: Shaughnessy for O'Kane (58), Roofe for Ekuban (80) and Grot for Alioski (88). Leeds won 2-0 with goals by Saiz (23) and Alioski (45+ in injury time). Attendance was 16,399 including 4,513 Leeds fans.

This morning before I set off I sent a couple of tweets:

Come on Leeds believe in yourselves.We can do this! Marching on Together! Positivity makes a difference. The key is don't go there expecting to be beaten.We can do this!

Thinking back to times gone by, we were already beaten many times when we went to Old Trafford until we had the belief we could go and win, such as when Beckford scored! I stand by this and it was great to see the belief today.

With Wiedwald back in goal today, I knew we would play a different way and, no disrespect to Lonergan, I was looking forward to seeing how the game would play out. Oakwell is always a tough place to come to and they always raise their game when they play us, so I wasn't underestimating them. We were attacking the opposite end of the ground but the sun was so strong and bright it was hard to see. I put my glasses on but that meant I couldn't see well enough to take photos, so in the end I took them off. I could see the players but not make out the names on the backs of their shirts. We started off very well and won some corners although nothing came of them. Barnsley were quick with a counter attack, and Jansson fouled one of their players, only to get booked more or less with his first touch of the ball! Although some balls went astray and didn't reach our players, we did start to play as a team, keeping the ball on the floor. Alioski repaid Saiz with a great pass through and Saiz ran at the defence and let fly with a shot that beat their goalie to put us into the lead. That meant great celebrations in the Leeds end, and despite the recent news about bans for anyone with the flares, a couple went off. I wasn't expecting the 'bomb' though and can well do without those. I feel this took the pressure off us somewhat as we

carried on playing some good football. At one point Phillips was rugby tackled and even though we played on, their player did not receive a booking for it when play stopped. I didn't feel too worried in the first half about Barnsley because our players were backing each other up and on the whole managed to deal with them quite easily. Although we hoped for a second goal, it came really unexpectedly in injury time at the end of the first half. With our attack, Ayling passed the ball for Alioski to put a cracking shot into the net to double our lead. That was brilliant timing and would give us a little breathing space for the second half.

When I got below the stands there were plenty of young Leeds fans going 'mental' as I headed to the ladies. The first thing I noticed was that the floor was wet through so I assumed they'd been visited by the lads again. I couldn't see any damage or why the floor was wet but as long as no one damages them deliberately that is all I ask. After I was asked why I hadn't put any photos of damage to the toilets at Wolves, I replied because I never saw any damage!

The second half saw a really fast half with end-to-end football, but surprisingly I wasn't too worried. We had a couple of attacks before Ekuban was through, but unfortunately he took too

long with his shot which then hit the side netting. He played very well though and was very fast and getting stuck in. We came close a couple of times and had another shot on target as the closing minutes came. I went down to get my banner and took a photo of some young kids. When I went to take a second one I had to wait whilst one took his coat off so he could have his photo wearing his Leeds shirt. I love these young fans who take pride in wearing their Leeds colours and it's good to see them being brought up right! Just after Alioski was subbed it went quiet on the terraces for a couple of minutes and I didn't want a nervy finish so was glad when the Leeds fans carried on singing. Barnsley hadn't given up, but we were able to see the game out and get the three points! I had to do a video with a report which will be sent to Sportsline for Monday evening, but as the Leeds fans were singing Marching on Together I had to join in. In fact after the win I kept breaking into song as I was so happy (I repeated that a few times in my video). In my last interview with BBC Radio Leeds I kept repeating 'you know' too many times-oops! When you've got to think on your feet though it's not a surprise!

As the team came off the pitch, Wiedwald came over to give someone his shirt. It was only after the game that I found out that one of the Shropshire Whites had given Wiedwald his cap to wear as the sun was so bright. That's one thing I can always remember Gary Sprake wearing regularly and I'm surprised it wasn't thought of beforehand. I don't think it will be a forgotten item in future.

On the coach after the game and for the second day running, I knocked my cup of coffee over! There's no hope for me I reckon! I'd like to say a big thank you to my best friend Sue for buying my latest book *The Sleeping Giant Awakens*. As always, my grateful thanks are given. It was great to have a very short journey back to Leeds so I was looking forward to going Christmas shopping and ended up going back into the club shop and taking advantage of some bargains! Just as I got to the club shop, I was talking to someone from our coach and saying we play a different way with Wiedwald in goal and, no disrespect to Lonergan, then someone shouted out as we passed them on the corner, saying that's exactly what they were saying! Later on it was good to be able to see my banner on the seats behind the goal when watching the highlights!

Our next game sees the visit of Aston Villa next Friday with another live Sky game and another large crowd. Just carry on the same way Leeds, and fingers crossed we can build once again by getting another three points. See you there – LUFC – Marching on Together!

CHAPTER 6 – DECEMBER 2017

ASTON VILLA (H) – 1ST DECEMBER 2017

With another game moved for Sky, I decided that an early start after work would be best. After picking my granddaughter Laura up, who was very giddy and excited about going to the game, we headed onto the M62 at Brighouse. There were immediate signs saying an obstruction in the road but still saying 50mph. We had only gone a short while when the car in front of me stopped as a lorry was bearing down behind us, which had my heart in my mouth for a few seconds. The broken-down car was on the inside lane trying to manoeuvre off the motorway, whilst one behind him tried to come into our lane. I felt really sorry for them as it was a scary thing to happen but glad we got past safely. I was surprised the signs didn't have that lane blocked off though unless it had only just happened.

After a trip to the White Rose we arrived at the ground in good time and we headed to the Peacock. As we passed MacDonalds a lad shouted my name and asked if I had my camera with me so as usual I obliged by taking a photo. As Laura said, though, if anyone talks to you, you always take a photo! Out of the mouths of babes - oh dear I think she knows me too well lol! We'd only just got into the Peacock when I saw Gary Edwards and he asked me to go outside to talk to a film crew from America who had been following him around because the girl had the same name as

me! They'd been filming his wife today, getting her reaction to Gary's near-on, 50-year consecutive game commitment of following Leeds. Laura screamed so she could see the sound monitor moving then went all shy when they asked her to sing a song, so I had to sing with her. 'Pontus's magic hat' and 'Last Christmas' got an airing, although may not make it to the final film lol.

We got into the ground just before kick-off as the ground was filling up nicely once again for this Friday night game just before Christmas. The team today were: Wiedwald, Ayling, Berardi, Jansson, Cooper, Vieira, Phillips, Saiz, Alioski, Hernandez and Ekuban. Subs were: Roofe for Hernandez who went off injured (42), Sacko for Ekuban (83) and Grot for Alioski (90). Attendance was 30,547 including approximately 2,443 Villa fans, who had possibly sold out their allocation. The score was a 1-1 draw with Jansson scoring the Leeds goal on 19 minutes.

Although we were at home today, I will never ever forget my first visit to Villa Park on 11th October 1972 for the League Cup third-round game. Getting there right on kick-off for the 1-1 draw, we didn't see any trouble. We had to walk through a group of Villa fans on a street corner after the game to get to our coach, but as we'd hidden our colours there were no issues. I think our Wallace Arnold coach was the only one there that game, and all of a sudden we came under attack when we were stuck in traffic. Out of the blue, bricks were thrown at the coach until after the eighth one hit the window next to me it eventually went through. With two large windows put through and a further one cracked, it meant a very cold journey home as well as a terrifying episode for us fans on the coach. As trouble always happened there it wasn't a nice ground to visit as a Leeds fan.

Despite Villa being above us in the table I wasn't too worried about playing them. Having turned the corner after the run of defeats, we set out with great determination. Our players were fighting for the ball and putting Villa under pressure. When we won a corner, it looked like our new coach had been working with them on set pieces as a bullet header from Jansson put us into an early lead. We continued to play some good football and I don't think Villa were really in the game in the first half. They had a couple of attacks, but luckily we managed to clear the ball as we kept them at bay. Hernandez had been injured a couple of times and was then subbed just before half time when Roofe came on to replace him.

In the second half there were some challenges, especially from their number 21, that went unpunished. From the amount of fouls he committed, he should have been booked long before he was. When I think of some of the things we've had players booked for as of late and Vieira's recent sending off at Wolves, their player should have been long gone! Although Villa had a couple of chances we came very near to doubling our lead when we had three players lining up to put the ball into the net, but somehow it missed them all. When the ball was headed into the net in front of the Kop, I suddenly saw the ball being kicked out of the goal and play carrying on. It was only then that I realised the goal had been disallowed, apparently for offside. That was such a shame as I feel it would have put the game out of reach for Villa. Just after this, the referee seemed to have had a whisper in his ear because all of a sudden he was letting fouls go on us then giving free kicks to Villa. With an attack just in front of the Kop, Ayling was fighting for the ball and he kept it in between his feet, only for the ref to give a free kick to Villa. What was that all about? Ayling hadn't fouled anyone so why it was given against us I've no idea. It wasn't the only thing that went against us in a spell of at least 10 minutes. It was no surprise when Villa pulled one back to equalise, but they were very lucky, getting the rub of the green when the ball fell for them every time. A long-range shot hit the post and went in, beating Wiedwald sadly. I'd forgotten the Villa fans were there to be honest as they'd been very quiet up until then. It was disappointing that they'd equalised, as it would have been good to see the game out without them scoring. There were a few times when it looked like Villa may get the winner but the game ended in a 1-1 draw, which overall was probably a fair result. The positive was not getting beaten after being in the lead and one point is better than none!

Laura had gone down to the toilets just before the end of the game, and as fans were starting to leave I thought I'd better get down the steps to make sure she didn't get lost. Unfortunately, as I got to the bottom there was no sign of her. Luckily one of the men who stands near me pointed out that she had gone back up into the stand, so I went back up and found her straight away.

We bumped into my daughter Dani and her boyfriend as we were leaving, and just as we got to Billy's statue Laura saw the police horses and wanted to stroke them. I immediately had to grab her as we realised something was kicking off. There were loads of police standing outside the car

BILLY BREMNER

1942 - 1997

LEEDS UNITED

1959 - 1976

"WE'VE BEEN THROUGH IT ALL TOGETHER,
AND WE'VE HAD OUR UPS AND DOWNS,
WE'RE GOING TO STAY WITH YOU FOREVER,
AT LEAST UNTIL
THE WORLD STOPS GOING ROUND "

MARCHING ON TOGETHER

park entrance opposite and I couldn't work out if they were Leeds fans being moved on or Villa fans. Laura had heard someone shout 'he hasn't done anything'. I could hear a group of Villa fans coming down the road behind us and suddenly realised we were right in the middle of their fans. There was a young Irish lad standing next to me so we had a conversation, and I just said, 'as long as Laura is alright that is all that matters!'

It didn't feel like a Friday night and with no football tomorrow now, I'm sure I'll get my days mixed up once again! The good thing is I don't have to get up for work in the morning so I got my blog done, even though I kept falling asleep whilst writing it.

Next week sees us travel to Loftus Road for our game at QPR. Our 7.00am start gives us a good run down with a pub stop on the way and should be another good day out. Keep the faith lads and lasses, we will get there in time.

Don't forget to pick up my books, they'll make a great Christmas present for the football fan in your life! See you at QPR – LUFC – Marching on Together!

QUEENS PARK RANGERS (A) – 9TH DECEMBER 2017

Up at the unearthly hour of 5am can only mean one thing, a football away day with Leeds United. I daren't have that extra 25 minutes sleep before my alarm was due to go off just to make sure I didn't miss it. It was going to be a cold one today before all of the snow heading our way tomorrow, according to the weather forecast. After defrosting the car, I saw it was minus two so I was glad I had many layers of clothes on.

7th December saw the sad 20th anniversary of the death of my hero Billy Bremner, and today would have been his 75th birthday. He epitomised what being Leeds was all about, always giving 110% and showed me the love and loyalty for following my team. He was a legend for Leeds United and my thoughts go out to his family. It was nice to see his youngest daughter and family went to visit his statue, which will always see his name live long in the hearts of Leeds United fans. Also, it's great to see that the club are going to have Bremner Square around the statue, so I'm hoping Father Christmas will be kind to me and bring me a stone! A shout out too for WACCOE, the message board I frequent, for putting flowers with King Billy down at the statue. They looked great and brought a lump to the throat.

The anniversary of his death also saw me appear on Radio Yorkshire with Darren Harper on fan Thursday, alongside Kevin Markey and Andrew Wrigglesworth. Andrew, who sang a solo of the Ballad of Billy Bremner when we were recording our cd recently, gave a fantastic rendition of it for the show too. He had grown men nearly crying and well done to him.

We also had the draw for the third round of the FA Cup during the week, and this means it's a new ground for me with the away trip to Newport. Personally, I'm glad we get the chance to go there because the league cup game earlier in the season that should have been at Newport was changed to Elland Road due to their pitch being re-laid. I was gutted to think I'd missed that one, as for once I was missing a game because I had an opportunity to go with my family to Disney World, having never had the chance to do that before. We were also refused permission to play Newport in a friendly game when they had financial problems, which was silly as we'd have taken loads of fans. As it is, we will have just over 1,000 fans there on the day with the tie being beamed back to Elland Road hopefully.

With our visit to QPR today, great memories return of us being crowned First Division Champions in 1974. The tickets for this game were meant to go on sale at the end of the last home game, but due to absolute chaos in the West Stand car park, plus the crushes that occurred, the tickets went on sale the next day at 9am. That meant we were back queuing outside the ticket office at midnight,

making sure we were at the front of the queue. We had a 'nice tarmac bed' outside the West Stand Ticket office. We got our tickets, enabling us to celebrate with the team. My friends Carole and Margaret were drinking champagne on the pitch at the end of the game!

We had a nice stop in Uxbridge before getting to the game, where we had a good laugh reminiscing about being banned from games, but remembering Leeds fans overcoming the obstacles and still getting to them. We got to the ground just after 2pm and then had the long walk around the ground to get into the upper tier. After a quick search I got through okay, although it was a squeeze through the turnstiles with my bag - or maybe the amount of clothes I was wearing contributed to this too! It was only after that some female fans complained that the female steward who searched them had inappropriately touched them and they were not happy. An official complaint will be going in about it. Also I can't believe the women's toilets were already not working before the game even kicked off. There aren't many of them anyway and we even found a man caught in the women's loos - you know who you are! I won't name you to ease your embarrassment.

I went to hang my banner up first and I wanted it near to where my seat would be, so put it up next to the Sky camera that was cordoned off at the top of the stand. A couple of our Norwegian

fans helped me hang it up. I was ready to thread the ties through a beam when I realised that one of the lads had tied it to a hook in front of it, so it was very easy to hang up. I had a chat with them and a big thank you to Rolf for buying my first book *Follow Me and Leeds United* and as usual, thanks for the support, which is appreciated.

I stood at the front of the stand to take photos, and once the team were ready to kick-off I went to find my seat but it was chock-a-block behind me by this time. I stayed where I was until the fans arrived to claim their seats then stood at the top of the steps with others for the first half.

The team today were: Wiedwald, Ayling, Cooper, Berardi, Jansson, Roofe, Saiz, Alioski, Phillips, Vieira and Ekuban. Subs were: Cibicki for Ekuban (38) who went off injured (he was on crutches at the end of the game and it could be a repeat of the broken foot that he had only just recovered from), O'Kane for Alioski (70), although at first they did say Cibicki was going off, and Pennington for Vieira (80). Attendance was 15,506 including 3,149 Leeds fans. Leeds won 3-1, with Roofe getting a hat trick, scoring on (63, 68 and 90 + 4).

QPR set off on the attack, but for some strange reason I felt quite calm. They were a lot stronger than us in midfield for a while, but we more or less held our own and limited their scoring chances. The nearest one I think went wide of the post. The flag went up for offside as the ref blew his whistle, but the QPR player carried on to put the ball into the net. The lad behind me hadn't seen the flag up and thought they'd scored and was glad to hear all was okay. When someone thought we weren't doing so well I said remember last season, we were already a goal down within five minutes so I'm happy scores were even at half time. Unfortunately, Ekuban was injured but the ref played on for ages. He tried to get up before going down again, and Ekuban was then allowed treatment. At the time I wasn't sure if it was a precaution or not, but Leeds subbed him immediately. With Cibicki coming on to replace him it meant that Roofe went to centre forward. As this is his strongest position I wasn't too fazed that we were forced to make the change, although I was sad for Ekuban as he looks like he has a lot to offer in that position too. As we changed shape slightly, we seemed to overcome the midfield issue and ended the half strongly. We were very unlucky not to go in with a goal lead when Roofe had a great chance, but the QPR defender recovered to make a crucial tackle to get the ball away.

At half time I went downstairs but as there wasn't much room down there I didn't stay long. Having not had to show my ticket to get into this part of the stand before the game, it seems the stewards had gone into overdrive. I had to show my ticket and was then told I couldn't stand where I had for the first half and should get to my seat. As a third smoke bomb had gone off, it looked like we were getting the brunt of their displeasure despite us having nothing to do with it. I raised my eyebrows and said I would move and find my seat, but I said I couldn't get to it from there anyway. I stood at the top of the stand talking to the same fans I had earlier and one said his seat was underneath the cordoned off area for the TV camera! The row I was on wasn't accessible from here either. The next thing I knew, the steward came rushing up to tell me I could still get to my seat from there and shouted at another Leeds fan asking him if he was asleep. I asked the fans in the seats to let me past, although this was further down the stand on the wrong row. I realised then that I would have to climb over the seats to get to my row, which was two rows behind this one! I was initially going to try and get my leg up and climb over but decided to stand on the seat instead. Luckily a young girl stopped me falling off as the seats were very flimsy and I hoped they wouldn't break underneath me. I then also had to climb over another row, not very good organisation QPR and a health and safety issue really. Luckily I'm agile enough but it would have been no good for some of our supporters to do that.

I was then standing with the usual fans around me, who are also a good bunch. My mate Andrew who sang the Ballad of Billy Bremner so brilliantly on our Yorkshire Radio interview this week was standing behind me. In the second half Leeds got a strong grip on the game and started putting some great attacks together. We were still a bit frustrating at times, as when we got near the goal we were trying to walk the ball in when a shot would have been a better chance. We put ourselves under pressure by passing back to Wiedwald a couple of times when we should have turned and passed the ball out instead. There was a fantastic cross between Saiz and Alioski and it was fantastic to see this bond growing between them as it was a pinpoint pass. Leeds had taken the game by the scruff of the neck, although the ref started ignoring some fouls on us. When one time he ignored the foul on our player I hoped it wouldn't mean them getting a goal as that has happened so many times. When he booked Alioski I thought he shouldn't have done that as it wasn't a booking in my eyes and it was no wonder Alioski got upset. Leeds took the lead with a great goal taken by Roofe after a fantastic cross from Alioski. Roofe got a second goal with another great cross, this time from Cibicki, to send the Leeds fans into raptures. 'Jingle Bells, Jingle Bells, Jingle all the way, oh what fun it is to see United win away' rang out from the stands but I didn't want to sing it too early and jinx the score line. Christiansen brought on Pennington to shore up the defence and took Vieira off to try and maintain our lead, but I also thought it was to prevent him getting a second booking and being sent off.

We made a couple of defensive mishaps, one passing the ball back and also kicking it out for a corner. With five minutes left, I had to climb over the seats as I was going to get my banner down. Unfortunately, I kneed someone I knew in the back and as I apologised he said that I should stay in my seat until the end of the game. Sorry but no, I make sure I get my banner before the end of the games to ensure I don't get delayed getting it down. I found some of the SLI lads there in front of it so I took a photo of them. We were all discussing how many minutes of injury time would be put up (I said four or five and someone else said seven) when out of the blue the ball was put forward in a QPR attack and the ball bounced in front of Wiedwald as he came out for it, misjudged it, only for it to bounce high over his head. Even though he scooped the ball out and away, unfortunately it had gone over the line to give QPR a lifeline. The next minute he redeemed himself with a great save with a one on one that denied QPR an equaliser. As I looked at my watch only a minute had

passed. Leeds then put the game to bed when Saiz ran down the middle towards us with another Leeds player on each side of him. He passed the ball to Roofe for him to claim his hat trick. Game over and three points to Leeds and an excellent win!

On our way out of the ground it was nice to get some great feedback about my blog and the fact fans were looking forward to reading it later tonight. I also did a video for BBC Radio Leeds, but just as I got my phone out to do it the battery died! Luckily I had a battery charger with me, although when I plugged it in it said it was 32% charged. Damn thing! As we were walking back to the coaches I told one of the Keighley Whites that I'd got a photo of him earlier. It was nice to hear that he is receiving my latest book as a Christmas present and he will bring it for me to sign at a game. As always, I am happy to autograph any that are bought for fans, you only have to ask!

We had a very good journey home and didn't stop so were back in Leeds by 9.30pm. Luckily by the time I got home at 10pm, although we still had snow it had kept off falling some more. According to all the weather forecasts (we'll see how right they are), tomorrow is going to be bad so I'm glad I can stay at home and watch it from the warmth of my house.

Next week sees the first of two home games before Christmas with first Norwich and then Hull City. Keep going Leeds I'm glad you listened to my tweet this morning saying believe, you can do it lol! Just keep playing to our strengths and let the other teams worry about us. Getting as many points as possible into the New Year will set us up nicely for the run in until the end of the season and you never know, we may sneak that automatic place!

Don't forget to pick up my books, they'll make a great Christmas present for the football fan in your life! See you at Elland Road against Norwich – LUFC – Marching on Together!

NORWICH CITY (H) - 16TH DECEMBER 2017

After an extremely busy week and with only one more week to go until Christmas, it was nice to be heading back to Elland Road for the first of two home games in a week. I was going in early with my daughter Danielle and granddaughter Hannah, as I'd arranged to meet up with some fans who were buying my new book. Although the temperature was below freezing, the sun was shining so I made sure I had plenty of layers of clothes on again.

The first stop was Billy's bar but I was surprised to see that no under 18s were allowed in, but as I don't normally go in there for home games I suppose it was understandable. They let me in with Hannah as I said I wasn't stopping, only handing my books out. As usual my thanks go to fans Kev from Ripon, Susan and also to Lynsey and Katie, who also bought a book after the game, for their support. The Chiltern Whites

were in there too and I took a photo of them as well as some lads from Halifax. As I was going out of Billy's Bar a fella shouted me and said he'd stood next to me at Hillsborough when we played man u in the FA Cup semi-final. He said there had been a lad with a beard with us, and I had to cast my mind back to the game itself. I thought at first it was Collar but then remembered we'd waited for Mac from Shropshire to arrive so assume he was the one with us. Hannah asked me why I know so many people as I always stop and talk. I said it's because I've been going for a long, long time to see Leeds United and I've met so many fans along the way.

As we headed to the Peacock I found I'd missed Terje On Tour Hansen. Today is Terje's 200th consecutive home game, which is a fantastic achievement considering he travels from just outside Stavanger in Norway for every game. We have many fans who have also made fantastic achievements following Leeds, and I salute each and every one of you and am proud to have you as friends. It was nice to meet up with Aidan Montague, who was over from America and there with his brother and a friend (a Southampton supporter). Of course, I had to mention our 7-0 win didn't I lol! I met Aidan in Ireland with his sons a few years ago at our pre-season friendly, where I took the usual obligatory photo as we walked to the ground.

We got into the ground in good time ready for kick-off. I felt that we would be okay today and wasn't too worried, but I got the feeling some of the Norwich fans aren't happy with the way things are going. I've seen something mentioned on one of the message boards but as usual can't remember what! After falling asleep once more whilst writing my blog I realised I'd better get a move on. Some fans are waiting patiently for me to post it but they also fell asleep waiting for the blog to appear on the internet last week!

The team today were: Wiedwald, Ayling, Berardi, Cooper, Jansson, Roofe, Phillips, Vieira, Alioski, Saiz and Cibicki. Subs were: Hernandez for Roofe (78), Grot for Saiz (81) and Pennington for Cibicki (85). Leeds won 1-0 with a goal from Jansson on 41 minutes. Attendance was 30,590 with 997 Norwich fans. Today was the first time we had the virtual advertising boards on all four sides of the ground and along the middle of the East Stand.

Norwich had a lot of possession in the first half. Although I wasn't particularly worried, some of this was our own making due to passes being short and not having enough power to reach our players. The first half wasn't the best and it seemed to drag but our hopes were raised when Berardi had a shot that went wide. Chants of 'if Berardi scores we're on the pitch' rang out. We had a couple more chances before Phillips made a crucial tackle to deny Norwich a scoring chance. He was also unlucky not to score at the other end when his shot hit the post. To be honest things were quite even on the pitch until just before half time when we won a free kick out on the right. Having recently got a free kick specialist helping to train the team, it looked like this was paying off when Jansson rose to head the ball into the net off the post. As he celebrated, first in front of the West Stand, he came down to the Kop end and immediately tried to raise the bar with the atmosphere. This worked and we ended the half on a high despite Norwich ending up on the attack. Prior to the goal it had been pretty quiet on the terraces too in comparison to recent games, even Hannah said so and I said we needed to be the twelfth man and we also needed a goal, which obviously worked. My friend Carole said exactly the same thing at half time; great minds think alike.

In the second half it was noticeable that we were guilty of trying to walk the ball in when we should have had a go instead. This half passed a lot quicker though and the atmosphere was so much better and that's how I love it to be. We had a couple of chances, as did Norwich, with them having a shot that clipped the top of the crossbar. Wiedwald was called on to make a few saves before it looked like we were going to put the game to bed when Saiz won the ball to bear down on to the Norwich goal at the Kop end. As the Leeds fans cheered, this turned to groans as the ball came back off the post to be cleared. That was such a shame as he deserved to score. When Norwich came close as we waited to bring Hernandez on, I was just glad they didn't score in the meantime. As Pennington was brought on I knew we were going to see the game out, which the team did. There were a few doubts at times but I think we were learning all the time and making sure we didn't concede in the last few minutes after taking the lead. There were six minutes of injury time, and loads of people around me were agreeing that the South Stand keeping the ball had contributed to this. If we are only leading by a small margin it feels counterproductive. We got the three points with the win at the end of the day, even though it was tough at times. Having been asked to take a video at the end of the game again for both BBC Radio Leeds and Sportsline, I decided to film before the final whistle so I could capture the reaction from the fans.

Before I finish my blog tonight, I would like to pay my respects to David Zaman who was one of the fans who took part in our recent CD recording with his mum Gwen. She sadly died a couple of days after this took place, but she will always be remembered as being part of the group of fans making history by doing this. Unfortunately for those fans asking, we will not be able to get the CD out for Christmas. Getting everyone together to finalise this has been difficult but also I feel we need to get this right so won't rush it. As soon as there is any news, you can be certain I will share this with everyone.

Next week sees Hull City at Elland Road, who have just got a new manager. As usual I've no idea who it is but let's hope we can go into the Christmas period with another win. See you next week – LUFC – Marching on Together!

HULL CITY (H) – 23RD DECEMBER 2017

Before I start my blog today, with the Christmas period upon us and my favourite time of the year I want to wish everyone who follows my blog, all friends, family, acquaintances and Leeds United fans all over the world a very Merry Christmas and a Happy New Year. For those of you going through difficult times or not with your families through no fault of your own, my heart goes out to you all. Please remember, though, Leeds United has a big family with lots of fans who are prepared to listen and who have big shoulders if you need to talk! Our celebrations start tomorrow with our German tradition of Christmas Eve celebrations and despite the few utterings around us today, I am proud of my heritage so Frohe Weihnachten und herzliche Neujahrsgrüsse!

After a very busy week at work I can look forward to a good two-week break, which sees Leeds play five games before heading back in. I also attended the LUFC v Leeds United Trust Quiz on Tuesday with my daughter Danielle. It really was a great night, enjoyable with plenty of laughs, although we were home later than we thought due to Eunan O'Kane turning up about 45 minutes late! I spoke to Andy Lonergan while I was there and told him I was one of the few who thought Wiedwald should not have been dropped as I could see what was trying to be done. I also said that

was no disrespect to him though! I look forward to more of these in the future, as well as the West Yorkshire Sports Quiz.

A very high crowd was expected for the pre-Christmas fixture, which was good to see. In the past the gates just before Christmas used to be very low across all clubs, as people went Christmas shopping instead. As Leeds fans buck the trend this year, it was also good to see the SS5 (South Stand) initiative taking hold on social media over the last few days, where fans were encouraged to wear scarves for the game. As someone who loves the memories of being part of the Kop in the seventies when we used to sing and raise our scarves above our heads, it was something I was looking forward to. This was also backed by the club today, and as I arrived at Elland Road with my daughter Danielle and granddaughter Laura, it was so good to see fans wearing their colours and being proud to show who they support.

The Peacock was our first stop, and as the other two had gone up into the garden I decided I would go and take a few photos. As it was a few fans I knew shouted me for photos and after I took a photo of the Barrow Whites flag, I was asked to take photos of the group of fans from Barrow who it belonged to. It was also lovely to catch up with Andy Ramshaw, one of my lads from the Selby branch of the Leeds United Supporters' Club. Although I stopped running the branch in 1992 and it's that long since I saw him, it seemed like yesterday. Memories will always be there and we had some great times from 1985 travelling everywhere with Voyager International and Ben our driver (unfortunately now deceased, RIP). Taking three coaches to the semi-final at Hillsborough and then to the play-off final at Birmingham will always stick out in my mind despite the results.

On the way into the ground I stopped to wait by Billy's statue for Kev, who had bought my book *The Sleeping Giant Awakens* last week. He had come back for a couple more as friends who had their photos in the book wanted one too. Thank you once again for the great support and promotion of my books for me. Also, earlier one lad said he wanted to buy all four of my books and I look forward to sorting those out for him shortly.

The team today were: Wiedwald, Ayling, Jansson, Cooper, Berardi, Phillips, Vieira, Alioski, Roofe, Hernandez and Cibicki. Subs were: O'Kane for Phillips (46), Lasogga for Roofe (76) and Pennington for Hernandez (90). Attendance was 35,156 including 1,794 Hull fans. Leeds won the game 1-0 with a goal by Hernandez (29).

As the teams came out of the tunnel they were met with a wonderful sight from all four corners of the stadium of scarves being waved and held aloft. It was spectacular and brought back lots of lovely memories and it was great to see. This is one thing that I am happy to see resurrected. It also added to the atmosphere and kept that twelfth man in place for the majority of the game. It was Laura who spotted Father Christmas sitting in the Director's box and she said did I know that Santa was a Leeds fan? Of course, I said to her! He had come to watch the game and also to check that all the children were on their best behaviour before he set off tomorrow to deliver presents!

As the game kicked off though, we struggled to get a grip as Hull took the initiative and saw plenty of the ball to attack us. Some of our passing was woefully short again, which does impact on our game. As we were under the cosh I was still very calm and said we would be okay, we had to let them have their first ten minutes and tire themselves out. Okay it was maybe more than that before we got a bit of a grip on the game but we just had to keep going. We had an attack at the other end of the field in front of the South Stand, and I couldn't believe it when the ball was sent to their goalie and we just sat back and let the ball reach him. We need to put pressure on any back passes. Not long after I'd said that, the ball was passed back again and I shouted to Roofe to keep going, put him under pressure. Then Roofe did run at him (obviously he'd heard me from the Kop) causing their goalie to make a mistake and pass the ball straight to Hernandez. He ran straight at him, chipped the ball over his head and into the net to put us into the lead. It was a super taken goal, although at first, from the Kop, it looked like it had gone straight over the top rather than an up and under!

The scarf waving went into a frenzy once again all around the Leeds stands as the fans celebrated the goal. Although we didn't add to this goal in the first half, we nearly let Hull back into it with a shot that hit the upright and went out for a goal kick. I had thought that was in so it was good to know it wasn't and we went in at half time in the lead. Talking to my friends Carole and Margaret at half time, it was good that we were all on the same wavelength about Roofe closing the keeper down. It just shows that great minds think alike but as we have all supported Leeds for over 50 years, it isn't a surprise really when you think of the amount of live football games we have seen between us.

The second half saw a change when O'Kane came on for Phillips, which I'm assuming was for an injury. This wasn't a very good half from a football perspective on our part, but we were frustrating Hull in their attempts to attack us. Hernandez should have hit a long-range shot instead of trying to control the ball, which enabled the Hull players to clear it. A lad next to me said that he didn't like the fact that we sat on a one-goal lead again. I know we can't do what the good old Leeds team did in the late sixties and early seventies as they could defend for their lives. In fact, we expected that team not to drop many points in those days, and I know I was privileged to be there and see it for myself; we were spoilt in many ways. Now we are getting better at doing this, and Christiansen is learning to change things by bringing on a defender near the end, although we were beginning to think he had left it very late today. Maybe it's because the game wasn't passing by as quick for some reason. We didn't agree on subs though, as he thought Alioski should have been taken off and Roofe put on the wing. Alioski had made some great tackles, and although all didn't come off he was doing well, plus Roofe is no good on the wing in my opinion. We did have a great chance when Pontus dribbled round the Hull players with ease and started an attack, which had three Leeds players bearing down on the Kop goal. Unfortunately, Cibicki's shot went over the top when maybe he should have passed the ball instead. Lasogga brought a save out of their goalie in the last minutes of injury time, but we were able to see the game out to claim another three points and the win. At the end of the day, that's what counts. I don't agree with the fan who sent a text into BBC Radio Leeds saying that was the worst game he had ever seen! I can assure you it wasn't anywhere near the worst! The fans ended the game the same way as they started, with the scarves being waved and held aloft. Some things are worth preserving from the earlier eras and that is certainly one of them and I look forward to seeing this more and more this season.

Tuesday sees us travel to Burton for the live Sky game, which I am happy to say remains as a 3 o'clock kick-off! Not before time, but at least the travelling fans are thought of as well as the rest of our worldwide fan base who are able to see the game too. Last season the away game at Burton saw our hopes of the play-offs die off completely as we dropped out of the top six. Today a win will see us climb into the top six again. My mantra is that we should still aspire for the top two as anyone can beat anyone in this division, and just like our last few games, with a winning run behind us, it shows how quickly things can turn around in this division.

It was nice to have fans saying they love my blog and my books plus my appearance on the recent LUST Podcast. The new feature on my website www.followmeandleedsunited.co.uk of a slideshow for the photos instead of having to scroll through every one has made it easier to see them all and thank you for the feedback. Stay healthy and happy and enjoy the next couple of days and I'll see you at Burton on Tuesday – LUFC – Marching on Together!

BURTON ALBION (A) – 26TH DECEMBER 2017

I hope everyone has had a great Christmas. Following the visit of Santa to Elland Road on Saturday, our kids got the surprise of their lives when he turned up on Sunday at our Christmas Eve celebrations on the way to deliver all his presents. Knowing Santa is a Leeds fan and the fact that he was at Elland Road the day before meant he got a fantastic reception! When I got my present of a stone in Bremner Square titled Heidi Haigh, Follow Me and Leeds United from my family, all I could do was cry as that was exactly what I would have put. I'd come home from an away game and said I was going to get one only to be told an emphatic NO! I guessed I was getting one but the emotion I felt when I opened my present was captured on video when I burst into tears. There will always be a part of me at Elland Road once I'm long gone.

After the weather being so mild yesterday I was surprised to find ice on my windscreen

from sleet when I set off, which was a complete contrast. It did try to snow on the way to Elland Road though, but luckily it was too wet for anything bad on the roads. Seeing a sign saying the A58 was closed at Wyke and I needed to do a detour was all I needed. I knew there had been a burst water main last week, but the road had still been in use on Saturday. I thought I'd keep going until the road was totally blocked, as did other cars, and lo and behold it was open all the way to the motorway!

As I got to Leeds I felt as weak as a kitten once again but have decided it's down to dehydration. We had a relatively short journey as we were stopping at Chesterfield today, but that didn't stop me falling asleep three times, only waking up to do the football card, golden goal and pay for my coach fare. Whilst stood at the bar I did nothing but yawn, despite the sleeping, but after a pint of coke, a pint of water and three lattes (free after the first one so why not?) I should be able to stay awake during the game lol! When we got back on to the coach I found out I'd won £20 on the football card. Having said I never win but did it anyway, I've had to eat my words, so thank you Preston.

We got to the ground in good time and got dropped off right outside it. I went past the standing part for the away fans and heard my name shouted. Even though I'd seen Kev at the last two games, I'd forgotten to pick my membership cards up from him so today it was third time lucky. As I got in the stand I hung my flag up in the corner of the seating area in readiness for the start of the game. I spent time taking photos and was able to go near to the dugouts and the tunnel.

A couple of women next to me were waiting to take a video of the match ball sponsors, and I said if there were any photos I'd taken that they wanted to save they could do. To remember my name I was added to the end of their video too. The game had kicked off as I headed to my seat and the ball was kicked into touch just above me, but I still ducked. I also had to sign my book that Phil Thumbs Up Cresswell had bought - thank you for the support. He had some good-natured banter thrown at him from some of our fans, which was funny.

The team today were: Wiedwald, Ayling, Berardi, Cooper, Jansson, Alioski, O'Kane, Hernandez, Roofe, Cibicki and Vieira. Subs were: Lasogga for Cibicki (75), Phillips for Vieira (77) and Pennington for Alioski (90). Attendance was 5,612 including 1,730 Leeds fans. Leeds won the game 2-1 with goals from Hernandez (free kick 61) and Roofe (64).

Leeds started on the attack towards the Leeds fans (opposite to last season) and were playing some good stuff down the wings, with both Cibicki and Alioski involved in a lot of the play. We had some chances too but they weren't on target, although we had a lot of possession. Roofe was guilty of missing a couple of good chances but was getting closer when his shot went past the outside of the post. It just shows how you need to take your chances because all of a sudden we were a goal down, against the run of play. The ball was hit from the right side of the goal and one of the Burton players was on the left to poke the ball over the line. That was gutting and there was a déjà vu feeling amongst the fans. Burton hadn't won at home in seven games and with it being a small ground that has a non-league feel about it was it going to be a banana skin? It nearly was after we'd had a free kick and immediately Burton went on the attack as they won the ball near our penalty area for what looked like a breakaway goal. Lucky for us the final shot was wide as it looked odds on that they would score. The whistle went for half time with a bit of a free for all going on at the far left-hand side of the pitch. Although Jansson was going berserk, it looked like it was something to do with Berardi, but as I'd taken my glasses off I couldn't make out what had happened. The linesman down our side was constantly getting offside wrong, with the men in front of me saying he wasn't fit enough to keep up with play.

The second half still saw us with a lot of possession. Vieira had a really bad tackle made on him and he was down for a while, so it was good to see him get back up and carry on. We started getting into the game and won a free kick on the edge of the penalty area. As the fans chanted for Hernandez to take it, I was interested to see what would happen as the recent addition of our free kick or corner specialist (I can't remember which) could make a difference. It was funny seeing the reaction of the Burton goalkeeper; he was going nuts behind our players who stood in front of him. He couldn't get a clear look at the wall in front of him and the next thing the ref went over and booked him. As soon as we went to take the kick our two players ran back on side as Hernandez sent a fantastic shot just inside the post to equalise. What a cracker of a goal that was! Three minutes later Roofe ran onto a through ball and this time finished it properly by putting it into the net to put us into the lead, sending the Leeds following wild! What a turn around that was,

but also a relief to be in front. I don't think anything untoward happened, but all of a sudden I saw the stewards taking someone out to the left of me and realised it was Aaron Cawley. For the rest of the game we were fine when on the attack, but then decided to play about with the ball across the back line, thus inviting Burton to attack and put pressure on us. Our best form of defence is attack, Leeds - and don't forget that! Although we had some more chances, it was Burton who ended up on the attack when six minutes of injury time was put up. With one attack it was battle stations in our penalty area, and it was good to see us overcome this attack to keep the ball out and get the win plus another three points! It has been a good Christmas period so far and keeps us up near the top of the table in the top six There were plenty of happy smiling faces at the end of the game because of the win, which was good to see. Also, although I hadn't realised it, this was the first time in over a year that we had come from behind to win a game. Our coach driver also broke his hoodoo as it is the first time we've won with him driving as far as I'm aware.

Saturday sees our second away game in a week with our visit to Birmingham before starting the New Year with a home game against Nottingham Forest. The latter is also on Sky with a 3pm kick-off. I would love that to become the norm; being on Sky but with a 3pm kick-off even on a Saturday! LUTV were also streaming the game live to 33 different countries - such is the pull of our fantastic worldwide fan base! See you on Saturday – LUFC – Marching on Together!

BIRMINGHAM CITY (A) – 30TH DECEMBER 2017

Could I just put out a plea for as many fans as possible to send a birthday card before 5th January to little Toby Nye, the Leeds United fan suffering from cancer. Toby will be five and as he was diagnosed with Neuroblastoma on his 4th birthday, his family and friends want to make this birthday a special one for him. Cards can be sent to Toby Nye, The Hope Inn, 74 York Road, Leeds LS9 8ES. I've got mine ready to send so let's get as many cards to him as we can!

After all the snow we had yesterday, it was good to see that it had melted in readiness for our trip to Birmingham for our last game in 2017. Although I'd glimpsed a magpie out of the corner of my eye, I thought I'd ignore it, only to see a little bugger sat on top of the traffic lights as I got off the M621 at Elland Road. If I hadn't have seen people saying Birmingham were bottom of the league I wouldn't have had a clue and I just hoped we wouldn't see a banana skin today. I'd done a small voice message preview for Adam Pope and BBC Radio Leeds yesterday and I said that as long as we don't lose that was the main thing but I wouldn't make a score prediction as I always get them wrong!

We had a good journey to the Bottle of Sack in Sutton Coldfield, where we've stopped many times. As usual I'd slept most of the way there, but maybe the antibiotics I'm taking had knocked me out. We had a good two hours there and as I went upstairs to find the loos a man asked me where we were playing. I had to think again before saying Birmingham. He was a Nottingham Forest fan but followed the blues when he moved over here. We had a really long chat as he said he always had a soft spot for Leeds and he'd met Billy Bremner and had got his autograph. He also agreed that Clough should never have come to Leeds. As usual the reason he spoke to me in my opinion is because I was wearing my Leeds colours with pride.

When we got to the ground, I woke up with a jump as yes, you've guessed it, I'd fallen asleep! As we got off the coach and through the bag/body search, which didn't take long, I heard someone say they couldn't take their bottles in the ground unless they removed the lids. I volunteered to put a couple of bottles back on the coach till after the game for them as they had travelled by car. I hate clubs doing this because I think it is very unhygienic and you don't want to drink everything at once. As I waited outside the turnstiles the team coach arrived but sadly without the players, having dropped them off already. On my way in a couple of riot police wished us luck. I'm sure that one day I'll get stuck in the turnstiles as trying to get my bag through with me was a challenge! A couple in the ground complained about having to take their bottle tops off. They were able to get their bottle into the ground as the lady was ill but they had to get permission from their top steward. They could have brought it in the ground in a paper cup though so what actually is the difference? As it was, when I was standing in my seat later all of a sudden a pool of water appeared in front of the seat next to me. Obviously someone's drink had been knocked over. I was just glad that it hadn't gone into my bag and I certainly wouldn't have wanted to stand in a pool of water all game. That's another reason why taking off bottle tops is not a very good idea.

As I went into the stand to hang my flag up I was going to put it up right behind the goal but was told I couldn't put it there as I'd be covering the advertising. As I went to get my flag at the end of the game, lo and behold there were a few flags over the advertising, so I could have put mine there! I put it up nearer the tunnel where the away dressing room was in the opposite corner from where they come out for the actual game. It was nice to get some feedback about my latest book *The Sleeping Giant Awakens* from a lad looking for the Keighley Whites. He said he was going to look at it for 10 minutes and looked at the photos first. Two hours later he was still reading it as he couldn't put it down. He said it was great and what I'd written was exactly as it had happened. That was great to hear and I thanked him for the feedback, which was appreciated. As I went under the stand onto the concourse I met the Bournemouth Whites. They knew they were in the book and I found out one of my near neighbours is their friend and they couldn't believe it when they heard they were in the book loads of times. Hearing some more fans have either got the book for Christmas or are getting it soon for their birthday, and that it is very popular is really great, and a big thank you to everyone for their support. Lots of fans were also queuing up to have their photos taken so as usual I was happy to oblige.

The team today were: Wiedwald, Ayling, Berardi (playing his 100th game and also Captain for the day), Jansson, Cooper, Shaughnessy, Alioski, Phillips, Hernandez, Roofe and Cibicki. Subs were: Saiz for Cibicki (55), Klich for Phillips (69) and Lasogga for Alioski (85). Attendance was 21,673 including 2,484 Leeds fans. Leeds lost the game 1-0 with Birmingham scoring in the 83rd minute.

Leeds were very slow out of the starting block today as Birmingham, despite their position at the foot of the table, raised their game as they were playing us. They wanted the ball more than us and were constantly on the attack. We struggled to get going as Birmingham kept attacking and winning corners, but luckily for us their finishing was poor. The ref was terrible, giving free kick after free kick the other way and in the meantime letting fouls go against us. I always think this gives the other team the impetus and the ball just kept running for them. We had one shot on target in the first half and were hoping for more from the free kick from Hernandez just outside the penalty area, but unfortunately we weren't able to emulate the goal we scored at Burton with the ball being hit too high. The only good thing was us going into half time on an equal footing. Apart from 'keep right on to the end of the road' being sung by the Birmingham fans, they were pretty quiet, despite their team being on top for most of the half. I realised pretty early on that Shaughnessy was playing in midfield due to Vieira and O'Kane being injured, which surprised me. His strengths are at centre back which is where we should be playing him and not putting square pegs in round holes. That said, he defended really well and won plenty of headers for us, the only bad thing in my opinion was that Birmingham were winning the midfield battle, which wasn't his fault.

At half time I saw Charlie from Harrogate who said our centenary match in 2019 should be against Club Atletico *Independent* of Buenos Aires. When we were robbed by Bayern Munich in 1975 in the European Cup final, the World Club Championship in 1975 never took place. Bayern Munich turned down the chance to play the game so the title has never been won. Leeds should get the chance to win this rightful title by playing the game at Elland Road. Watch this space as I will put the suggestion forward!

One of the Birmingham stewards told one of our fans that Birmingham usually played well in the first half but faded in the second half, but for some reason they decided to play for the full game today! I actually feel sorry for their fans that they have failed to do this for most of the season so far as they showed what they can do. I missed the half-time announcements of the Birmingham fans that have died (not sure if it was during the whole year or this season). My friend Sue said it was very poignant, especially as there were quite a lot who were younger than us.

When Saiz came on as sub on 55 minutes I was hoping we could start getting into the game more. He did have some impact; we had a great shot that was saved, hit the crossbar and was our best chance in the game which gave us a bit of hope. Just as I decided I would make my way to the front to get my flag, Birmingham scored after a Wiedwald save was put into the net from the rebound. I had been hoping to at least get a point out of the game, despite not playing well, but unfortunately it wasn't to be and we ended up on the losing side for the first time in a few games. Not a good ending to the year but not totally unexpected when we failed to get a grip on the game and resigned ourselves to the defeat. The consensus from some of our fans on the way out was that Birmingham wanted it more than us and that our team selection was all wrong. To be honest, we are getting so many injuries, I wonder why and whether it is happening on the training pitch. Is it modern football boots causing issues? Obviously I don't know what the answers to these questions are, but I still maintain we should play to our strengths. It will bring some of our fans down to earth as they were predicting that with a win we could have been two points away from second place, but as usual we fall down at the last hurdle. We can still aspire to a top-two position, but it won't be easy and we'll have to play a lot better than we did today. What I can't understand either is why they got rid of the reserve league, as players on the fringe of the first team would get match practice. Hearing that once they've played in the first team they can't play in the under 23s just doesn't seem right. Apart from going out on loan, that's the only way they'll get that match fitness.

With the transfer window opening next week, I'm not sure what we will do as a club. If there are players who aren't getting a look in who are on loan, I'd be inclined to send them back and look for different ones. I don't expect us to go all out and pay silly money for anyone but we do need to strengthen. Whether it is a loan who we can buy at the end of the season or a gem that can be the final cog in the team, we will have to wait and see. With another game on New Year's Day at Elland Road against Nottingham Forest, we need to get back to winning ways and at least turn up on the pitch. There's still a long way to go until the end of the season and you never know what will happen between now and then. I prefer to wait and see where we are nearer the end of the season but getting as many points as possible will go a long way to securing our future. I started writing my blog on the coach and fell asleep in the middle of it, only waking up at Meadowhall. I always say that travelling to the football is my chilling out time, apart from the football or lack of it in the middle!

In the meantime, I would like to wish everyone who reads my blog and Leeds fans all over the world a very happy and prosperous New Year. See you next year – LUFC Marching on Together.

CHAPTER 7 – JANUARY 2018

NOTTINGHAM FOREST (H) – 1ST JANUARY 2018

I hope everyone has had a happy New Year, a great night seeing in 2018 and are not feeling too rough today. Luckily for me, I stopped drinking alcohol over 30 years ago so I don't have that problem, but I had a lovely evening with my eldest daughter and family: I laughed that much my throat hurt! I also wish my sister Erica a very happy birthday for today too.

When we set off from home the sun was shining and it felt like good football weather, but that soon changed once we got to Leeds. My daughter Dani, granddaughter Hannah and I didn't arrive at Elland Road until 2.10pm but then sat in the car a while listening to BBC Radio Leeds. Having done a preview of the game for them we wanted to listen to it, but once again it wasn't played whilst listening to the programme. At 2.45pm we gave up and went into the ground as the rain started, so I've no idea if it was played at all. My mum, sister Karin and friends Carole and Ashley had heard the one I did before the Birmingham game, but I'd missed that one too. I do have the recordings myself anyway so I can listen to it again so never mind.

I was taking photos before the kick-off and a steward came up to me asking me to move. I said I was taking photos for my blog and would move at the start of the game. Just as I was getting ready to move to my seat one of the stewards I knew came and spoke to me. He'd been told there was a woman taking photos and he said it's okay it's Heidi! Thanks for the support.

The team today were: Wiedwald, Ayling, Berardi, Jansson, Cooper, Roofe, Hernandez, Phillips, Saiz, Alioski and O'Kane. Subs were: Anita for Ayling (26), Lasogga for Alioski (46) and Sacko for Roofe (80). Attendance was 32,426 including 917 Forest fans. The game was a no score draw (0-0). Forest had sacked their manager the day before so I hoped it wouldn't be another one where the opposition raised their game.

As the game kicked off I felt that Forest were there for the taking as we had our first attack. If we thought Forest were going to lie down and die for us, then unfortunately we were sadly mistaken. We were nearly a goal down when their man was through on goal, only for Cooper to make a fantastic tackle at the last minute to deny them a shooting chance. We had a goal scoring chance at the other end when Jansson's header was cleared off the line, and as the ball rebounded to Roofe he hit it over the bar. Forest were getting to grips with the game as we tried to break them down. Ayling went down after a tackle from our former player Bridcutt caused him an injury. We'd seen Bridcutt go and say something to Ayling but didn't realise he was the one who had fouled him in the first place and cut him by the sounds of it. He was treated and got up to carry on but was still limping. It wasn't a surprise to see him go down again on 26 minutes and he was then subbed, with Anita coming on. Straight away Berardi swapped to right back - his correct position - as Anita went to left back. It took a while for Berardi to settle down in that position in my opinion as he is so used to playing at left back. We didn't play particularly well in the first half, but it wasn't as bad as the Birmingham game, going in 0-0 at the break. I thought Saiz was a lot quieter but thought that was because he had come back from injury at the Birmingham game.

My friend Carole said we would be okay and the second half would be better. Lasogga came on at the start of the second half in place of Alioski. The second half was indeed better, with Saiz back to his normal self, but it ended up being a half of frustrations. We were unlucky not to take the lead after some great play from Saiz on the right-hand side of the goal, when he passed the ball to Roofe. As we waited for the ball to hit the net, it hit the crossbar instead and rebounded to be cleared away. A short while after, Roofe should have repaid the favour and passed the ball to Saiz or Lasogga as they ran through the Forest defence alongside him. As there was a gap in front of him, he shot instead and the ball went over the crossbar. That was probably a chance missed unfortunately. It could also have proved costly as Wiedwald had to make a fantastic save to tip the ball over the crossbar and prevent Forest scoring against the run of play at the other end. This gave Forest impetus to attack us and Wiedwald made another save to keep them out. We had a couple of chances with headers from both Jansson and Lasogga (didn't have enough pace on his) but their goalie was leading a charmed life and saving whatever came his way. The referee at this time was making some atrocious decisions when our players were being rugby tackled and he let Forest get away with it, then he was pulling us up for innocuous challenges. The home crowd were up in arms at this stage and the linesmen were no better as one foul on the left of the pitch was right in front of one of them. It looks like they should have borrowed my glasses as they were terrible decisions. My fear at this late stage was that Forest would steal a winner, but they didn't and it looked like the game was going to end in a 0-0 draw. I was right in my thinking when another six minutes of injury time was put up, and although we attacked some more we had to settle for the draw and one point. The positive is that it is better than losing, but it was an extremely frustrating game for us Leeds fans. The ref got some stick at the end of the game too which he deserved for an inept performance.

It was disappointing to only get a point overall from the last two games but we are still in the top six, although it is very tight from 2nd place to 9th; Wolverhampton Wanderers being an impressive nine points ahead of 2nd at this stage of the season. Obviously things can change very easily in this division but we are still in the mix.

Next week sees us visit Newport County in the FA Cup third round. I have a message for Leeds United, especially after hearing Thomas Christiansen say he would change the team for the visit. Please do not treat the FA Cup with disdain and disrespect the Leeds United support, who will be getting up at silly hours to travel the miles to get there. I hold the FA Cup dear to me and am a traditionalist along with many other fans. Winning breeds winning and after the debacle at Sutton last year, something I would never forgive Monk for, I don't want the same to happen next week. I've no problem with a few changes but we don't need to change the whole team.

Having had the privilege of seeing Leeds United win the FA Cup at Wembley in 1972 and seeing my hero Billy Bremner get handed the cup from her Majesty the Queen, I can honestly say the feelings of winning were out of this world. It is also a chance to get into Europe. If by any chance we do not manage to get into the play-offs or go up automatically (which we should aspire to do), we can still build on things by having the European games ahead of us next season if we actually win the FA Cup. It may be a pie in the sky moment but you never know, and I'll be optimistic providing we take the challenge seriously. As the club hierarchy seems to be looking at challenging for promotion next season and not this, I do believe we should still try to get there. Other fans are looking at us strengthening the team in the January transfer window but obviously time will tell if we do or not. As it is, I am looking forward to visiting a new ground next week and look forward to progressing in the FA Cup. See those of you going next week – LUFC – Marching on Together!

NEWPORT COUNTY (A), FA CUP THIRD ROUND – 7TH JANUARY 2018

Up at 4am to travel to Leeds to get the coach to Newport shows the lengths us Leeds fans have to go to when following our team. For once some of the Thames Valley Whites will be setting off later at around 10am as this game is relatively close for them, so really I have nothing to moan about as early set offs are a regular occurrence for them and others. As usual I didn't sleep well knowing I had to be up early so thank goodness I am able to sleep on the coach. Having to defrost my car before setting off meant it's going to be a cold one today too. At least the early morning set

off meant not much traffic on the roads, so even taking it steady I got to Elland Road by 5.20am.

Going back 12 months, I will never forgive Monk for throwing in the towel at Sutton, who deserved their win on the day. Our visit to Newport is along similar lines and will be a big test for Leeds, especially as some of the fringe players will be involved. The FA Cup is still important to me as I am a traditionalist and I am privileged to have been at Wembley in 1972 to see my hero Billy Bremner lift the cup. A good cup run will do us the world of good and yes my hopes of winning the cup may be unlikely, but I live in hope that we treat this game with respect. Also the fans who are travelling there today want to be treated with respect too and seeing the team give everything to come away with a win is all that is asked. That said, I decided to tweet the club yesterday with my comments about respecting the FA Cup and the fans, and I just hope it didn't fall on deaf ears.

I am looking forward to adding Newport to my list of grounds visited. I had a conversation in McDonalds about all the new grounds there are now in comparison to grounds we have visited in the past. With Maine Road and Ayresome Park having bitten the dust, they are two grounds I was glad to see the back of, as they were the two worst grounds to visit as a Leeds fan in the seventies because of violence.

After a good sleep, I woke up just before we arrived in Monmouth for a short pub stop along with the Harrogate Whites. It was a nice break despite it being short, and as I left I took some requested photos of the Harrogate Whites outside the pub. We arrived in Newport in plenty of time for kick-off, getting dropped off right outside the turnstiles. After hanging my flag up behind the goal I made my way to the side stand where my seat was as I was in the auto cup scheme. It was nice to see decent facilities for a small ground, which puts some others like QPR to shame. The sun was shining and warmer than I'd dared hope for in the side stand. The ones behind the goal weren't as lucky as they weren't in the sun and Sue said the biting wind didn't help either.

The team today had nine changes, which I wasn't happy about as that was too many in my eyes. They were: Lonergan, Berardi (captain), Shaughnessy, Anita, Borthwick-Jackson, Klich, Lasogga, Grot, Sacko, Cibicki and Phillips. Subs were: Cooper for Borthwick-Jackson (60) and Saiz for Grot (74). I had no problems with our four youngsters being part of the team on the bench today to give them the experience of being involved (Liam Kitching, Tom Pearce, Oriol Ray and Jack Clarke). If we had been a few goals up then that would have been the time to introduce one of them, but not otherwise. The attendance was 6,887 including 1,040 Leeds fans, although there were many more in the home ends. Leeds lost 2-1 with Berardi scoring his first goal for Leeds (10). (Sue and I shared the golden goal prize of £20 on the coach, having been put down with the initials TT which we correctly worked out as the Terrible Twins - something my mum always calls us too!)

What I wanted more than anything was for Leeds to take this game seriously and not underestimate Newport. The game was fairly even before we had an attack and Berardi, playing in an unfamiliar place in the middle of the back four alongside Shaughnessy, let fly with a shot from

177

outside the area (apparently hitting Lasogga on the way in) to score his first goal for Leeds. I was so pleased for him as he ran to the fans behind the goal to celebrate, only to get a booking for it, which was a harsh decision in my opinion. What's wrong with celebrating your first goal for crying out loud? That was an unexpected bonus though and I hoped we could build on that goal. Today's game was also a big test for me to see if the club had the same ambitions as I did. Although we didn't shine for the rest of the first half we more or less matched Newport, who didn't give up but they also came close to an equaliser.

The second half saw the Leeds fans behind the goal and those of us in the side Bisley Stand creating an atmosphere between ourselves, which caused a lot of laughs. Meanwhile on the pitch we were very lucky to keep Newport out as they kept on attacking us. Although we had a couple of shots on target, I was frustrated when we went backwards instead of attacking as we only invited Newport to put pressure on us. They came very near two or three times when I was convinced they had scored but luckily they hadn't. When we went forward we couldn't get any decent crosses in to give us a clear shot at goal. I wanted us to add to the goal as the longer the game went on the more chance Newport would have to pull one back. The equaliser came when Sacko messed about in front of us and allowed Newport to win the ball back, and it ended up in the back of the net to give them hope when it deflected off Shaughnessy. Instead of us going for the winner we allowed Newport time and space to keep on attacking us. Saiz came on for Grot but hardly touched the ball. I felt the sub hadn't worked and I'd have given Grot the full 90 minutes, although Sue thought he may have had a knock. As Newport came close again there was only one team who was going to win it and it wasn't us. Lo and behold that is exactly what happened in the closing minutes of the game, to leave the Leeds fans reeling, gutted and, as one lad said to me afterwards, embarrassed by the showing we had put on the pitch. Many others were downright angry as once again the fans and the FA Cup had been shown disrespect.

Never mind saying we were never going to win it - why not? We won't unless we try that's for sure and I'd rather give it a good go and get the feel-good factor going, together with hope, than to not give a damn. Winning breeds winning and if we don't get the chance to go up automatically or get in the play-offs this season then once again it is an opportunity lost to keep the fans onside. Also, the chance of getting back into Europe is a factor. I for one, along with others, long to see the day we win the FA Cup again, and for fans to say the FA Cup doesn't matter, well sorry but it should. It's a shame the club chose to ignore my video I sent through yesterday because after Berardi scored, there is no way we should have lost that game. We should have battled for everything and built on his goal. Saiz also got sent off after their winner with those around me in the Bisley stand saying it was for spitting. Sorry but if that is the case it isn't acceptable under any circumstances as it is disgusting. As I got to my flag some fans were mystified as to why he'd been sent off so I told them what the reason was according to those around me in the side stand.

At the final whistle I did both a video for Sportsline (Made in Leeds), so will be ringing them

tomorrow evening, and a voice message for BBC Radio Leeds - West Yorkshire Sport, which should have been read out after the game. To say I was disappointed is an understatement, with many others very angry at the don't-care attitude of many of the players. It's a real low again knowing we have been beaten rather than getting something out of the game.

There are no excuses now, Leeds, for not turning up for any games for the remainder of the season. Putting weakened teams out is flawed in my opinion and shouldn't be allowed. Fine teams if they do, but I think the greed of premiership money has changed football beyond recognition. Arriving home at 7pm meant a round journey time trip of 15 hours. Thanks for the no show Leeds! Once again our support is tested to the limit with our loyalty taken for granted, but then once we've slept on it our eyes turn to the next game. Next week sees us travel to Ipswich for another far away game but at least it is on a Saturday. See you there – LUFC – Marching on Together!

IPSWICH TOWN (A) – 13TH JANUARY 2018

After last week's disappointing effort and result at Newport, which ended with me having swollen legs after that 15-hour round trip, the dread of having to go to Ipswich with half of the team injured made me want to forget it and not bother. Of course, it turned out to be a fleeting feeling. All thoughts of not wanting to go went out of my head on hearing the sad news that Eric Carlile had died. Eric was at the forefront of the Leeds United Supporters' Club for 50 years and my first memories of him was enrolling me as a postal branch member in the early seventies. Eric did a lot for us fans over the years with the all-ticket games and he will not be forgotten. I kept in touch with him by sending Christmas cards and he will be sadly missed. Leeds United fans, led by Mick

Hewitt and the LUSC South Kirkby Branch, raised a glass to Eric in the Corn Exchange in Bury St Edmunds at 12pm. RIP Eric.

Having done my good deed for the day by picking Gaz and Ella up (thanks for the breakfast), I answered a plea on WACCOE to bring some tickets down to Ipswich and declined the offer of a bottle of booze. As the lad could no longer make it, he didn't want to let his mate down, who he was meeting at the ground to give him his tickets. I met him at Elland Road at 7.30am with his baby boy to get the tickets from him and can confirm they were promptly delivered to the right person on arrival at Ipswich. This is what Leeds United fans are about, always helping each other out when they can and I will always do that willingly if I am able.

As well as doing a voice message for BBC Radio Leeds, I have a message for Eddie Gray. Eddie is 70 on Wednesday so happy birthday. It doesn't seem two minutes since he was tearing Chelsea apart at Wembley in 1970 and it's such a shame we never got our just desserts in that game. If we'd avoided the replay they wouldn't have had chance to put Eddie out of the game with a brutal tackle. That display was fantastic and always stands out in my mind. You are a fantastic ambassador for Leeds United, not only for the club but for us fans too. Always willing to take part in events or in my case did the foreword for my first book *Follow Me and Leeds United*, which I am very grateful for. I used to love the supporters' club events at Menwith Hill which all the team came to. I've a confession to make, I never did drink that crème de menthe you bought my friend Carole and I after telling us we had to drink it, I gave it to Carole! So sorry!

I would like to say something to the fans who were in the pub near Bury St Edmunds and whose behaviour stopped them from serving beer just before we were leaving. By all means have a good time, have a drink, but take responsibility for your actions. You had been asked to stop swearing when singing and it quietened down for a while but then you did it again. I know that I asked some lads to think about it earlier. Although I don't use the men's loos I believe these weren't left in too good a state either. Just remember that this reflects on every Leeds fan and this pub is one we have been going to for years without any issues, and possible we won't be allowed back. There were plenty of families in there and some had walked out - maybe without the swearing they wouldn't have felt so intimidated.

We were still 10 miles out of Ipswich when we received the start of our police escort before pulling into the services. There were at least 15 coaches in the escort, which took my memories back to the eighties. It was great in those times seeing the long line of coaches, sometimes 30 strong, full of Leeds fans. We were then escorted to the ground, getting there at 2.30pm just at the same time as the couple I was meeting. I was standing chatting to a couple of lads and, what a coincidence, they had all met up last week at Newport! It's a small world! The next thing we heard was a commotion and saw a load of scarecrows coming down the street. I'd heard that some of the SLI had dressed up today so I took some photos. They did look good though! The only disadvantage of everyone arriving at the same time was that the stairs into the stand were jam packed with fans. After putting my flag up I headed to my seat just after the team had come out. Thanks for the Selby Whites flag photo Andy Welford!

The team today were: Wiedwald, Berardi, Cooper, Jansson, Anita, Roofe, Hernandez, Alioski, O'Kane, Phillips and Cibicki. Subs were: Sacko for Cibicki (injured 29), Shaughnessy for Alioski (46) and Lasogga for Anita (78). Leeds lost the game 1-0 with a wonder goal from their player in the 67th minute of the game. Attendance was 18,638 including 3,537 Leeds fans.

Portman Road is never a good place to come to and Ipswich have often been a bogey team for us over the years. I remember our FA Cup run of replays that ended up being played at Filbert Street, Leicester, on both the Tuesday and Thursday with Ipswich eventually winning the tie. I also remember coming here in the seventies and getting ambushed in the Sporting Farmer pub. Having arrived at 12pm on a freezing cold coach, 15 of us went to the pub and were spotted by about 40 Ipswich fans who ran down the road and followed us in. Our lads let me sit between them near the bar, which was a good job as I'd have fallen down with fear from the intimidation. I then spent two and a half hours shaking like a leaf. They went out after a couple of hours, only to return 100-strong and start singing IRA songs to us. I thought our time was up and it was only because the landlord stood up to them that the pool table full of bottles didn't descend on us. After they went, a load of Leeds fans turned up so I felt safe but not something I wanted to happen in the first place.

As the game kicked off today it was fairly even. Some of our passing wasn't very good, but we had a chance and it's a case you have to take chances when they are there. We were passing the ball across the back four a lot at one point, which frustrated me, and so we slowed everything down as no one was taking ownership of the ball. After Cibicki went off injured Sacko was brought on as sub. Many fans would have preferred Dallas to have come on as he was back from injury. For

the rest of the first half I could see why fans were worried as it looked like he needed someone to tell him what to do with the ball once he had it. We started playing out from the back, Sacko was through with the ball and Alioski was screaming for the ball at the far side of the pitch in a great position, level with the defence with them on the back foot. When Sacko slowed down and waited for everyone to catch up with him and we eventually lost the ball, it looked like he had no idea what to do with it and no awareness of other teammates on the pitch. That should have been a great chance for us, but we didn't even get near their goalie to put him under pressure. The ref had already shown his true colours: when Pontus was fouled he'd ignored him and then Cibicki went down. Pontus then started getting very angry. Whilst the trainer was on the pitch Jansson went across to the bench as Christiansen was shouting to him but it looked like he was ignoring him. He did go back to him then but Christiansen kept his hand in front of his mouth when talking to him, which had me wondering why he didn't want anyone lip reading his comments? We had another attack and as O'Kane was following their player to the bye line fighting for the ball, the lad next to me shouted don't foul him. When their player went down I thought damn he did. The next thing he was shown a red card and sent from the pitch. I was astounded as I never saw anything untoward, only someone trying to challenge for the ball. Is this not allowed anymore? Others around me said he had nutted their player and he had to go. On video evidence later on it looked like a case of their player conning the ref, yes he got pushed but I don't think it was a sending-off offence just their player going down like a sack of spuds. If indeed it is found that he cheated then the red card should be rescinded for O'Kane and given to their player! That's only fair in my eyes. When their player had a tantrum he was only spoken to by the ref, although when Jansson had a tantrum he was booked. I was worried that Jansson was losing it though and he is no use to us back in the dressing room. As usual, double standards by the ref and if we had a player all over us it was our player backing in, whereas Ipswich players falling like flies got a free kick! The red card came on 37 minutes and I felt like we were losing by the time half time came, especially as Ipswich had a couple of late chances. One direct from a corner hit the post, then another hit the crossbar.

At the start of the second half it took me a few minutes to realise Shaughnessy had come on and had to work out that it was Alioski that had been taken off. We actually played better with 10 men than we did with 11, although it took us a while to get on top. Anita, who had been quiet in the first half, looked a lot better and was getting in some good tackles and played well in front of us. It seemed to go against the run of play when Ipswich scored an absolute screamer of a goal, which proved to be the winner. There was nothing we could do to save it, but we gave their player too much space. I bet if he tried that again he wouldn't score in a month of Sundays so that was a pain. We brought Lasogga on as we tried to get an equalizer, which we nearly did when their goalie made a great save from him to prevent us getting something out of the game. I think a draw would have been a true reflection of the game, but as always the score says otherwise and we came away empty handed. The fans let the ref know their feelings at the end of the game, but the team were clapped off the pitch. Our fans had been singing for most of the game but 'you only sing when you're winning' came to mind for the Ipswich fans as they'd been quiet for most of the game.

We're at home next week against Millwall and their fans have had their ticket restrictions lifted so we will see if they bring more fans to Elland Road. I've also been asked if we can get the atmosphere in the Kop going with flags and scarves again, trying to recreate days gone by. I feel sure once our CD comes out - apologies for the delay but it's got to be right - there will be a fair few fans relishing singing some of the songs again. In the meantime if we get it right on the pitch, the stands follow suit with the atmosphere. We can be the twelfth man and help the team. I do realise how disheartened some fans get as I was very disappointed last week. Despite the loss today I felt more heartened that we didn't lie down and die and showed some great attacks, but unfortunately the final balls didn't put their goalie under pressure. Once again, though, we have another injury and that is something that concerns me greatly. Can we go back to traditional football boots please and see if that makes a difference? I do wonder why it is happening so if anyone has any other ideas please let me know as I'd appreciate their input. As usual time will tell how we will recover from the defeats over the last two weeks.

I'm still annoyed about the FA Cup run, and for the second year running if we'd have got through to the fourth round of the FA Cup we'd have had a big pay day with home ties against Arsenal and Spurs respectively. Why we would turn down the chance of a good cup run I've no idea? I don't agree with those fans who say we are never going to win it anyway and promotion is the be all and end all; you never will if you don't try! Winning breeds winning and if we don't get in the top six by any chance, it would have been nice to have something to shout about by progressing in the cup. At this moment in time we feel a long way away from a promotion side but as things can change very quickly in this division, with any team capable of beating anyone on their day, then you never know. We're not out of things yet and we just have to 'keep fighting'. See you next week LUFC - Marching on Together!

MILLWALL (H) – 20TH JANUARY 2018

Today I was heading in early to Leeds with my daughter and granddaughter following later. My first stop was at the Peacock to meet Rob, who was joining me at BBC Radio Leeds for an interview regarding a community project. Big congratulations to Katherine Hannah and her husband on the birth of their baby girl, and I look forward to seeing her back at Elland Road with a new Leeds fan! After this, I headed back to the Peacock to meet a couple of guys from a media company in London, COPA90, to do an interview about why both clubs are hated. I've no idea how I will come across as you have to think on your feet but I didn't agree with the comments from a couple of Millwall fans who they interviewed last night. They said that we were the Millwall fans of the north - I don't think so! The one thing I did forget to mention was about us getting ambushed at the services by Millwall fans on our way back from Fulham in the eighties. They had come over to our

side of the motorway at Leicester Forest to wait for us. As I went and hid in the ladies' loos, they were returned to the other side of the motorway pronto by the Leeds fans, with some even risking their lives by running over all six lanes of the motorway! After completing my third interview for All Leeds TV I can honestly say that I've been in demand today! I was asked what I thought the score would be today, but I said I wouldn't predict anything as I always get it wrong but hoped for a win. When I was told that Millwall hadn't won away all season I immediately said, 'that's the worst thing to hear because it always works out the other way once it's mentioned!' I'm positive that they'll raise their game to play us too. When Dani and Laura arrived later I headed up to the White Rose to pick them up, having a quick chat with my friends Sue and Paul on the way before going straight into the ground on our return.

There was great news for little Toby Nye this week. Through the pleas of the club, everyone including fans and players had done a fantastic job and raised the £200,000 for his next treatment for his Neuroblastoma. Saiz donated the last £25,000 after his recent misdemeanour at Newport for spitting to reach the total. Well done to everyone involved and I'm proud to see this has been achieved. Toby was also going to make his last appearance at Elland Road today before starting the treatment next week. It was lovely to see him being carried out by Liam Cooper before getting the chance to run about on the pitch. Good luck little man and I look forward to seeing you back at Elland Road in the near future.

The team today were: Wiedwald, Berardi, Cooper (sent off straight red), Jansson, Laurens De Bock (making his debut at left back), Roofe, Lasogga, Hernandez, Phillips, Vieira and Alioski. Subs were: Pennington for Vieira (43), Dallas for Roofe (74) and Shaughnessy for Lasogga (83). Attendance was 33,564 including 1,285 Millwall fans (bubble trip removed for this game). Millwall won 4-3 with Leeds scorers Lasogga (46, 62) and Roofe (55).

The first pass from De Bock was fantastic, right across to the far right of the pitch to the feet of our player. That was an impressive start in my eyes. Wiedwald was called into an early save before we had two great chances to take the lead in the opening minutes. Lasogga had two clear chances to score, the first one a header straight to the goalie and the second one saved by the advancing goalie, where a chip over him may have resulted in a goal. I can't even pinpoint where things changed because all of a sudden Millwall took charge. They scored a goal and, as they celebrated, the Leeds fans started cheering as it was disallowed. My fear then was they would come back even stronger because of all the jeering. Sadly, that turned out to be as they scored another goal more or less straight away - well it felt that way! How Morison our ex-player got away with antagonising the Leeds fans in the Kop and North East lower I will never know. When Berardi got booked for celebrating his first goal at Newport the other week with his own fans, how could someone who was deliberately goading the opposition fans to get a reaction be ignored? Morison was never good enough for us and swapping Becchio for him was the worst deal ever at the time.

They then got a second wind when they were stronger, bullying and intimidating us. A push in the back by Phillips was silly and gave them a free kick, but I expect consistency from referees, and as usual, two that happened to us were ignored. I didn't realise until they had a corner how tall some of their players were, with one being 6ft 7in or so, I heard after the game. We were struggling to contain Millwall by the end of the half and then a third red card in three games was given when Cooper made a late challenge on their player. I don't think he'd been having a good game, but Millwall players immediately surrounded the referee, which then resulted in him being shown the card. The Millwall bench also took off to our bench, although I didn't see what or how this happened, but both teams had an assistant manager sent to the stands. It baffles me how we have had straight reds for fouls when others just get a yellow card for doing the same thing. Down to 10 men once again, and to make matters worse, just as we were looking to make a sub, they scored a second goal. Morison once again goaded the fans with the referee completely ignoring his behaviour. This is yet another time when we were going to bring a sub on and the opposition

It is with great pride that Leeds United can announce that the funds for Toby Nye's Neuroblastoma treatment have been successfully raised.

scored. We looked down and out as the half-time whistle blew after three minutes of injury time. To be honest I expected about six!

At half time I think my friends and I were a little shell shocked as there was no answer to the way we had collapsed. As I was going back into the stand Susan said a 2-2 draw will do and the lad next to me agreed that a 3-2 win would be better.

Well our 10 men stood up to be counted in the second half, as within 30 seconds Lasogga had scored to pull a goal back. That got the fans revved up, and our players and the fans on the terraces joined forces to rack up the pressure. I suddenly realised that Berardi had gone back over to the

left-hand side of the pitch. He had been playing in his normal position at right back now we had cover at left back and Ayling was out injured. We started playing with vigour and putting some great attacking football in. Whatever Christiansen had said to the team at half time, it worked. Although Millwall hadn't given up at this point, with Wiedwald called into action we got an equaliser after a massive scramble on

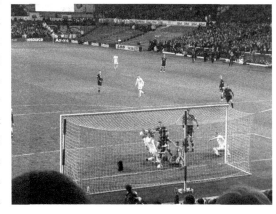

the goal line after their goalie spilled a shot. The noise ramped up to a crescendo all around the ground as Leeds fans celebrated. We had the upper hand at this stage and the Leeds fans were sent delirious when Lasogga got his second goal of the game to put us into the lead. We had played better with 10 men than with 11, and to score three goals in this way was unbelievable. I just hoped we could keep going. Roofe was subbed first and then Lasogga, who had been fouled earlier, went off too. For me it was too early to defend a lead with seven minutes of normal time left and four minutes of injury time. Our best form of defence had been attack, and this depleted our attack so personally I wouldn't have brought a defender on. Someone fast up front to run at them would have taken the pressure off us. Unfortunately, this proved to be our downfall as Millwall got their equaliser and then deep into stoppage time they won the game with a deflected goal.

Although the first half had been horrendous for us, this was another game where we didn't deserve to get nothing out of it. Having 10 men in the end probably cost us. Despite the result, we have shown what we can do and have to learn to do this for 90 minutes and not 45. Keeping 11 men on the pitch would be good too, although you can't help but think referees have an agenda against us! For those who think the Kop doesn't sing, well I can assure you every Leeds fan did their job in the second half, creating the fantastic atmosphere which is something I love. Eddie Gray got his rendition of oh, Eddie, Eddie, Eddie, Eddie, Eddie, Eddie, Eddie Gray by me on the 70th minute, and others a few minutes later. We may have been beaten in the end, but I saw hope today that we aren't dead and buried even though the score line says we lost. I'm proud to be a Leeds fan as always. With no game next week due to the FA Cup fifth round, the Leeds team are having a break in Murcia I think Christiansen said. Hopefully the warm climate will do some healing as despite the players being out through suspensions (with Phillips joining them as well today), we seem to be thin on the ground.

As an aside and I know I mention the ladies' loos in the Kop don't have seats, but I think we can add leaking toilets and locks missing to that too. I look forward to the day I don't have to moan about this!

Time will tell what happens next with the rearranged game at Hull coming the day before the end of the transfer window. See you there – LUFC – Marching on Together!

HULL CITY (A) – 30TH JANUARY 2018

Well what a week it's been as a Leeds United fan. The club launched a new crest that was underwhelming due to it being a Leeds salute, and this went down like a lead balloon with the fans. Now don't get me wrong, I love the Leeds salute and it's something I do all the time, but it is definitely not what I want to see on the club badge. By the time I'd finished work and been on Radio 5 live, a petition was doing the rounds that had nearly 70,000 signatures, so I certainly wasn't the only one who didn't like it. By the time I finished my interview it had gone up by 1,000 names. Wow just wow, but when our support works together we are a force to be reckoned with. I'm

glad to say the club had a rethink because of the number of fans against the badge, and now it is in our hands to design the new one. I have seen some fantastic designs on the web and I have to give a mention to Jacko on WACCOE for the ones he has done as they are superb. I look forward to seeing what happens next.

With the funeral of Eric Carlile this week, who was a great ambassador for the Leeds United Supporters' Club and was on the Board of the Club for a while, fans have asked for a 50th minute round of applause to take place at the Cardiff game in memory of him. I hope all Leeds United Supporters' club members past and present, plus everyone else, will give him the sendoff he deserves.

Last week saw another sad loss with the death of Jimmy Armfield, the manager who took Leeds to the European Cup final in Paris in 1975. Jimmy was a lovely person and he said if all fans were like us there would be no problems. After a game under his watch against man u at Elland Road, their fans had left graffiti all around the ground; well there was no way that was staying! A group of us then borrowed cleaning materials from the groundsman and got rid of it all, so we were well thought of because of that gesture. We also helped Jimmy by getting a petition signed by fans and players of the club to appeal our four-year ban from European football. He took it with him to the appeal and it was reduced to two years. I spoke to Jimmy on the telephone when we last played Blackpool as I'd been asked to deliver a photo of him with his World Cup-winner's medal. Dave Cocker, the son of our old trainer Les Cocker, had asked me to deliver this to him

and I was happy to oblige. You were a gentleman Jimmy and we will always be Champions of Europe. I feel like part of my youth has gone this last couple of weeks with these deaths, but sadly that is a reality we cannot change.

Tonight saw us head to Hull for the rearranged game because they still had an FA Cup game last Saturday. I actually had a chilled-out weekend for a change as I knew I had a busy week ahead. I got up at 5.25am this morning to organise a big event at work, but despite the early start it made me feel good when everything went like clockwork. I also got a pat on the back for a new work resource I created - it received good feedback which was great. I was already falling asleep waiting for the coach to arrive and hoped I'd be wide awake for the game. I thought I'd get some sleep on the way across but we seemed to be there before I knew it. We arrived at 6.20pm and found the turnstiles weren't even open, so as it was cold we decided to stay on the coach for a while and I had forty winks then.

We went into the ground at around 7pm and I headed straight to the front of the stand to hang my flag up. It's the first time for yonks that I was asked for my fire certificate, which was in my bag. I had a chat to little Jack from the Worcestershire Whites (I hope I've got that right?) and whilst we were standing chatting Jansson took off his kick out racism t-shirt and threw it to Jack. He was chuffed to bits, especially when he found out later that Jansson had signed it too. He went back to find his dad further up the stand, and I stayed at the front and one of the Leeds trainers (or the ball collector) came over and shouted to me. He asked me to go and find the lad with the t-shirt, as Pontus had left the orange bib inside it and wanted it back. I went and got it for him and as he came back to collect it, I tried throwing it to him but my throw was very poor and it landed on the floor in between the stand and the advertising hoardings. Luckily he got it back when some of the stewards helped him out. I was very disappointed at the end of the game though when Jansson came to throw his shirt into the crowd but went to the fans behind the goal instead. He could have let me have it for getting him his bib back lol!!

The team today were: Wiedwald, De Bock, Berardi, Jansson, Shaughnessy, Alioski, Roofe, Lasogga, Hernandez, Vieira and our new signing Forshaw from Boro making his debut. Sadly we lost Shaughnessy to a serious injury very early on, just as I was looking forward to seeing him play in his proper position at centre back. This gave Dallas his chance to get back into the side (5). Our other subs were: Sacko for Alioski (86) and Cibicki replacing Roofe just before the end of the game (90). The game finished as a 0-0 draw. Attendance was 17,237 including 2,097 Leeds fans.

Hull put us straight under attack and within a few minutes got the better of Shaughnessy, who went down injured after he landed awkwardly and ended with him being stretchered off. Wiedwald was called into action, making saves to keep us in the game. From my point of view this was his best game for us as he was also coming off his line and catching the ball a few times. He did misjudge one though, when he ended up outside the area, but managed to redeem himself luckily for us. We were actually making Hull look good at times as our passing today was absolutely atrocious. I know we had to make a sub early on, but, to say the team had just spent a week in Spain bonding in the warmth, they looked as if they had never seen each other before! Hernandez and Vieira constantly gave the ball away which put us under pressure. Hernandez did a terrible back pass that we were lucky to get away without conceding a goal. He put Wiedwald into an awkward situation, but he managed to get the ball away with their player nearly on his toes. That was a dicey move that could have been prevented by remembering the best form of defence is attack. Roofe looked so lightweight tonight too, and to be honest it's a good job Hull couldn't put any of their chances away.

The second half started off with more of the same; Leeds did start to get into the game more with some good attacks, but to be fair we didn't put their goalie under too much pressure. The closest we came to scoring was a powerful shot from Lasogga that went past the post. Alioski had the best chance of the game for us when he got into a fantastic position, only to fail to connect with the ball and miss it. I thought he had played very well in this second half with some delightful footwork to get past the Hull players along the wing in front of us. A couple of blatant fouls on our players in the second half that the ref let go made the lad next to me say that you can tell him what you like but there was an agenda against Leeds United. When our player was literally rugby tackled and thrown to the ground and this was ignored, I can't blame anyone for coming up with those thoughts. At least Hull were very bad at shooting too as they missed an absolute sitter in the second half, probably the miss of the season.

It was a disappointing game and result but I took the positives from it. We didn't lose, we got a point away from home, Wiedwald had his best game for us, De Bock played well and I thought Forshaw made a good start to his Leeds United playing days. Wearing the same number four that my hero Billy Bremner wore, I'm hoping that Billy's never-say-die attitude will rub off on him.

Cardiff at home on Saturday is a must-win game for us now, so nothing but three points will do. See you then – LUFC – Marching on Together!

CHAPTER 8 – FEBRUARY 2018

CARDIFF CITY (H) – 3RD FEBRUARY 2018

Yesterday saw a big gathering of Leeds United Supporters, who came together to say goodbye to Eric Carlile. With fans arriving from Norway, East Anglia, Wellingborough and many other places, it showed how well-respected Eric was for his service of over 50 years to the Leeds United Supporters' Club and to our members. With standing room only and people not able to get into the crematorium, he got the sendoff he deserved. The amount of fans who first met in the seventies and were there shows what an incredible fan base Leeds United have. The camaraderie shown yesterday will never be beaten in my opinion. Eric also got a 50th minute

applause at the game today by the whole stadium and a big thank you to everyone for showing him the respect he deserved. The game also started with another round of applause to show respect to Jimmy Armfield and had WACCOE ringing out around the stands; thanks for the memories, we will always be Champions of Europe. RIP Eric and Jimmy.

It had been snowing all morning and I wasn't looking forward to the cold, but luckily none of it was sticking to the ground. It was a good job because we got as far as Hipperholme when I asked Dani if she'd got her season ticket and she realised she hadn't! She's definitely her mother's daughter as I did the same a few seasons ago when I left our Rochdale tickets at home. At least now with us both doing it and having to go back home I can't be given any stick!

I'd got my positive head on today as everyone was writing us off and I said we'd win. Even the magpies came out in twos and fives so we thought we were onto a winner!! How wrong could we be? I am feeling very downbeat at the moment and will try and put everything into words but where we go from here I really don't know. For those shouting for TC to go, I really feel it won't make a difference

whoever is here. I want stability and want continuity to go into next season but I also realise that my aspirations of going up automatically have gone plus possibly even making the play-offs. Although there are still many points to play for, I can also understand why many fans are asking are we going to get any more at all? My quandary is that I so want my way to work, but without a crystal ball to see into the future only time will tell what will happen next. I do feel this will be the last 30,000+ crowd for this season as I know many fans walked out before the end and some left at half time. I always stay to the bitter end ever since the early seventies when I missed a cracking goal by Peter Lorimer, plus I like to see things in person to make my judgements. It feels like I did that with a heavy heart today though.

The team today were: Wiedwald, Jansson, Pennington, Berardi, De Bock, Forshaw, Vieira, Hernandez, Alioski, Lasogga and Roofe. Subs were: Dallas for Jansson (who was carried off on a stretcher) (30), Sacko for Lasogga (73) and Grot for Vieira (86). Leeds lost the game 4-1 with an own goal from Bamba. Attendance was 30,534 including 624 Cardiff fans.

With Neil Warnock and Sol Bamba back against us, I really hoped we could put one over them after getting beaten when we played in Cardiff. The trouble was Cardiff came to bully us off the park and when the ref played on after their first foul on us he set the tone for the whole game. With them getting the first free kicks, they went from strength to strength and within minutes they had the ball in the back of the net in front of the Kop. To be honest it all looked so easy as

my heart sank. I thought come on Leeds as we tried an immediate response with a fantastic shot from Lasogga that brought out a great save from their keeper. We also had another great chance with a scramble in their penalty area, which saw them get the rub of the green when Lasogga hit the crossbar and we couldn't put the ball into the net. After another attack, Jansson was left in a heap at the other end of the pitch as Cardiff won another free kick nearer our penalty area. Apparently it was a foul from Bamba that ended with him getting stretchered off. As Dallas came on to replace him I said at least we still had 11 men on the pitch. I should have kept my big gob shut because the ref, who showed favouritism towards Cardiff, gave Berardi his marching orders for a second bookable offence. What really gets to me is the fact that some of the Cardiff players committed

foul after foul and didn't get booked, yet we got the early bookings once again. All I want is a level playing field, which unfortunately once again we did not get. Cardiff had already scored a second goal and then just before half time put their third in to give us a mammoth task for the second half.

Talk at half time wasn't happy, but we all thought if they sack TC we will still be in the same boat unfortunately. Knowing it was always going to take time didn't help either. Could we have another second half comeback? Plus we played better with 10 men so we might as well start with a man down! (I don't mean it really). As I was going back up into the stand, Soggy from Halifax stopped to talk to me so I was late getting back to my seat and the second half had started, not that I missed anything. My granddaughter followed me a few minutes afterwards and as she went past my seat I lost my balance and nearly went backwards into the row behind me. Luckily for me I managed to right myself but jarred my back in the process!

The 50th minute applause for Eric got to Bamba as he put the ball into our net to pull us a goal back. That was when I got hope that we could do something this half. We looked better as a team in the second half, although Roofe looked so far out of it at times it was painful to watch. My daughter also wanted to go and pull his socks up as he wears them at half-mast for some reason. We were trying and were at least attacking, but then Christiansen made his second sub taking off Lasogga and bringing on Sacko. The only thing I could think was that he was looking at both Roofe and Sacko being fast (which he said on BBC Radio Leeds after the game) but sadly all this substitution did was take the sting out of the game. With Lasogga being the only one who looked likely to score, many fans took their displeasure out on TC by singing 'you don't know what you're doing'.

JIMMY ARMFIELD
1935-2018

All that happened was Cardiff got their fourth goal of the game and we were outplayed, outfought and a shadow of the team we saw at the start of the season. What with suspensions, injuries etc. our team depth looks terrible so I can understand why lots of fans are reacting badly to this further defeat. I take each game as it comes and my coping mechanism is forgetting how bad things really are after sleeping on it. That said, today feels completely different and it will take more time to see things more positively.

We have an early kick-off at Sheffield United to look forward to next week; that's if we even have a team we can play, as I've lost count of who will be available and who won't! Hands up those fans on the terraces who want to bring their football boots, as you may just get a game lol! See you there – LUFC – Marching on Together.

SHEFFIELD UNITED (A) – 10TH FEBRUARY 2018

Well it's certainly never dull being a Leeds United fan after another week of turmoil - sacking our manager and getting another one in. I know I was wavering last week after the defeat against Cardiff, but I so wanted to see stability and things work out and knew it wouldn't happen overnight. The lad standing next to me at the Cardiff game had said to me make sure you get a photo of Christiansen as it will be his last game. On hearing on Sunday evening that he had been sacked, it was a case of here we go again. Social media went nuts with the news, with lots of fans glad that he had gone, whereas I was sad that it had to end like this once again. One thing I will say thanks to Christiansen for is the great start to the season that we had. There was some fantastic football played and it was such a shame we couldn't keep going that way.

Monday saw the leaking of names as our next manager with Grayson, McLaren, Stam and Hughes to name a few being bandied around. Whilst I like Simon Grayson and thought he should have stayed at the time he was sacked, I don't think going back was an option. I didn't want any of the others either. The next name to come out in public, Paul Heckingbottom the manager of Barnsley, left me feeling very underwhelmed. We recently played Barnsley at Oakwell and I saw comments he made about hating Leeds, which didn't go down well with me, plus he had only seen one win in 16 games, whereas Christiansen had not won in only 10 games, so it didn't make sense to me.

I deliberately stopped looking at all the comments from fans as there were many with the same opinion as me. Others were saying he was a young manager and he'd been fighting a bit of a losing battle at Barnsley with his best players being sold. I actually felt so down and the worst I've felt as a Leeds fan for a long, long time. My best option was to sleep on things as they never seem so bad afterwards. He was indeed signed as our next manager so now he is here I have no option but to get behind him as I always do. As the week went on I only really listened to what he had to say after Adam Pope interviewed him on Thursday, and I'll admit he did come across well, plus it was easy to understand another Yorkshire accent! I don't want to jinx anything but I am hoping that he does indeed manage to turn things around for us. He will have to hit the ground running as proof of the pudding will be in the eating for me, and with a Yorkshire derby on Saturday against Sheffield he couldn't get a better baptism to show what he can do with the team.

Bramall Lane has lots of good and bad memories for me. 'We took the Shoreham easy, easy' - that chant will have many memories for Leeds fans who went there in the seventies. We got there early and just went in their end. By the time their fans started to arrive it was full of Leeds fans and they went back out of the stand very quickly and left us to it. The following year the police let a lot of our fans into their end again but then decided to stop the rest of us queuing up outside. As we were all sent to the away end instead, my friend Carole had a horse stand on her foot. Those Leeds fans in the Shoreham that year had a torrid time in their end as they were seriously outnumbered. I was glad I was in the other end but didn't like seeing the fighting taking place. One good memory was when we won the league there in 1992 when we won 3-2 with some bizarre goals. Liverpool then beat man u in the later kick-off and Leeds United became the last champions of the old First Division! What a day and what great memories!

Today will be the first game with our new manager once again, Paul Heckingbottom. It was pointed out by some of our fans last week that they didn't realise the club sponsors 32Red meant we were actually trying to receive that many red cards throughout the season. They also said they hoped that his surname wasn't a bad omen and we were going to end up bottom. No! It reminds me of when we were relegated with the sponsors Bet24. So to make sure it doesn't happen I've decided to go with the name Hecky instead, and all I could think of was (H)ecky thump for some reason! I hope it means we could thump some goals in.

Joking apart though, I've had time to calm down now and will look forward to what the rest of the season has to come. As always, I go by what I see on the pitch in the flesh. As our under-23 side had a great win yesterday, something that seemed to be lacking for most of this season as they built a brand-new side, I am looking forward to the first team emulating that score.

Heading off for the dinner time kick-off, I am grateful for Em's taxis this morning. Thanks to my daughter Emily for helping me out as my car has been playing up and needs some tlc today. We got to the ground in plenty of time for the coach and arrived at Bramall Lane in good time for the early kick-off. As we pulled up outside the stand, I'd seen a shop near it so Sue and I decided as there was a bitter wind to warm up with a Costa Coffee before the game. The female steward who got on the coach prior to us getting off was all for us winning today as she supported the other team in Sheffield.

After a quick chat with some of the stewards outside the turnstiles, I needed to be a contortionist to get through the turnstiles with my bag. Why the heck they make them so tiny I cannot understand. I had to have my bag by my head and came out backwards. At least I got through it, but I'm sure one of these days I won't make it! After putting my flag up by the corner flag and chatting to a few people, I went up to my seat, but not before seeing Peter Lorimer coming onto the pitch with Tony Currie. It was good to see Peter looking so well as he battles his illness and nice to see him back at a game. It was also the first time in ages that Radrizzani was back at a game too. With everything going on this week, it wasn't a surprise. As 'you can do magic' by Limmie & The Family Cookin belted out from the tannoy that took me back to the seventies, and I hoped it meant we could somehow get something out of this season after all.

The team today were: Wiedwald, Dallas (playing right back), Pennington, Jansson, De Bock, O'Kane,

Phillips, Roofe, Alioski, Lasogga and Forshaw. Subs were: Hernandez for Roofe (45), Sacko for Alioski (75) and Ekuban for Phillips (77). Leeds lost the game 2-1 with Lasogga (47) scoring for Leeds. Attendance was 27,553 including 2,236 Leeds fans.

We couldn't have got off to a worse start as we were a goal down within a couple of minutes when ex-Leeds player Billy Sharp volleyed the ball from the edge of the area straight under the crossbar and into the net. Here we go again came to mind as my heart sank! For a while we were under the cosh and struggling to get a grip on the game. Roofe sadly once again was failing to make an impact, but playing on the wing is a no, no for me. At times it felt like we were playing with 10 men once again as he was that poor and a weak link. After getting an early booking for Forshaw with his first tackle, I also thought it was another referee showing his true colours again. We managed to get a shot on target and Lasogga came close, but we struggled to get any momentum going. Roofe went down injured as some fans chanted for Hernandez to come on, but then carried on. He eventually went off just before half time and we were down to 10 men before eventually Hernandez replaced him. I hoped we'd have a more balanced side now as Roofe has been ineffective in my opinion. We were very unlucky not to get back into the game as our free kick came to Jansson who was clear in the area, only for his header to bring a great save out of their goalie to deny us an equaliser.

I went downstairs at half time and when I was asked about what would happen in the second half, I said we had 45 minutes to do something about it to which one lad replied, 'no chance'! As I went back down the steps it was packed with fans, and I thought I'd better get back to my seat because if we scored I'd end up at the front of the stand. No sooner had I got back to my seat than we did exactly that. A lovely cross from Hernandez saw Lasogga connect with the ball to head it into the bottom corner of the net and send the Leeds fans behind the goal into raptures! That gave us a heads up and got us back into the game. We started playing better and battled more as the game went on to give us some hope. We had a short spell as we grew into the game that saw some great passing and forward play as the players tried to get something out of the game. At that time, I was hopeful we could go on and get a winner but then we had the wind taken out of our sails once again when they were awarded a penalty. We were slow off the mark with their free kick and it looked a cast-iron penalty from our end as O'Kane took their player down at the other end. I've heard plenty of conflicting reports for and against this so would like to look at it again. Wiedwald went the right way but wasn't able to save, Sharp scoring his second goal of the game. This goal ended up being the winner and, although I would have taken a draw, this wasn't to be. It was a disappointing result, and there is a lot to be done team wise. As I wondered why Roofe had been given a starting position (I'd have him as an impact sub), I realised that everyone had been given a chance today.

With our next game not until next Sunday and another live game on Sky against Bristol City, Hecky has a lot to do between now and then. Never mind if the players look good on the training

pitch, it is how our formation does or does not work on the main field of play that counts. There was the positive of not giving up in the second half, but once again we got off to a slow start and conceded the early goal. We have to learn to play for 90 minutes and are fit enough to do that. As the lad behind me said, and I agreed, why do we pull all 11 men back into the penalty area to defend a corner? We need to leave someone on the half-way line, which will take at least a couple of men out of the attack. We also agreed that the best form of defence is attack, so if anybody from Leeds United reads this blog, I would be grateful if this message can be passed on to Hecky for me please! As someone who has watched Leeds United for over 50 years and seen the best team ever play for us, I do know what I am talking about in this respect.

We are where we are, and there is nothing us fans can do about it apart from support our team. Unfortunately, as we are back to square one it is going to take more time to turn things around. At least if it had to be done, the sacking of Christiansen wasn't done at the end of the season because I want to go into next season fully prepared for it. Some fans are saying the season is over, but it is never over until the fat lady sings. What I will say though is that I wrote my last book *The Sleeping Giant Awakens* last season as it was the first time in years when the season wasn't written off in October! We are now in February and it's up to the team to stand up and be counted like the fans do week in week out. It's over to them! See you next week – LUFC – Marching on Together!

BRISTOL CITY (H) – 18TH FEBRUARY 2018

After a week of feeling lethargic, irritable and generally not feeling well, it was a relief when my daughter Dani said she'd drive us to the game today. With it being a silly kick-off time of 4.30pm, courtesy of our usual change for showing the game live on Sky TV, we called in at the White Rose Centre on our way there. Once parked up at the ground, I left Dani and Laura my granddaughter in the car so she could have a sleep. I felt that way myself but after a Costa to give me some energy I headed to the Peacock.

When I got into the pub there was a surprise in store with an atmosphere already in place, probably due to the amount of time some fans had already spent in there. Although some of the songs weren't to my taste, it was very loud and I hoped this would transfer on to the terraces. We need to be the twelfth man as that always makes a difference. I'd already forgotten that this would be Hecky's first home game, and it seemed so long ago since his first game at Sheffield for some reason. It would also show how the rest of the season would go today, having already been written off by many fans, which was unsurprising really. As I stood at the bar I was talking to Kev and Karen, who asked if I had any photos of me and my friends walking about with our flags outside the ground, from our early days of following Leeds. As soon as I showed them the front cover of my book *Follow Me and Leeds United* they bought it, and as usual I am very grateful for their support. Also my appreciation goes to those fans who thanked me for sharing my blog and photos as they look forward to reading it. Those little things actually mean a lot and make it worthwhile for me.

There had been a lot of complaints about the cost of the tickets for the Bristol supporters today and whilst I agree they should be cheaper I want to praise the loyalty of the Leeds support. We had our loyal fans travelling from Bournemouth, which they do every game, along with the Devon Whites. We had some of our Norwegian fans in attendance as usual and some fans putting in great efforts just to get to the game - Norwich to Leeds via Portsmouth and a taxi to London from Farnborough as no trains ran early enough for the 8am coach to Leeds, plus a Leeds fan travelling from Inverness for the game. I could go on as there will be many more who deserve the accolades too. I also want to give a big shout out to a good friend of mine Gary Edwards for his 50 years of not missing a consecutive competitive game following Leeds United. That is a fantastic achievement and I know there are a few more fans who are nearing that record too. As a fanatical Leeds supporter I know the efforts our fans go to when following our team, and I don't think there are any other fans who can touch us!

By the time I headed into the ground I felt a lot better. One fan stopped me to thank me for my blog, and another one stopped to talk to me. He knew I took the photos but he had no idea of the lengths I go to by writing my reports too. I chatted to another fan about the game ahead of us today. We both take each game as it comes and I will make my judgement on what I see happening on the pitch. After getting my usual photos as the teams came out I headed to my seat to see what we had to come as the game kicked off.

The team today were: Wiedwald, De Bock, Jansson, Pennington, Anita, Hernandez, Dallas, Lasogga, Ekuban, Forshaw and O'Kane. Subs were: Sacko for Dallas (64), Roofe for Ekuban (64) and Phillips for O'Kane (73). Attendance was 28,004 including 536 Bristol City fans. The game ended in a 2-2 draw with Lasogga (72) and Roofe (80) scoring for Leeds.

Well once again all I can say is the first half was painful, very painful in fact. We got the first shot in, and when the ball came back to the Kop end, which we were defending, I just said that we shouldn't concede first at any cost. I suppose once again that I should have kept that big gob shut because within 16 minutes we were two goals down, with the Elland Road faithful shocked to the core. Not again - I shook my head. The first goal conceded was Wiedwald's fault as he missed the cross completely and then was out of position as Bristol slotted the ball into the net. The second one was an own goal from O'Kane, although I didn't see how that one went in. We failed to defend from the long throws, effectively gifting Bristol the lead. As someone pointed out, we had conceded 10 goals in recent home games which was a terrible stat to have. Although the atmosphere had started well on the terraces, this knocked everyone for six. It wasn't long before the players were getting jeered at: for example, at Wiedwald when he caught a ball and at Pennington after kicking the ball out of play, as frustrations began taking over on the terraces. The play was that bad in the first half I literally couldn't believe what I was seeing once again and just kept shaking my head. Laura did the best thing and lay across the seats and went to sleep! Wiedwald did make amends later on when he made a great save to prevent the game being put

beyond us. We had a shot across goal that Ekuban, I think, just missed. With us two goals down at half time, the team went off to loud boos from around the ground. I had my coping mechanism head on and tried to push how bad we'd been to the back of my mind. I wasn't the only one who thought it had been painful either! We are on the same wavelengths some of us that's for sure!

Downstairs we had our usual meet up behind the betting desk, which created a laugh with some lads. All of a sudden I saw Trampas there too, so had a chat to him. We were discussing the Bremner stones we had both been bought and one lad said he was going to be laying of the stones around Billy's statue. It was only as I said my name that one of the lads realised I was the one who wrote the blogs that he reads all the time! At least many of those who spoke to me today about liking my blogs will find their photos included in this one!

As we went back into the stand for the second half, Carole said that the last time we had a comeback it was as soon as we got back to our seats. We were discussing scores, I said 3-2 and the lad next to me said 4-2 and we also had a 4-3. I don't think at that point anyone thought we would score but we were hoping that Hecky's half-time talk would have had an effect on the team. As it was it took time for us to get to grips with the second half. We also had Wiedwald to thank for keeping us in the game. When a double substitution of Sacko and Roofe was made for Dallas and Ekuban, I felt underwhelmed. Although I did say that I preferred Roofe as an impact sub rather than playing for 90 minutes, the good thing I thought was he was playing upfront. As the frustrations with the fans were starting to creep onto the terraces once again, we showed the world why we have the best fans in the world. A bit of gallows humour crept in, with us singing Leeds are going up and then cheering the ref for actually giving us a free kick. As the noise picked up we started a fantastic WACCOE (We are the Champions, Champions of Europe) all around the ground and an equally as loud 'Marching on Together' ringing out loud and proud! I thought if it didn't pick the team up, us being the twelfth man, then nothing would. As Hernandez got the ball, instead of passing out to the wing where I expected it to go, he whipped the ball across to the far post where Lasogga got his foot to it and put it into the net to pull a goal back. I was made to eat my words (which I didn't mind) when Roofe got to the ball first to score our second goal to equalise. Cue immense relief around Elland Road as the frustrations turned to celebrations. You could see Bristol wilting at this moment in time and it is why I would love to see 90 minutes of singing and chanting regardless of what is or is not happening on the pitch.

Leeds were very unlucky not to win the game with the last kick when Lasogga nearly got a second goal and his attempt came back off the crossbar and was cleared. What a winner that would have been if it had gone in, although I did capture the second goal on my recording. The second half papered over the cracks, but we did show a fighting spirit that needs to be there for the full 90 minutes and not 45. Whilst the booing isn't nice and not something I joined in with, fans are still entitled to make their own minds up. What happens or doesn't happen on the pitch will always mean fans have different views whether I agree with them or not, although I don't agree with telling other fans of ours to go and support someone else. Sorry, once a Leeds fan always a Leeds fan, regardless.

I would also like to say that being Leeds can be very special, which is what this second half showed today. Experiencing this atmosphere and support was phenomenal, going from gallows humour to a fantastic noisy support in minutes to completely change the game! I'm always proud to be a Leeds fan though.

One downside today was when I heard about a Leeds fan turning on another in a cowardly way because they objected to how they supported our team - all I can say is shame on you. That isn't what being Leeds is all about and I will never condone that sort of behaviour.

With our away game at Derby on Wednesday before our home game against Brentford on Saturday, this could still be a make or break week for us. I still live in hope that we can rescue this season, although a lot can depend on the other teams around us. I never bother looking at other teams' results though so have no idea half of the time what is going on around us. Talking of not knowing things, in the recording I was doing near the end of the game I couldn't even remember who scored first or second for us! My memory is terrible but at least I can laugh at myself! See you on Wednesday – LUFC – Marching on Together!

DERBY COUNTY (A) – 21ST FEBRUARY 2018

For once, this game worked in my favour as the holiday period timed in with me not being at work this week. Arriving at Elland Road in time for the coach departure, I headed for Billy's bar but then did an about turn after seeing they had some new bags in the club shop window. Having been looking for one that is slightly larger than the one I have, which will fit my flag and books in, they had just the thing. I then retraced my steps, only to find Billy's bar shut when I thought it would be open, but everyone had congregated in the Peacock anyway. Despite heavy traffic most of the way, we seemed to arrive in Derby in no time at all. I think I fell asleep whilst on the M1 and woke up at the ground, so it was no wonder it felt like a quick trip. It looked like the turnstiles weren't even open, so initially we didn't want to get off the coach, but it wasn't long before the lights came on so we went straight into the ground. On our way to the turnstiles the Leeds United photographer stopped us for a photo, so for once I was on the receiving end of one. After a bit of banter, with a Leeds fan saying I didn't get to many games, he got his photo taken by me. When I went through the turnstiles the steward who checked my bag questioned me when I said I was an author and my books were in my bag. She was very impressed when I showed them to her and it was nice to get the praise for writing them, which was appreciated.

I managed to get my flag put up in a good spot at the top of the stairs then went to talk to Nikki and her companion as well as Rita her dog. We had a good chat before I went back downstairs, chatting to other Leeds fans before the game. The next thing, Derby fans started banging on the partition between the stands before a Leeds fan responded doing the same. He got escorted away

by another Leeds fan to save him getting into trouble, as the Leeds fans let them know we were there by singing instead.

My scarf has been washed, so I hope to have got rid of all the bad luck and rubbish that has been happening recently. I am going to be positive instead. I was trying hard not to be superstitious, but I remember with our 29-game unbeaten run in the seventies my scarf only got washed when we were beaten at Stoke, as not washing it kept our run going. Although that was opposite to my thoughts today, old habits die hard in one sense. When I eventually got to my seat, guess who had forgotten the game was live on Sky, even though I'd seen the camera below us? As daft as it is, I didn't twig for ages that that was the reason for the camera being there, so there's no hope for me really lol!

The team today were: Wiedwald, Berardi and Cooper (both back from suspension), Jansson, De Bock, Vieira, Hernandez, Lasogga, Roofe, Dallas and Forshaw. Subs were: Saiz (back from suspension since Newport) for Roofe (54), Phillips for Vieira (62) and Alioski for Hernandez (76). Leeds drew 2-2 with goals from Lasogga (34) and Alioski (79). Attendance was 27,944 including 3,152 Leeds fans.

I didn't know what to expect today, but the Leeds fans immediately got behind the team and sang for the whole game. It had been ages since this happened at an away game, but it carried on from Sunday's home game against Bristol City. What I did see from the team, despite being under the cosh for a lot of the first 30 minutes, was some fight in them. We could have been three goals down and out of the game but as we rode our luck I hoped it would be a good omen. I felt even better when, against the run of play, Cooper put over a fantastic cross from the left-hand side of the field near his penalty area over to Dallas on the right. His perfect cross for Lasogga to head the ball into the net put Leeds into the lead and sent the celebrating Leeds fans into raptures. This was the first time we had taken the lead for a while I think. The game had been very fast and we'd had a lot of defending to do as Derby carried on with the pressure. Just when we thought we could go into half time in the lead as another attack ended with a rebounded shot being flagged for offside, we let Derby in with an equaliser. They sent a high ball into the area, which Cooper got to but sadly the ball came backwards to a Derby player just in front of our goal, giving Wiedwald no chance. That was disappointing but at least it was 1-1 and they weren't in the lead.

At the start of the second half, we were under the cosh once again and I said we needed to change it. Luckily, Heckingbottom saw what I did and Saiz came back for his first game since he was sent off at Newport for spitting. Immediately he made a difference as we started attacking, playing some nice passing between us and upping the tempo. There was a lot of end-to-end play from both teams as we were caught out of position, having to race back to cover when an attack broke down. For a neutral fan it was a good advert for football because when we had attacked they responded by counter attacking. It also meant the game passed by really quickly and didn't drag. When Alioski came on, the lad next to me said he'd have to do something, and I replied saying he would as he'd got Saiz back and they played well together. Sure enough it wasn't long before Saiz put Alioski through and although their goalie saved his initial shot he headed in the rebound to send Leeds into the lead once again and the Leeds fans into exuberant celebrations! At that point it looked like we might steal the win as droves of Derby fans streamed to the exits. As the Leeds fans sang is there a fire drill, it didn't stop loads of their stands emptying as the incredible noise coming from the Leeds fans continued. Unfortunately for us, plus it shows you shouldn't leave the game until the final whistle blows, Derby got an equaliser in injury time again. That was such a shame for us as it would have been good to get the away win and three points. Still, that has to be one of the best fighting spirited games we have played there, and getting a point should be seen as a good result, especially as we have never played well at their new ground. The Baseball ground is another matter as we had some good results there in the past. Those of us who remember going there and standing in the Pop side will also remember that horrible narrow ginnel all the Leeds fans would be sent down at the end of the games there. Thousands of us crammed into a narrow space, it's surprising that more often than not we ended up unscathed from that experience!

When I got back to the coach it was good to meet up with a Leeds fan from India, who was with the Thames Valley Whites. At least he got into the game this year after apparently being denied entry in with the Leeds fans last year as they didn't agree he'd come to watch Leeds! How anyone can do that is beyond me, especially with the worldwide support Leeds United have!

Take a bow Leeds United fans as our atmosphere was brilliant tonight, getting behind the team all game, plus we don't need a drum! Seeing social media after the game, there were a lot of unhappy Leeds fans because we didn't get the win and blaming players etc. What I will say is that normally this would have been a good result but because games are running out for us, fans are up in arms that it wasn't three points. From my point of view, though, the season isn't over yet, things can still change and I haven't given up as yet. My positives after our recent bad run are that we have shown if we give Lasogga the right service he will score, we scored two goals away from home and took the lead twice. We can build on this and if the fans remain the twelfth man until the end of the season, maybe, just maybe, we can sneak into that final play-off spot. See you at Elland Road on Saturday for the Brentford game. LUFC - Marching on Together!

BRENTFORD (H) – 24TH FEBRUARY 2018

As we set off for Elland Road today, despite how cold it was, the sun was shining and the sky was blue. In my eyes this was a perfect setting for playing football in. When we got into the Peacock I said that I was expecting a win today seeing that we had been beaten and had two draws since Heckingbottom came to Leeds. As always, I go to games with an open mind and wait and see how things pan out on the pitch. A lot of Leeds players have come in for criticism recently on social media due to errors made which meant we conceded goals. Whilst I can understand the frustrations, I am hopeful that many players will be able to turn things around. I feel our fitness has been lacking and maybe the training methods will change now. Despite Wiedwald being on the receiving end of this too, I feel that with proper coaching he can turn things around too, even if my views are in a minority. Being able to communicate with his defence, together with being able to come for a ball comfortably at corners, will make a heck of a difference to his game.

As we were walking into the ground it was nice to catch up with Andy, who I hadn't seen for a while, and his friend. He mentioned us turning up to see Jimmy Armfield at his house in Blackpool in the seventies and whether I remembered it. I certainly did and said I'd shared the photo I'd taken at the time of Andy, Carole, Linda and Jimmy with the Blackpool Gazette on his recent death.

The team today were: Wiedwald, Cooper, Jansson, Berardi, Anita, Saiz, Alioski, Lasogga, O'Kane, Phillips and Dallas. Subs were: Ekuban for Lasogga (73), Sacko for Dallas (83) and Vieira for Saiz (90). Leeds won the game 1-0 with a goal from Cooper (31). Attendance was 28,428 including 539 Brentford fans.

The first 30 minutes saw Leeds on the receiving end of pressure for a lot of it. Our passing was poor, whereas Brentford's was very good, with their players often in loads of space. By giving them the ball all the time, it contributed to us not getting going in the right direction. The referee once again showed his true colours when he booked Anita for his first foul following this up by booking Alioski. Now admittedly Alioski went for a header and his arm was out, but I'm positive there was very little contact, not that you could tell as their player fell down as if he'd been hit by a missile! As he got up very quickly after the booking I would say that the referee was conned. Unfortunately, once the referee had shown his true colours by just talking to their player when he fouled us just after this, he didn't get any better. We had Wiedwald to thank for keeping us in the game when he made a superb save to deny them the opening goal.

We eventually got a free kick on the left-hand side of the pitch and I said that we needed to make the most of this. With a fantastic cross from Alioski's free kick, Cooper headed the ball into the net to put Leeds into the lead. It was possibly against the run of play, but even though Brentford had had lots of possession they hadn't scored. I said, once we got a goal it would take the pressure off us a bit and it did. We started to play, with Saiz stepping up, showing how we've missed having him in the team, working well with Alioski before Lasogga's shot was saved by their goalie. It was nice going in at half time in the lead.

The second half saw the officials really rile the Leeds fans up by being the twelfth and thirteenth men for Brentford. The linesman in front of the East Stand surpassed himself. After seemingly never up with play and always giving Brentford the benefit of the doubt with offside in the first half, he had no problems using his flag this half. One of his decisions, which was only inches into the opposition's half, was just baffling. Both he and the ref missed a blatant arm around Saiz that pulled him back and instead said play on. The worst decision was when Saiz passed the ball out to Lasogga, who was bearing down on our goal with just their goalie in his sights, and instead of giving us advantage he pulled us back for a free kick! It really does seem like their own personal feelings take over from their professional judgements because once again the officials are not treating both teams on a level playing field.

Prior to that chance, we did put some lovely play together with Saiz, Alioski (he did a lot of running today) and Lasogga who was unlucky not to score. I hadn't felt worried that Brentford would score as it looked like we had worn them down, but when they got a free kick just outside our penalty area in the last minutes, my stomach churned a little bit. There were gasps as Wiedwald made the save but probably more because he punched it out and we were able to close them down enough for the rebound shot to go over.

We are back to winning ways for the first time with Heckingbottom, but I'd also forgotten that it was our first win since Boxing Day. We can build on this and need to go to each game just getting as many points as we can. As I said last week, you never know and I will still stay positive. It was nice to bump into the Norwegian Whites on my way back to the car so got a customary photo.

At this moment of writing my blog, I am hearing sad news that a Leeds fan was knocked down after the game after pushing a young child out of the way. Until this is clarified I am not going to speculate on what happened and how he is as there are different versions and I wouldn't want to spread any wrong news. It does put things into perspective though.

Onto Middlesbrough on Friday night for another televised game. I will be going straight from work and I'm sure that will be so for a lot of our fans. With the snow forecast for this week, as long as it doesn't affect our travel arrangements I will be happy as I really don't like driving in it. See you there – LUFC – Marching on Together.

CHAPTER 9 – MARCH 2018

MIDDLESBROUGH (A) – 2ND MARCH 2018

Well what an end to the week with horrendous weather from the Beast from the East which saw heavy snow hit the north of England and Scotland. Storm Emma headed south yesterday and caused further havoc. In amongst these was a football game that was taking place tonight at Middlesbrough. Will it be on? Will it be postponed? Those questions were doing the rounds but I knew that this would be played despite the conditions because it was being televised for Sky. I did think a decision would be made today as long as there was no more snow, which turned out to be the case. Whilst I'm happy the game was going ahead, especially when I was on my way there, I had a lot of sympathy for those fans with tickets in the sell-out away end that can no longer go due to the snow. Our Bournemouth Whites, South Wales Whites, Bristol Whites to name a few have been unable to travel now which is a shame and I feel for them. I'm not sure if Inverness White got down either as everything he was trying was getting cancelled, but it was good to see our Lincolnshire Whites were able to make it. We had Peter flying over from Canberra, Australia, to see his first Leeds game with help from David who met him in Australia, so I'm hoping to catch up with him at the game. Whilst it may be a consolation that the game is being screened live, there is still no better feeling than watching a game in person and being amongst other Leeds fans! As I'd found out I wasn't in work this morning after all, at least it meant I could have a leisurely trip over to Leeds instead of a mad dash after work to get there for the coach.

Everyone met up in the Peacock where the Shropshire Whites had stopped for a quick pint before carrying on their way. When I took a photo of them one of them said that every time I take a photo of them we lose; something tells me he was right! That's it lads tell me to go away next time please! We heard that many fans had already arrived at the ground after a good trip so hopefully our journey will be the same. We were picking some fans up at Green Hammerton then heading straight to the ground and after a police escort arrived there at 7pm. We also heard there'd been some trouble in Middlesbrough itself before the game and our coach was showered with snowballs on arrival. I wasn't looking forward to the cold and looked like Michelin man with that many layers of clothes on. The wind was going to be the worst thing and outside the turnstiles it certainly was blowing a gale. I felt sorry for our stewards who had been out in that from 4pm. At least it looked like we would be sheltered inside as the wind was hitting the stand we were in.

After putting my flag up it was nice to see Simon, one of our Southern fans, had made it after many hours of travelling. I went back downstairs to find Peter, our Canberra White, and David – I was presented with a T-shirt especially for me, which was really nice. Peter reads my blog every week in Australia as I share the posts on Facebook and this time he will find he is part of it too. Cato from Norway was there as well.

The team today were: Wiedwald, Anita, Jansson, Cooper, Berardi, Dallas, O'Kane, Phillips, Lasogga, Saiz and Alioski. Subs were: Forshaw for Alioski (46) Vieira for Phillips (46) and Ekuban for O'Kane (68). Leeds lost 3-0 with the attendance 27,621 including 2,987 Leeds fans.

The snow started coming down again as we kicked off, but at least we had arrived safely, although I worried about getting home afterwards. If we got back to Elland Road okay at least McDonalds was open for 24 hours! Luckily the snow didn't stick and everything turned out fine from that point of view.

From a footballing point of view, this performance was a total disgrace. No passion, no commitment, no trying, no nothing. It looked like players were square pegs in round holes once again and I've no idea what formation we were using; neither did the players from the look of it! We were being run through time and time again and to be honest I'm surprised it took 31 minutes for them to score their first. Things were that bad that I don't think we even had a shot on target. Apart from a free kick, there was very little to talk about amongst ourselves. This was made even worse when they scored a second goal just before half time and nearly got a third.

Talking to others at half time, we all could accept a defeat but what we couldn't and wouldn't accept was the laying down and dying. Just because it was cold, that was no reason for the team not to turn up. The fans as usual had done their bit, getting behind them and singing all the time. Even all those hardy souls taking off their shirts and being bare chested put more effort in than the team! Those fans whose coach and relief coach broke down on the way to the game only got there at half time to find we were already two goals down.

The second half saw Forshaw (who missed the game last week as his wife was giving birth) and Vieira come on. Forshaw, playing against his former club, was the only one who stood out even though he only played for 45 minutes. To be honest the half carried on where we left off, being poor and not looking like we could score in a month of Sundays! I feel Anita isn't good enough for us and there is something about the way he runs/his stance that I cannot stand. In fact, he reminded me of Gregan in that way as I couldn't stand his stance either! As much as I've stuck up for Wiedwald in the past and despite the fact we only have Bailey Peacock-Farrell to challenge him due to Lonergan's injury, he has to lose his place in the team. I could go on because for once I felt there were no positives to take from this game. As much as I said we'd win and get something out of the game to push on for the play-offs, the reality is much different. We are light years away from having a settled side that can challenge for the Premiership. All the hope and stuffing were knocked out of me today, and I have to accept that this season is over for us. What makes it stand out as a bad defeat was this day was the anniversary of our League Cup win in 1968, when we did have a team to be proud of! When we went three goals down I know fans were upset, but smashing seats does no one any good, least of all us. I challenged a young lad telling him to pack it in, and to give him his due he did stop. However, the older chap with him took exception to me having a go at him and wagged his finger at me. I said that it reflects badly on us all and I will stand by that. I know everyone is entitled to their opinion but causing damage is something I hate.

I went down to get my flag on 80 minutes and it was nice to be offered help from the Boro stewards to take it down. I stayed there for the last few minutes and chatted to a fan, who said he worked with Boro fans. He follows me on Twitter and reads my blog so he is another one who will find himself in it. Another fan who reads my blog had also been standing near my seat, which is nice to know as it makes it worthwhile, even though I keep falling asleep whilst writing this up! Another thing that was pointed out was Leeds need to ditch the black kit on an evening as they blended in too much with the crowd. No wonder they couldn't pass the ball between them!

As I reminisce of the past once again, my first ever visit to Middlesbrough was to Ayresome Park for Bill Gate's testimonial in May 1974. A dozen of us went up on the train, changing at Darlington, and to say that we hadn't played them before or not for a long time, I couldn't believe the hostility of their fans. That was something that got worse every time we went there, and along with Maine Road they were the worst grounds to visit as a Leeds United fan. I even left a game at 4.15pm at Ayresome Park one year as the trouble was that bad. These episodes in the seventies are all recorded in my first book *Follow Me and Leeds United* for those fans who want to find out what we as a fan group had to put up with to follow our team.

As we have Wolves at home to look forward to on Wednesday, hopefully the weather will have warmed up so it won't affect the fans travelling to Elland Road. This really is the last chance saloon for the team to show they can perform but there will have to be wholesale changes. Give our youngsters the chance to shine and show what they can do as they certainly can't do any worse than that performance, if you can call it that. See you then – LUFC – Marching on together.

WOLVERHAMPTON WANDERERS (H) – 7TH MARCH 2018

I was on BBC Radio Leeds this morning before heading to work. I was asked how many points I would give Heckingbottom out of 10 since he has been here. Maybe I surprised myself and did him a disservice, but I said none although I did say he could have a point after our recent win! I wanted the team to go out and fight tonight as it was a last chance saloon for many fans.

After a full on day at work I felt like I had a thick head and was looking forward to taking my mind off things as I headed to Elland Road with my daughter Dani and granddaughter Hannah. After arriving just after 7pm having had a good run there, we called in the Peacock first. A girl from Ireland was attending her first game here today, and also Peter from Australia was attending his first-ever Leeds game at Elland Road. After seeing our defeat and the way we lost at Boro, I was hoping for better things. A big thank you to Peter for buying my second book *Once a Leeds fan, always a Leeds fan* and, as always, thank you for the support it is appreciated.

The team were: Bailey Peacock-Farrell (playing his first game for a couple of years), Berardi, Jansson, Cooper, Anita, Forshaw, Sacko, Saiz, Lasogga, Dallas and Phillips. Subs were: Pennington for Cooper went off injured 36, Hernandez for Sacko 46 and Ekuban for Lasogga 73. Attendance was 26,434 including approximately 1,250 Wolves fans. Leeds lost the game 3-0.

All we want as Leeds fans is to see the team giving 100% and take pride in wearing a Leeds United shirt. After the diabolical display at Boro, we didn't start the game very well at all despite having the first attack of the game, and their goalie made a save. After approximately 15 minutes we started fighting for the ball and looked up for it. We got a corner and then wasted it with a silly short one that ended up with us losing the ball. A weak link was down the left-hand side as Wolves attacked the Kop end with Anita and Sacko not combining well at all. Anita was either out of position or beaten time after time. One time, Sacko was standing in the middle of the pitch leaving their man on his own on the wing in front of the East Stand, and by the time he had woken up their player had the ball in acres of space and set up another Wolves attack. We had Peacock-Farrell to thank for not being at least three goals down in the first 20 minutes! We were at sixes and sevens all over the pitch, and I've no idea who was supposed to be marking whom, as wave after wave of Wolves attacks showed them in loads of space time after time. We weren't closing them down at all and it was no surprise that they scored, taking the lead. The Leeds fans had been trying to up the tempo once again, getting behind the team, but then everyone had the stuffing knocked out of them when Wolves took the lead. With Peacock-Farrell denying them a second goal, I was hopeful we would be able to get something out of the game. Lots were hoping for an upset against the top of the table team but that took a dive when they got their second goal just before half time. After a great save from Peacock-Farrell they were first to the rebound, scoring their second goal of the game. My only disappointment was just before they scored the South Stand kept hold of the ball and wouldn't let it come back into play. Now if we were a few goals to the good, that may be an opportune moment to waste a bit of time, but sadly for us by the time we got the ball back into play we were a second goal down as Wolves went straight down to the Kop end and scored!

At the start of the second half I wasn't sure if I really wanted to go back up and watch the game, although I knew I would as I always stay until the bitter end! Hernandez came on for Sacko, and although the team tried we were really out of our depth and showed what a gulf there was between the two teams. We had a shot from Lasogga on target and a couple of other chances, but apart from that we were very poor. When Wolves got a third when they lobbed Peacock-Farrell as he came out of his area that was it - game over once again. Although that was a mistake from our young goalie, he was actually my man of the match as he pulled off some great saves, despite being let down from the players in front of him. What more can I say as we ended with another 3-0 defeat. I told Hannah that being a Leeds United fan is character building because it teaches you how to be a good loser! I don't know about the good part, but it is something we as Leeds fans have had to get used to over the years. At the moment things are as bad as I've seen them for a long time after such high hopes at the start of the season. There seems to be a lot that is wrong in the background, and, although I can't pinpoint anything with proof, a lot of fans have turned on the role Orta has in the club. Even listening to Heckingbottom on BBC Radio Leeds after the game, he said that things are different at our club. What I will say is that I don't think we are fit enough!

I've no idea what the goal keeping coach has been doing where Wiedwald was concerned, as things never improved over the season. As for the free kick specialist, I cannot for the life of me see any improvements on that score either!

Where do we go from here? With season ticket renewals out at the moment, I know I will renew ours, although I am waiting for the paper copies to arrive. I think the club have made two big mistakes: bringing them out so early, and also the fact that any season ticket holders who bought the half ones at Christmas or one for the first time have not been given the same renewals price as us long-term season ticket holders. In the past, if you bought a season ticket at the higher rate as a new holder, once renewals came out they got the same price as us. Sadly, this will definitely affect fans renewing plus also the very poor displays of late will impact greatly on sales I feel.

Onto Reading on Saturday, it is once again a case of going through the motions, enjoying the day out with our fans and trying to forget the 90 minutes in between. It is a coping mechanism that works for me as I forget how bad we are once I've slept on things. Will we get a win anytime soon, who knows? But as we slip down the table to 13th my aspirations of top two for this season are well and truly gone! See you Saturday – LUFC – Marching on Together!

READING (A) – 10TH MARCH 2018

Before I start my blog today, I would like to say the following: if any fan is interested in buying my books at a game, please note that I only carry one of each book with me on the day. If I know

more than one copy is required, I can sort this in advance if you let me know. Prices are as follows: *Follow Me and Leeds United, Once a Leeds fan, always a Leeds fan* and *The Sleeping Giant Awakens 2016-17* are all £12.99 each. *The Good, The Bad and The Ugly of Leeds United; Leeds United in the 1980s,* my joint book with Andrew Dalton, is £14.99.

As the loyal contingent of Leeds fans headed to Reading today the team had very little to play for but pride. I thought I must be bonkers when I got up at 4.50am! I posted that online before I left home and it was good to see comments from other fans doing the same thing. As usual the camaraderie of our fans is second to none.

After the snow had returned two days ago causing havoc where I lived for approximately five hours then disappearing as fast as it came, I was glad to have a clear run to Leeds, despite the

heavy rain and a damp, miserable start. This continued on our way down the motorway with some fog thrown in, but it eased off by the time we arrived at Windsor to have tea with Her Majesty the Queen! Well not quite, and we arrived just too late to see the changing of the guard. Having never seen anything like that in person before, I would have loved that opportunity. I'm sure Leeds United will always be in her thoughts though as she handed the FA Cup to Billy Bremner in 1972 after our win! We had a nice stay in the King and Castle pub and I chatted to other Leeds fans in there as well as taking photos. As we left the pub I managed to get a group from the Fullerton Park Supporters' Club coach together and a lad asked if I wanted him to take a photo for us. He said he wouldn't run off with my camera and actually supported that club across the Pennines, to which I chanted, 'There's only one United!' Thanks for taking the photo though! I managed another sleep on the coach and woke up just before arriving at the ground. Although it was an hour before kick-off, it took us about 20 minutes to get dropped off but at least the weather was fine and we even saw some sunshine! As the stewards checked my bag one was astounded to learn that we had travelled five hours to get here as he didn't know where Leeds was! I did feel quite weary as I went into the ground, with the early start catching up with me, but luckily I soon perked up.

Inside the ground, although there were plenty of Leeds fans all standing around watching the TVs it was quiet and orderly. When I watched the TV, I saw Allan Clarke's goal at Wembley in 1972 and Eddie Gray's goal against Burnley and I cheered the goals as if I was still at the games as old habits die hard! Going into the ladies was treacherous as it looked like they had only just finished cleaning the floors. They were wet and slippery and stayed that way even until the end of the game. Maybe it was the dampness that made it stay that way. Once again, we had plenty of our male fans deciding to walk into the ladies to use the loos which upset some of our female fans. I had a quick chat with Phillip Thumbsup Cresswell before putting my flag up at the front behind the goal, and it was nice to catch a glimpse of it later on TV during replays of the game. Just before the game kicked off, the singing under the stands had lots in a jovial mood, showing that the Leeds fans had turned up once again - but would the team?

The team were: Peacock-Farrell (retaining his place), De Bock, Jansson, Berardi (captain), Pennington, O'Kane, Saiz, Alioski, Hernandez, Ekuban and Forshaw. Subs were: Lasogga for Ekuban 77 and Dallas for Hernandez 85. Attendance was 19,770 including 3,467 Leeds fans. Leeds drew 2-2 with Jansson (43) and Hernandez (56) getting our goals.

It was disappointing to see that Leeds didn't have a mascot again. It is a shame considering all the young fans that were at the game. The Leeds fans were in good voice, giving the team backing with plenty of WACCOE chants and scarf waving. Despite that, within 16 minutes once again we found ourselves a goal down, despite having an early chance when their goalie saved from Alioski. Reading were suspiciously beating the offside trap every time despite looking to be in front of our men. That said, they ran at us causing lots of problems with their speed and won the battle to score their first goal. We had Peacock-Farrell to thank for saving a long-range shot that was dipping just under the bar and another good save later on. We then had another scramble off the line with Pennington and Peacock-Farrell battling to keep the ball out, then Pennington blocked the rebound as we got the ball away. I thought that could be our saving grace and give us a chance to do something with the game. That happened just before half time when we equalised with a goal from Jansson after a corner was punched out by their goalie and hooked back into the box from Forshaw. It seems ages since we scored a goal.

At half time I went downstairs and had to gingerly pick my way down the steep steps in the stand, which were frankly dangerous. That showed when we scored as fans went hurtling down them. It was no wonder Reading stewards were clearing the gangway regularly. It was also precarious underfoot, and as I realised I had no grip on my soles I had to gingerly step over puddles on the floor from spilt drinks, which wasn't good. At least I didn't end up on my backside in a puddle! Taking plenty of photos, the Midland Whites from Derby, Leicester and Birmingham have to get a mention today for their great support and it was nice to say hello! A big thank you to Allison for buying my second book, your support is appreciated.

The second half hadn't been going long when Leeds took the lead with a shot from the edge of the area from Hernandez. Sadly, this lead only lasted a few minutes as once again down our left-hand side, we left a Reading player in acres of space and they were able to equalise. Whitby John who stood next to me thought I'd lost the plot when I looked at the scoreboard and said, 'oh it says 2-2, when did we score two?' I'll blame it on the early morning start and tiredness, having forgotten our first-half goal even though I'd taken a photo of the scoreboard at 2-1! Silly me! We came close a few times with the post getting in the way of a goal for us plus Alioski brought a great save from their goalie, although I thought we grew into the game as a team. We still had some worrying defensive mishaps but at least they didn't score a third. I felt slightly disappointed that

the game ended quietly, but it was a point rather than a defeat which I'll take as a positive. One of our young fans took a chance at the end of the game, getting Hernandez's shirt, and my heart was in my mouth when I saw him jump over the wall and run across the pitch to grab it!

Once again, a big thank you to all the fans who wanted their photos taken today and say they read my blog. As always, I do this as a fan for the fans! We had a great run back to Leeds, only to look like we were being diverted once again as the M1 was shut at Barnsley. Luckily we got there just before it was completely shut and ended up getting back onto the carriageway and on our way. That was a relief and despite sleeping a lot of the way home, as well as many others, getting home sooner rather than later was a bonus!

With Sheffield Wednesday at home next Saturday, I want to get in to Leeds as early as possible as I want to renew our season tickets first. A glutton for punishment that's for sure, but even if this season does turn out to be a big disappointment on the pitch, hopefully things in the background will now have stabilized. I'm sure that things have been a mess but we need stability to move on in the right direction. Mistakes have been made and the club should never take our support for granted, because we have been beyond loyal despite everything that has gone on in the past 15 years! See you then – LUFC – Marching on Together!

SHEFFIELD WEDNESDAY (H) – 17TH MARCH 2018

Today saw a poignant day for my family as we should have been celebrating my daughter Charlotte's birthday. Despite her short life of 17 days when she was taken from us suddenly and unexpectedly, she found fame as a Leeds United fan. She attended her first game against Crystal Palace at six days old. On the day that she was born we played Arsenal at Highbury, which meant I had another priority that day and didn't make it to the game. Charlotte made headline news that day as her birth was announced live on TV just after half time by Greavsie. He said I'd seen more action that day than Leeds had! She will never be forgotten and will always be in our hearts.

Waking up to snow once again that had settled in the garden, it was nice to see that it was only flurries and the roads were clear. The icy wind chill and the fact the temperature was hovering around zero degrees or below meant it was going to be a cold one that's for sure, even though the sun kept coming out.

With another crowd above 30,000 expected, our support once more shows how extensive our worldwide fan base reaches. I was meeting DJ from Singapore coming to his first Leeds United game having arrived yesterday, and a big thank you to him for buying one of my books. Also, we had Sam and his wife arriving from Australia, and other fans in attendance from Norway, Sweden and Ireland. BBC Radio Leeds said we even had some fly in from Iceland, such is the pull of the name Leeds United. It's just a shame that our team cannot match this fantastic support sadly.

The team were: Peacock-Farrell, Berardi, Jansson, Pennington, O'Kane, Forshaw, Dallas, Alioski, Hernandez, Ekuban and Tom Pearce making his debut at left back. Subs were: Lasogga

for Ekuban (59), Grot for Pearce (77) and Phillips for O'Kane (78). Leeds lost the game 2-1 with Grot scoring the Leeds goal (86). Attendance was 31,638 including 2,039 Sheffield Wednesday fans. It was good to see that the scoreboard now has the teams, score and time on it!

Although I wouldn't make any predictions of the score line, I still had high hopes at the start of the game that we could turn things around after our bad run of results since Boxing Day 2017. Talking of turning around, it was the first time we've changed ends at the start of a game for a while. We didn't get off to the best of starts though as we let Wednesday have the run of the pitch, giving them early chances to take the lead. Passes from Hernandez were badly placed at least three times, but all of a sudden it looked like he upped his game as we started to gain more and more possession. We won a free kick at the edge of the box and, as I had my camera poised, our free kick didn't go where we all expected it to and we were unlucky not to score. We got in another scoring position and Ekuban should have done better as he blasted the ball over the top of the goal when he would have been better hitting it low and hard. I thought Alioski was working hard and getting some crosses in and when someone shouted the opposite of my thoughts I said he was running around a lot. The lad in front of me turned around and said he'd run around a bit for £20,000 a week! As I said, I don't think he's on that much, but I did take his point of view on board. Despite having lots of possession, I just turned around to get my bag to go downstairs at half time when I heard the Wednesday fans cheering as the ball ended up in our net. As my heart sank, the Leeds fans started cheering as the linesman put his flag up for offside. That was a relief as it meant we

were still level pegging going in at the break.

As I came back into the stand, I couldn't believe what I was seeing with the snow and swirling wind. For some reason I was thinking the worst was over, even though I'd seen severe weather warnings on the way to the ground. The two lads who stood in front of me and the lad to the left of me (he was expecting a defeat), didn't come back into the stand for the second half. The game itself wasn't a spectacle so I suppose it wasn't a surprise that they hadn't come back up to their seats. That lad to the left of me said Wednesday were very poor and so were we, and if we couldn't beat them there was no hope for us. At that point I couldn't see us scoring as we have to learn to take our chances when they are there and we hadn't.

In the second half Alioski was getting crosses in, and although we came close it wasn't enough to put their goalie under pressure. They did have a chance earlier but then, against the run of play, the taking your chances when they are there came back to bite us on the backside. Wednesday attacked and the ball came off the crossbar and they put the rebound into the net. There was some time wasting after that as they took ages to get back to the centre spot. I had that sinking feeling again as we had to come from behind once again. As the weather deteriorated into a snowstorm the team looked down and out. It wasn't until we made two subs that we looked like an attacking side, and four minutes from time, with a second chance of a cross from Hernandez, Grot was on hand to head the ball into the net to equalise. At that moment in time I'd have taken a draw and a point. When six minutes of injury time was put up, the Leeds fans cheered as I shouted come on Leeds because I believed we could go on and win the game. Sadly I was very wrong as Wednesday broke away and got the better of Pennington to stick the ball into the net for the winner. Why oh why can we not stop conceding so many goals? My granddaughter Laura hadn't wanted to come to the game today as she was tired after sleeping at a friend's house last night. As her fingers and toes froze at the end of the game and I was shivering so much I couldn't hold my camera straight, I could understand her reluctance to be there!

Talking to a few fans as we came out of the ground, all they can see is a downward spiral for the team and the worst position and performances for a long time. Having renewed our season tickets before the game I know I'm in it for the long haul, but I feel sure many fans are going to question their loyalty. Having got the great offer from Leeds United for the Bolton game of bringing a friend for free for season ticket holders, I am bringing my eldest daughter and all my granddaughters to the game. I've given up thinking we can rescue the season or can win, although it could get very close to survival even at this stage of the season. Thank goodness we had a great start because without that we would have been relegation fodder already! See you at the Bolton game – LUFC – Marching on Together!

BOLTON WANDERERS (H) – 30TH MARCH 2018

Heading for Elland Road after the international break, for once I was very grateful for the break because things on the park weren't going very well, with lots of fans becoming disillusioned about the fall down the table. I felt the break had at least rejuvenated me, plus whet my appetite, so I was looking forward to today's game against Bolton. I was in a happy mood, singing along to the radio on my way into Leeds. In between our last game and the break, I attended the LFU AGM (Leeds Fans United/CBS) where Angus Kinnear, the Leeds CEO, spoke about the ongoing talks between LFU and the Club regarding fan ownership. I was there to represent myself but also Jailhouse John's groups from WACCOE as he died over a year ago. I was asked to take over the communications

with the groups after his death and I was pleased to do this. Being seen as trustworthy and someone who would always do her best to look after the interests of fans in the groups, it was a proud moment for me. As for the meeting, this was very positive and I look forward to hearing the outcome of these talks in due course.

I'd gone in early as I was meeting Craig from the Johannesburg branch who was here with his friend Michelle. He was acting as a go-between to take three of my books back to Keith in South Africa. After first trying Billy's Bar, I found I'd just missed them in the Peacock but luckily found them in the Pavilion. Bobby from Coventry bought a book from me too after stopping me to chat. As usual, I want to say a big thank you to Keith and Bobby for their support, it is appreciated. I look

forward to receiving feedback in due course once the books have been read. After bumping into Gary from my home village Carlton, Neil from New Zealand stopped to talk to me telling me he reads my blogs all the time. I had a few other people telling me they look forward to my blogs and looking to see if they are in the photos, so it is really lovely to know that these blogs serve a purpose with our worldwide fans. Thanks for the feedback from our Irish and Thames Valley Whites fans.

As I was on my way to meet two of my daughters Michelle and Danielle and my three granddaughters, I took a photo of some friends, and a couple of lads more or less stopped too so I asked did they want their photos taken? One said, 'but I'm a Bolton fan'! I said I'm happy to take photos of any fans for my blog so I did! I just managed to get into my position for taking photos at the start of the game as the teams came out. I'd already found Craig and Michelle again behind the goal to get some more photos. Today was going to be another great crowd due to the offer the club made for season ticket holders to bring a friend to the game for free. Recommended by the Trust, it was great to see this initiative taken up by the club which was also offered to Bolton fans. After hearing that Bolton fans had managed to have the Drysalters pub shut down due to incidents before the game, I was actually surprised to hear this. Having always been given plenty of tickets at Bolton and been made welcome in the local pub there, we haven't had any problems recently. Casting my mind back to when they played at Burnden Park though, we did have some trouble there if I remember correctly but I can't remember anything in recent years. Someone will possibly put me right on that score.

The team today were: Peacock-Farrell, Berardi (captain), Jansson, Pennington, Dallas (at right back), Alioski, O'Kane, Vieira, Ekuban, Hernandez and Lasogga. Subs were: Saiz for Lasogga (62) and Grot for Alioski (82). Attendance was 35,377 including 2,480 Bolton fans. Leeds won the game 2-1 with goals from Ekuban (4) and Hernandez (50).

Within four minutes of the start of the game Leeds found themselves in the lead with a goal from Ekuban after Lasogga's cross! Ekuban had looked very lively in the initial stages and he will have been glad to score as much as us fans were glad to see it. As I'd thought I couldn't see where the next win was coming from prior to this, that was a welcome goal to change my mind! When I thought there was something wrong with my eyes and I couldn't see clearly, I found out why when Danielle started laughing at me. I'd put my glasses on only to find out that the left hand lens had fallen out and the frame was broken, more money and yes I have just renewed our season tickets! And I've got to save the money for my away season ticket too. After an inspiring start from Leeds things quietened down, although we did threaten a few times which was good to see. I started to feel very weary courtesy of a stressful day at work and my sister's party at Drax the day before. For some reason that was when the game seemed to drag and I was looking forward to hearing the half-time whistle. We were very unlucky not to score a second just before the whistle went, but unfortunately Jansson's header hit the crossbar. With Bolton playing in purple, we managed to contain them most of the time but they did come close to an equaliser. One thing I noticed was that they had a couple of 'giants' playing for them!

At half time I surpassed my silliness due to being tired when I tried to make a cup of coffee for Keith only to realise I'd left it in the bag I'd handed to Michelle. Unfortunately they were in the family stand so he declined the hot water. I'd already left the flask behind with the girls when they were at McDonalds so it wasn't to be my day. At least it's the thought that counts!

The second half started off the same as the first did, with Leeds getting a second goal due to the persistence of Alioski on the left of the goal in front of the Kop. Hernandez was on hand to get to the loose ball in the penalty area to give us some breathing space, or so we thought. I thought the game might die a death as in the first half, but instead it was Bolton who pulled one back after they'd won a free kick and then stepped up their game. As the Leeds crowd got very restless we were very jittery and it took us a bit of time to settle down after Bolton scored. It was a case of déjà vu as the South Stand had just sung 'how sh*t must you be, we're winning at home'! I think the gallows humour should have been left until the end of the game when we knew what the final score was! Also singing 'Jansson, knock him out' ended up with him being booked along with the Bolton player not long after when they had a set too! It was one of those moments when you felt it wouldn't have happened if we'd not mentioned it. On the whole despite it being a large crowd the atmosphere wasn't one of the best. Things did improve on the pitch and we were very unlucky with a couple of great shots that were saved by their goalie. The second half raced by and it was already the 85th minute in no time at all, probably because there had been more action on the pitch. Luckily, we managed to hold out to get the win and the welcome three points.

After the game there was some argy bargy between some fans, with one getting dragged away by others. The police went over for a chat but as we came out of the car park instead of three fans there were five and he was still having a go! Whether he'd had too much to drink I've no idea but obviously something had got to him even though we'd won!

Tuesday sees us head to Fulham for the evening fixture that is live on Sky again. Luckily I'm off work now so even though it will be a late night, it won't feel so bad with not having to be up early for work. I'll take each game as it comes and yes it won't be easy that's for sure, but today showed we put up more of a fight so long may that continue. See you on Tuesday – LUFC – Marching on Together!

CHAPTER 10 – APRIL 2018

FULHAM (A) – 3RD APRIL 2018

Before I start my blog today I wish to pay my respects to the families and friends of our fans Christopher Loftus and Kevin Speight who were brutally murdered in Istanbul on 5th April 2000. Never forgive and never forget that they went to a football game to watch Leeds United and didn't return. Leeds fans are asked to turn their backs at the game tonight on 18 minutes to pay their respects to them as those fans at the game did 18 years ago. RIP Chris and Kev.

It's also 15 years since Marion, one of our Cockney Whites, died this week. Marion was a regular who only missed three games at home, away or abroad in 24 years and I've seen some lovely words from Greenie and her friend Tricia on Facebook regarding this. The whole week is a bad one and culminates in the anniversary of the sudden death of my baby daughter tomorrow. Life can be cruel with the best ones taken too soon sadly.

When I left home this morning I wasn't sure whether I'd be able to get to the motorway via the A58 or not as I'd had to turn back late last night due to flooding. I was also surprised to see my garden still full of snow when I got home, despite the torrential rain since the snow stopped at 11am. Having had at least 2 inches of snow yesterday in Halifax, all I can say is what a difference a day makes and thank goodness the game was today. There was no flooding to be seen on the A58 and I arrived at Elland Road just after 9am. A big thank you to Helen who I met straight away for buying my books *Follow Me and Leeds United* and *The Good, The Bad and The Ugly of Leeds United, Leeds United in the 1980s*. As always thank you for the support which is appreciated. The good thing about the game today was that I wasn't at work so even getting home late won't be an issue for once.

It was good to hear that my books are doing well in the club shop too and I look forward to seeing a dedicated book area after a six-week refurbishment that will take place shortly. Also for those fans who keep asking me about the CD we are recording with all the old Leeds songs, this is still in progress but unfortunately we have hit some technical issues. As we are trying ways to overcome the obstacle and I am waiting to receive it, it is sadly taking longer than I thought to sort out. It will be done but at this moment in time I don't have an end date for bringing this out so please bear with us.

CHRIS LOFTUS AND KEVIN SPEIGHT
WHO DIED TRAGICALLY IN ISTANBUL
APRIL 5TH 2000

THEY WILL NEVER BE FORGOTTEN

I woke up on the coach on the way there and thought we weren't going to get a pub stop as it was already 1.30pm before Sue pointed out it was an evening kick-off, oops. There's definitely no hope for me especially as I can't even blame alcohol for being a dipstick! At least catching up on my sleep is better than having a hangover that's all I can say lol. We arrived in Hammersmith for our pub stop prior to the game and found Leeds fans already there with some of the South Kirkby branch who had gone for a four-day trip to the capital. Unfortunately, one lad who was going on their day trip missed his lift as they were both waiting in two different places. He then spent another £80 to travel down by train as he hadn't missed a game so it had to be done, showing commitment and the things fans do for Leeds! We were joined by Mitch and Richard and as usual spent some time reminiscing about the past and having a laugh. One tale Mitch relayed was when they went to Ferencvaros. With the organised trips you were expected to share a room with another fan. He'd been woken up at 4am to hear his room colleague shouting he'd lost his teeth, but the funny part of it was them being found in a plant pot later in the day where he'd lost them after being sick, urghhh.

When we arrived at the ground we had a long walk from where the coaches parked and went straight in. Last year I'd struggled to get through the turnstiles with my arms full and came out backwards. This year I still had my bag with me, although I'd left my jacket on the coach and didn't have the same trouble there again. After a temperature of 2.5 degrees in the morning when I left home, it was 16 degrees in London – that's barmy. I went to hang my flag up only to be told the only place it was allowed to go was along the back of the stand. After showing my fire paperwork

I put it up at the back of the stand. Having a chat to some Sherburn Whites, it was a shock to realise that it was 30 years since I'd moved from Selby to Halifax. I then did my good deed for the day when I saw someone I knew was getting into an argument with a steward and was in danger of being kicked out. It was misleading as fans had been allowed in the right area according to the ticket but her seat was on the opposite side. One steward had allowed her in and this other one was kicking off about it and wouldn't let her go further down the stand. She did try though, so I quickly diffused the situation and said I would take her to her correct seat. Luckily that worked out okay. One of our disabled fans had also had issues with parking outside the ground. Having been in a disabled parking spot since 4pm, someone tried to get him kicked out of it and got the police involved. As he had a blue badge and was disabled, they said he had every right to park there! I also made a suggestion to the stewards in the ground that I asked to be passed on (not sure whether they will though): it's alright having notices saying the steps in the stand were uneven, but as I'd already missed my footing on the way down the stand and I was stone cold sober they needed something else to highlight this. I'd seen one of our fans with a walking stick nearly go flying too - it's alright having the steps painted yellow but they need a warning sign on them as it took you unawares when going down them. Going back up the stand didn't create the same problems but I'm sure there would have been many more who struggled with it.

The team today were: Peacock-Farrell, Jansson, Berardi, Pennington, Dallas, Hernandez, Ekuban, Vieira, O'Kane, Alioski and Saiz. Subs were: Phillips for O'Kane (22), Lasogga for Ekuban (72) and Grot for Alioski (72). Leeds lost the game 2-0 and the attendance was 21,538 including 4,003 Leeds fans plus 2,000 'neutral' fans with the majority being Leeds! Fantastic support once again, especially with nothing left to play for.

I hadn't realised that Fulham was on the banks of the River Thames, which ran at the back of the stand to the left. I think It has been dark every time we have been there recently or I'd just forgotten! There again when we played there for the first game of the season in 1985 there was only a crowd of 5,772, which included loads of our fans but I can't remember anything about the ground that day. I'd driven a minivan down with no seats in the back, if I remember right, with six members of the newly formed Selby Branch of the Leeds United Supporters' Club. Although it was another bad result, with us losing 3-1, the memory of that day that lingers in my mind was pulling into Leicester Forest services and being met by Millwall fans. They hadn't reckoned on some of our fans who were on the coaches taking exception to being 'attacked' and were returned to the other side of the motorway pronto! How those who ran across all six lanes of the motorway didn't get killed I'll never know!

We started off with plenty possession, but soon were overcome as Fulham had attack after attack, with a lot of this coming down the right wing. Dallas, playing right back, was struggling to contain their man as they used their speed to their advantage. I can't say I've enjoyed seeing Dallas play in that position as it is a square peg in a round hole situation once again. Why can't we

play to our strengths? Surely we have someone in the club who has this as their natural position? We were lucky young Bailey Peacock-Farrell was on form to prevent a couple of goals by making great saves. On 18 minutes the Leeds fans, who had been giving great support to the team with constant singing, paid tribute to Chris and Kev en masse. 'Turn your backs for Chris and Kev' was sung from the back of the stand and I shouted to those around me to do the same. A very touching moment to show we will remember them both always.

I suppose it didn't come as a great surprise when Fulham took the lead, although I don't think their man knew much about it. The ball struck him and went in with his back to the goal when we failed to defend a corner once more. We hadn't played well at all and had already had to change the team when O'Kane went off injured. Our play was slow and predictable, whereas Fulham were fast and putting us under constant pressure. One lad arrived in his correct seat just before the break as he'd gone to the wrong row by mistake. He told me off for not supporting him as I didn't agree with the seat number, sorry!

At half time I went down onto the concourse which was packed with Leeds fans. After taking some photos, including one of my 'adopted' daughter, someone said that Ralph Ineson, a famous Leeds fan, was nearby. I went across to find him for a photo and was introduced to some Nottingham Whites too. After introducing myself to Ralph I mentioned I was a friend of Gary Edwards and I had travelled with him on Wallace Arnold coaches in our early days of following Leeds. Ralph mentioned his dad (I hope I got that right?) used to drive the coaches in those early days of following Leeds in the seventies. We had some good drivers in those days who used to look after us so you never know he might have driven us to games. Of course, I did show him my *Follow Me and Leeds United* book as that is the name of my blog too and thanks for having your photo taken with it Ralph! He got the year right for the photo on the front of the book, which was taken by the *Daily Express* in 1975. He also showed an old war wound on his forehead caused by Jack Charlton. He was still in a pushchair and Jack was running, pushing him, but unfortunately he wasn't strapped in so went head first out of the pushchair, ouch.

The second half had kicked off when I got back into the stand and our row seemed to have gained at least four people. It meant that there wasn't much room, but Whitby John found himself in an argument with the lad next to him for encroaching on his space. Unfortunately, at football games these things happen but at least the argument died a death and I didn't need to intervene. I know it is frustrating when we are losing but we shouldn't be arguing or coming to blows with our own fans. Our fans were absolutely magnificent for the whole game and we don't need those silly clappers that had been handed out to the home fans that's for sure. We started to play better in the second half but still had to rely on Peacock-Farrell to deny Fulham a further goal. Alioski had the ball in the net, only for the linesman to put his flag up for offside. It's ironic but he didn't have the same reactions in the first half when Fulham were attacking the goal in front of us. We should have equalised with a great chance for Ekuban, only for him to hit the ball at their goalie when he

should have lifted the ball over him. That was a disastrous decision because Fulham raced to the far end of the pitch to put the ball into our net to give them a second goal and put the game out of reach for us. Alioski received some bad challenges and with just over 15 minutes of normal time left we made a double sub, with both Ekuban and Alioski making way for Lasogga and Grot. When Lasogga was brought down with a cynical challenge from behind by their player, who was also the last man, I was expecting a red card. Well of course he got a yellow card, but when I think back to our sending offs this season they were nowhere near as bad as this tackle.

We saw the end of the game out with nothing really to play for. I went up to the back of the stand to get my flag and didn't hang about after the whistle blew as I knew it was a long walk back to the coach. It certainly was for one of our fans as he struggled with the distance to get there. We were one of the last coaches away from the ground as another of our fans got lost when a policeman directed him in the wrong direction. We made it back to Watford Gap services in good time, although seeing a lorry with a car that had been hit in the slow lane of the M1, I just hope everyone got out safely. Just after we left the services one of our fans on the coach was taken ill with a medical episode but luckily, with the help of Keith and another couple of fans, they were able to sort him out. The story of Leeds fans lives happened again as we had to endure two detours off the motorway due to closures, but by going in a different direction to the diversions we ended up in front of the other coaches. Also, avoiding the M621 and going via Tingley roundabout helped too. All this meant that we didn't get back to Leeds till just after three and I eventually got home at 3.45am, a round trip of approximately 19 hours. The things we do to follow our team!

On the way back to Leeds on the coach I found that I couldn't be bothered typing up my blog. As I am not in work tomorrow I can type it up in the morning as I wouldn't be posting it till then.

As we hit the worst day of my life again, I can say that had an impact on the way I was feeling. Also I can't see a way forward at all for us as a club on the pitch at this moment in time. The hope that had been there at the start of the season that this was the year we made it back to the Premiership has been taken away big style. The last accounts under Cellino when Radrizzani came in as co-owner have now appeared, which shows the amount of money the latter has put into the club to buy it. I'm looking forward to Mike Thornton's analysis of the accounts which will help me understand more about the ins and outs of them. Radrizzani has done a lot in the background to steady the ship so to speak, which was always going to impact on us as a club. I only hope that he sees where things are not working and learns from this for next season.

Saturday sees us take on Sunderland so we need to get something from this game as we are at home. Whether we will or not remains to be seen. See you then – LUFC – Marching on Together!

SUNDERLAND (H) – 7 APRIL 2018

After I took a photo of the plaque at Elland Road on Tuesday remembering Chris and Kev, our two fans who were murdered in Turkey, I mentioned on the WACCOE forum that it was hard to read and asked whether there was anything we could do to remedy this. I'm very pleased to say that my message was picked up by the Leeds United Trust and along with the Don Revie plaques in the Kop they have now been polished and upgraded by them. Leeds fans looking after Leeds fans is what we do so a big well done from me. It is the least we can do to commemorate their murders and ensure we never forget them. RIP to both lads and thoughts are with their families and friends at this tough time of the year.

With nothing left to play for this season, we still were expecting a crowd of around 30,000 including a sizeable contingent from Norway of approximately 150 Leeds fans. I was meeting up with some fans before the game, but despite my best efforts of getting to Leeds early I found I was later than expected and rushing about. With an excited granddaughter, who will be celebrating her 8th birthday tomorrow, and my daughter Dani we left the car park, only for my bag zip to break and scatter the contents along the floor, which made me even later. Luckily, by the time we arrived at the Peacock the first person I saw was the person I'd been asked to take tickets for. I then had a chat with a couple of our Irish fans - and a big thank you Ken and Jack for buying my book *Follow Me and Leeds United* and Nick for buying *Once a Leeds fan, always a Leeds fan*. One of our Trust members I wished to thank for the plaque renovations was a little shy as he hid behind others when I took a photo! As we headed into the ground the rain had stopped so I was able to take photos of the flowers left for Chris and Kev.

The team today were: Peacock-Farrell, Berardi, Paudie O'Connor making his debut at centre back, Jansson, Dallas, Hernandez, Saiz, Alioski, Phillips, Vieira and Lasogga. Subs were: Roofe for Phillips (64), Ekuban for Lasogga (68) and Anita for Saiz (90). Berardi was sent off in the 90th minute with a straight red after a bad tackle. We drew 1-1, with Hernandez getting the Leeds

equalising goal (72). Attendance was 30,461 including approximately 2,200 Sunderland fans.

With Sunderland propping up the table and looking like having two consecutive relegations, I'd no idea what to expect from the game. We actually started off well and came close a few times but not close enough to make them count by scoring. We had most of the possession for a good while into the first half, and it was nearly a case of déjà vu when Sunderland had an attack and came very close to scoring. Luckily, for once it went our way as we were able to keep the ball out. As the half went on, things quietened on the terraces and we were going through the motions without any urgency. Once again, we were playing with a lone striker up front when we were at home - why? I don't think the system suited our players because the longer the half went on, the more it looked wrong. We had Dallas still at right back but had brought young Paudie O'Connor in at centre back, who played well. We had some mis-hit shots and gave the ball away too much and I couldn't wait for the half to end.

As I went back up into the Kop at the start of the second half, I found that I felt like a lead weight and had to literally drag myself back up to my seat. I thought at first it was because I wasn't looking forward to the second half but I still felt that way at the end of the game. This seemed more so when Sunderland put the ball into our net to take the lead within three minutes of the start. Sunderland were looking better than their place in the table suggested, but I think we were contributing to that, especially when they came close to getting a second. I felt that once we changed our system when Roofe came on we looked a different team. To say we have changed manager, Heckingbottom was still standing there with his arms crossed not getting involved and our tactics have remained the same. Why? As fans keep complaining about interference my thoughts are that we have a set piece coach and some other trainers so the team does the same thing regardless of it working or not. I found I was deflated and demoralised for a while in the second half because I couldn't see a way forward. When we changed the tactics it didn't take long

before we were able to get an equaliser when Hernandez got the ball in the penalty area and was able to score. We were very unlucky not to take the lead when Saiz brought out a great save from their goalie and hit the post with another shot. Sunderland hadn't given up either and we had Peacock-Farrell to thank again for another point-blank save to deny them taking the lead. We lost Berardi to a straight red card right on 90 minutes, so instead of trying to win the game we saw it out with 10 men once again. That was so frustrating and to be honest it felt like we'd lost again, although for once we'd got another point.

There were flashes of what we could do as a team but we weren't consistent enough. In the first half we have to make our chances count and play from the off for the whole game not just a few minutes here and there. I think that's why I was quite frustrated today because it didn't look like things were going to change in the long term and this is what we had to look forward to next year!

We have a further two away games next week with our visit to Preston on Tuesday and away at Villa on Friday. In my opinion I'd knock the lone striker on the head as I hate it because it doesn't work. As we have to change the team around again with Berardi's suspension, I have no idea who we have left to bring in, so will have to wait and see what happens at Deepdale. See you then – LUFC – Marching on Together!

PRESTON NORTH END (A) – 10 APRIL 2018

As we headed to Preston at 4pm, I thought we were going straight to the ground but luckily, despite the crawling traffic a few times, we managed an hour stop in Leyland. From there we got to the ground with a police escort just before 7pm. I was meeting Martin and his son who were over from Belgium, although they weren't going to be sitting with our fans. I always helped Martin out in the past by getting tickets for him as he was a regular who went everywhere. It was nice to meet up with him and his son after all these years and I recognised Martin straight away. On our way into the ground one of our stewards said this was his last away game as a steward, having been one for 18 years. He will just do the home games in future so he can have some family time - but well done.

Inside the ground I put my flag up and then went to look for Nikki and her dog Rita as I will be attending the LUDO end of season do on 21st April with my daughter Dani. As I got there I was introduced to a journalist from America who had decided to forego watching the Champions League game tonight and come to join us at Deepdale. He also bought my book *Follow Me and Leeds United* so a big thank you to him for that. John, who was standing on the row behind, asked if I had anymore books so he bought *Once a Leeds fan, always a Leeds fan*, so again I thank him for that as the support of fans is greatly appreciated. I managed to see loads of people I knew including Ian, who is Godfather to my eldest daughter Michelle. Ian was a regular on Wallace Arnold coaches with us in the seventies along with his friend Gary and we are still friends to this day. Being a Leeds United fan, the one thing I love is our unique bond and camaraderie that we have between us that stays forever.

The team today were: Peacock-Farrell, Anita, Jansson, Dallas, Hernandez, Grot, Roofe, Ekuban, Phillips, Vieira and O'Connor. Subs were: Hugo Diaz making his debut (replacing Jansson who went off injured) (57), Saiz for Roofe (67) and Alioski for Grot (68). Leeds lost the game 3-1 after leading 1-0 with Roofe scoring for Leeds (13). Attendance was 14,188 including 3,550 Leeds fans.

As soon as the team were announced before the game, people on social media were thinking it was a joke and that the real team would be announced later. Many were saying that if they'd known this earlier they wouldn't have bothered travelling to Preston. I was optimistic at this point and after seeing two magpies outside the Peacock I thought our luck was in. Talking of magpies,

my friend Sue found a live one in her house last week that must have been brought in by her cat. To say she was shocked was an understatement. Also, Brian from Wales was missing his first game tonight and said it would be typical of Leeds to win because he wasn't there, so I was hoping he'd be proved right. Obviously the reality was completely different and a tale of two halves once again followed.

As Preston attacked the goal in front of the Leeds fans they had a couple of chances as Peacock-Farrell was called on to make a save that went out for a corner. Leeds actually took the lead in the 13th minute when the corner came back out to Phillips, who then crossed the ball for Roofe to score! Immediately some Leeds fans sang 'How sh*t must you be we're winning away'. I just thought please don't sing that so early but wait until we've more goals under our belts. Instead that song came back to haunt us by the end of the game. It looked like we were playing with a front three so I thought just before we scored that maybe this would work. As it was, Preston did lots of attacking and came close to equalising. The one thing I noticed was their passing and control of the ball was superior to ours and also they kept creating so much space on either wing. Luckily for us though their shooting boots weren't on! We had a couple more shots on target which forced saves from their goalie before Preston hit the post just before the break.

I still thought we would be able to go on and win the game at this point but with the second half only a few minutes old, we had the stuffing knocked out of us when Preston were awarded a penalty after a foul by Anita. Peacock-Farrell went the right way but was unable to prevent the ball going into the net for the equaliser. The lad next to me said Gallagher, who was taking it, never misses and he was right. To make matters even worse, Preston took the lead a couple of minutes later after Peacock-Farrell had already denied them a second goal with a great save. Controversy followed as Jansson stayed down injured for a while and was then taken off. Loads of Leeds fans have slated him for going off as it looks like when the going gets tough he goes down injured. Doubts actually crossed my mind tonight. Young Hugo Diaz came on as sub and played well. We won a corner and O'Connor pushed their goalie over, who acted like he'd been shot. With that, the Preston players manhandled him and then fisticuffs started. The next minute it was all kicking off around us at the front of the stand where I'd stayed for the second half. Stewards including ours were in abundance as I saw one of ours was trying to calm down the lad who'd been stood near me. I got involved then as the lad was getting very agitated due to being held and to prevent him getting taken out I tried calming things down. Eventually we managed this between us all. He hadn't actually done anything wrong, only run towards the perimeter fence, but it was pre-empted that he was going to do something he shouldn't do. After things had calmed down and O'Connor was booked the game carried on. I'm not sure if any of the Preston players were booked for the retaliation, which would have been deserved, especially as one had him by the throat, but someone said no one was.

I went to get my flag but wasn't sure how many minutes were left, but it turned out to be at least 10 minutes. Their scoreboard at our end is terrible and I couldn't even look up there without getting dizzy so it was hard to work it out. As I got my flag I was talking to one of the Preston stewards who praised our fans by saying we always had a lot of fans both there tonight and at Elland Road. As we chatted, I said as long as Preston didn't get another goal so we were down and out that would be fine. Unfortunately that happened and it was indeed over for us. The penalty decision was the deciding factor and it will be interesting to see if our shout for a penalty in the first half should have been given or not. Whether that would have made a difference to the score I've no idea, but it really was a tale of two halves. Who could have seen that final score at half time? Why couldn't we defend a lead once again? It was so deflating for us all and you just end up resigned to it all. 'Orta out' was sung by many fans who are all convinced that he is the one dragging the club down. Personally I don't know what to think anymore, but the longer the season has gone on the more it feels like there is something seriously wrong at the club. I don't have any evidence but something isn't right. I'm still not convinced by Heckingbottom either as results and performances have not improved under him after the sacking of Christiansen.

The coaches were parked right outside the ground and we quickly headed away with a police escort. Instead of the quick trip to the motorway, we found we had diversions again as the entrance slip roads were closed! That wasn't the only diversion as apparently the exit road off the motorway was shut too plus we had roadworks to contend with near Rochdale.

I can't remember what got us talking about the Istanbul murders but I think I mentioned I was glad the plaque for Chris and Kev got cleaned and treated in time for the families to visit. John said that they nearly walked into the square as the attacks happened but were warned away from there by some shoe shine boys. As they headed downstairs to a bar slightly away from the area the small group of Leeds fans couldn't believe their eyes seeing the attacks being shown live on the TV. He is convinced that this was a set up because why would this be on the TV so quickly? Such an horrendous thing to happen. The next day all the hotels where the Leeds fans were staying were on lockdown and flights to Turkey cancelled so no more could arrive for the game. Incidentally, this game should never have been played because of what had happened, which is why all the Leeds fans turned their backs at the start of the game. John and his group were going to meet Phil Beeton to travel on his coach so they were in two taxis mostly wearing their Leeds colours. Unfortunately, the first taxi crashed into someone and it was then that things got very scary as groups of men surrounded the taxis and saw them wearing their colours. John had visions of them being attacked in there but luckily for them one of the drivers had rung ahead and two relief taxis turned up and got them out and to the hotel. As they got out of the taxis, no one could believe their eyes because no one had known there were any other Leeds fans out there for the game.

This got John talking about a couple of incidents that had happened in the past. One was at Newcastle when they were cornered on the steps of a building. There were about a dozen Leeds fans, including PC Barraclough. It was like the Alamo having to fend off all the Newcastle fans, with the baton being used in great abundance as well until the Newcastle police turned up to put a stop to it all. The second was coming out of a game at Chelsea to see their fans all holding up walking sticks. This was just after the Clockwork Orange film came out. It's not something he is proud of now but, in self-preservation, when a Chelsea fan lunged at him with the stick, he grabbed it and nutted him to stop him. I'm more than happy to leave trouble in the past, but unfortunately it isn't always the case that you can sadly.

We arrived back in Leeds just before midnight despite all the detours, and I'd found out we had a group of Danish Leeds fans travelling with us. As well as Norwegian fans there tonight, I feel for the Inverness White and Bournemouth Whites who have such a long way to travel back home. 'Why did he bother to make the trip?' was Inverness White's comments after the game, and I can't blame him. The detours didn't end there as I had another one on the way back to Halifax.

On Friday we travel to Aston Villa for another night game and live on Sky I think. I will be travelling in early for this one with Paul and Reuben, who have kindly offered me a lift. I am taking part in a Fan Girls documentary and will be doing some filming for it before the game. I've had to tell my seat number too so I'd better behave during the game lol! I really can't see us getting anything from the game but who knows. Always Leeds, Always Loyal is the Supporters' Club motto and one thing I do know is that at times Leeds United do not deserve our support but it's what we do! See you at Villa – LUFC - Marching on Together!

ASTON VILLA (A) – 13 APRIL 2018

I went early to the game today as I was meeting Harriet who was going to film me in an interview for a Fan Girls Documentary. Whether this will ever get into the public eye I've no idea, but it went really well and Harriet's comments later were that she had watched the footage and it was golden. Thank you for the opportunity to help! After the interview I was talking to some of our fans waiting for the team coach to arrive and we had our photo taken for LUFC. When we went back to wait for the coach Orta came and shook the hands of everyone in the group, including mine. This was the first time I had met him. I had also seen Angus Kinnear when I arrived and I'd told him what I was doing there. Thanks for being complimentary about my support of the club.

Because I needed to be at the ground early, I was grateful for the chance of a lift there and travelled with Paul, his son Reuben and friend Kenny. After lots of traffic delays near home we arrived at the ground for 4.50pm. Harriet did some more filming as I spoke to a few fans and we headed to the pub at the end of the street, but unfortunately they wouldn't let her film there so we parted ways. I suppose I could have stood outside the away end for a while because, due to health and safety reasons, she wasn't allowed to film me in with our fans which was a shame. Never mind.

As I looked around the ground, when I got to my seat I couldn't help casting my mind back to my many previous visits to Villa Park. The ground now, in comparison to my early visits, looks really good. The open end (to the right of the Leeds fans) was where we stood on my first-ever visit there for a 0-0 draw in the League Cup. That game turned out to be a bad one when we left the ground. We walked through Villa fans on the street corner, who asked us what the time was but we ignored them and got safely onto our Wallace Arnold coach. It was whilst we were stuck in traffic further down the road that the missiles and bricks started hitting the coach all down the left-hand side. One lad told me to get down in the aisle out of the way as we were in a terrifying situation. After a few minutes that felt like a lifetime with most of the windows smashed on the left-hand side, the Villa fans disappeared as quickly as they came. No police turned up either so we were left to carry on our way back to Leeds with no windows and it was freezing. Another time, as Leeds weren't playing I went to see Glasgow Rangers play Villa in a friendly game, with this one being abandoned 10 minutes into the second half due to trouble. I was standing in the Holte End for that one but ended up climbing on to the pitch and into the Doug Ellis stand to get away from the trouble. Memories!

Coming back to today, I wasn't sure what to expect from the game and would take things as they came, although I didn't think we'd win. With a bad run of results since Heckingbottom arrived at Leeds and our chances of the play-offs gone, I hoped that some of our youngsters would be given the chance to play. There again I couldn't remember a time when we had been hit so badly as a team with serious injuries and key players out. I'd be interested to see a comparison with old football boots against new ones to see if they had any impact. There again, they'd probably be too heavy for modern day footballers! Seriously though, it is a big concern of mine that we've had so many and I wonder what can be done to prevent this in the future?

The team today were: Peacock-Farrell, Pearce, Pennington, O'Connor, Dallas, Hernandez, Alioski, Roofe, Vieira, Phillips and Ekuban. Subs were: Saiz for Ekuban (45), Grot for Alioski (66) and Lasogga for Roofe (78). Leeds lost the game 1-0. Attendance was 33,374 including 2,400 Leeds fans. Apparently Villa needed over 38,000 there to go above us in the overall attendances and I knew they wouldn't get that after hearing they had their highest attendance of 36,000 for the visit of Wolves. That's why many fans had decided not to turn up then (tongue in cheek)! I can understand why many decided to call it a day today, but personally I prefer to see the game in person so I can make judgements about what I see. It was nice to see Ralu was over for the game from Romania again.

After an initial attack by Villa, Leeds started on the attack when Alioski unleashed a great shot which was saved by their goalie, giving us an early corner. I'd forgotten Snodgrass was playing for Villa even though one of our fans had told me he'd spoken to him outside the ground. Again we had to thank Peacock-Farrell for making some great saves to keep Villa out (this was also noted by Sky as he was chosen as man of the match at the end of the game). Leeds fans had given Snodgrass

a warm welcome but this changed when he won a free kick just outside the box by going down with a soft challenge. We were playing much better than we had of late with our youngsters Pearce and O'Connor also playing well. Unfortunately, Villa scored just before the half-hour mark with a header after we failed to clear the ball properly. That was a shame but the Leeds fans, who had been getting behind the

team with some great singing, carried on doing that. An incident happened in the seats behind me to the left when police started dragging a Leeds fan out and everyone was going mad. I've no idea why as I'd not seen or heard anything untoward, and my friend Sue said that the lad had his head banged against the wall which was out of order. Later on another fan was taken out and I also saw one I knew in the stand below taken out, again I've no idea why. No doubt I will find out in due course but it felt like things were well over the top. It was good to have a chat at half time with Derby Jim, Leicester Rob and Worcester Phil who have been mates since the early eighties. The club means so much to them, which especially shows as they are going through current traumas, and personally I know from experience that it is our fans who will help overcome these. It must be difficult as a Leeds fan being married to a Derby fan with a Derby ram tattoo on her backside though lol!

At the start of the second half Ekuban had been subbed for Saiz and we started off brightly and stronger. One thing that was apparent was our failure to pass the ball well, mostly falling short or not getting past the first man. The Leeds fans started chanting 'we all love Leeds,' getting louder and louder and getting behind the team, which they responded to. It took us singing to get the Villa fans to start getting behind their team but they didn't last as long as we did. They only had sporadic support in that area over the 90 minutes, and were only really loud when they scored, surprise, surprise!

The team responded in the second half and we did a lot of attacking, although we didn't have the final finish. Peacock-Farrell again showed how he has grown into the games with his run in the team, and he looked self-assured catching the ball and also making some great saves once again. As a mistake by us gave Villa the chance to get a second goal, Pennington timed his tackle well as he started playing better, to nick the ball off the Villa player's feet. When Grot and then Lasogga came on as subs, sadly they didn't make any difference and maybe even stifled our chance of an equaliser. Even though I didn't expect us to score, I was hoping we could sneak a last-minute goal to get a point out of the game, but that didn't happen.

I didn't feel so downhearted at the end of the game because the team had been trying and tried to play some attacking football in the second half. They were getting stronger, and, although some of the play showed that we need someone who can dictate the game more going forwards who can attack and score goals, I saw some positives. I have already said that we need to build the team around Peacock-Farrell, and I would be happy to see Pearce and O'Connor be part of this too. With Coyle to come back in at right back, we have a nucleus of youngsters and we then need to have quality with a few older heads and a few from the current squad to move forwards. I do disagree that this was the worst team ever after reading comments on Twitter after the game. I've seen some dross in my time of following Leeds and I don't think this team tonight comes even close to the worst, even though things haven't been good for a while! We have a long way to go I agree, especially as our hopes have been dashed so badly this season. The close season is going to be crucial and Radz, having made mistakes, is going to be key to how we move forward as a club. As long as he has learnt that we cannot do the bargain basement with lots and lots of players anymore and the way forward is quality over quantity then fingers crossed we will start heading in the right direction. Success will bring the fans back as today many fans voted with their feet and stayed away. Three away midweek

games in a couple of weeks have also taken their toll on the cash flow of some, but apparently we had more coaches here today than we took to Preston. Many must have travelled by different methods to that game!

Our next game is against Barnsley at Elland Road next Saturday, the team Heckingbottom was in charge of before us, and this could be a make or break game for him. He said on BBC Radio Leeds after the game that the players have all been seen now and given a chance to show what they can or cannot do. That means a cull is on the way, and we will know who hasn't made it by the players picked and on the bench next week. If things aren't working then give some more of the youngsters a chance.

As tonight showed, we are very lucky that once again we have some great youngsters coming through at the club, so things look brighter in that direction. Keep doing what we are doing with them and you never know life as a Leeds United supporter may do a u-turn and kick start next season. See you then – LUFC – Marching on Together!

BARNSLEY (H) – 21 APRIL 2018

The sun shone brightly in Halifax as I set off for Elland Road, making it perfect weather for a football game. Singing along to *The Greatest Showman* also made it a very happy journey. As I was meeting Dean at Billy's statue at 1.30pm for a live interview, I made sure I set off in plenty time to go to Leeds via Rastrick and Wakefield. First I picked up my granddaughter Hannah and then my daughter Danielle before getting to the ground right on cue. As my car was feeling poorly I was worried it would impact on getting there okay, but luckily it didn't let me down.

Thanks for the opportunity to do the live interview Dean, and, as always, I'm glad to be able to help other Leeds fans out. When asked if I was doing another book, I said I wasn't sure as I couldn't think of a title for it. 'A waste of time,' said Dean. Many fans who have had their photos taken for my blog throughout the year have also asked if they'd be in my next book so I feel I can't let them down. If the demand is there then another book would be based on my blog *Follow Me and Leeds*

United from this season, together with lots of photos as per last season's *The Sleeping Giant Awakens 2016-17*. Unfortunately, as this season hasn't gone the way we all hoped on the pitch, the title I would have picked isn't appropriate, that'll stay a secret and I hope it can be used at the end of next season instead! I'll have to get a move on with a title for this one if that is the case!

As it was so hot we didn't expect to get served in the Peacock, but as luck would have it most of the fans were outside so for once we managed to get a drink. We went up into the garden where we started chatting to a group of fans from Worksop and Airdrie. The latter who had travelled from Scotland for the game, Les and his son Donald, meant we had a good chat about the Scottish players that Leeds had playing for them at the start of the seventies. He also said Jim Storrie, one of our ex-players who played centre forward for us and helped Leeds win promotion to the First Division in 1964, was an Airdrie lad. Barry Bannan was a friend of his too (now playing at Sheffield Wednesday). Jamie had his dad to thank for buying my book *Follow Me and Leeds United* as a present for his 21st birthday. Enjoy the read. Getting into the ground, I was just in time to get in my spot to take photos and meet Debbie and James to give them my book *The Sleeping Giant Awakens,* so again thank you to them both.

The team today were: Peacock-Farrell, Pennington, Jansson (back after concussion), Pearce, O'Connor, Hernandez, Vieira, Phillips, Alioski, Saiz and Roofe. Subs were: Ekuban for Alioski (71), Forshaw (returning from injury) for Saiz (84). Leeds won the game 2-1 with goals by Pearce (17) and Alioski (50). Attendance was 30,451 including 1,663 Barnsley fans.

Leeds looked fired up from the start today after Barnsley had an early chance. They did create us a few problems, but I thought once we settled into the game that we could go on and win it. We were battling more and as young Pearce went forward with the ball he unleashed a long-range shot that took their goalie by surprise. The ball seemed to bobble along the floor on the way into the net as it took an age to end up in the back of it. We weren't the only ones ecstatic for him either and it was so nice to see the celebrations of the team with Pearce who was justified in his own joy of getting the goal. I was chuffed to bits for the lad. We didn't have it all our own way in the game though as Barnsley, who are in a relegation battle, kept putting us under pressure. After Pontus headed the ball out of defence well and did that a few times, he somehow nearly cost us a goal. He was going to kick the ball out of the penalty area then changed his mind at the last minute and it was a good job Peacock-Farrell was so alert to prevent the goal and make the save. Someone next to me thought someone had shouted,

but I didn't think it was the keeper as it took him by surprise. There was also another incident with Pontus that could have put us in trouble but again we were able to get the ball away. Unfortunately, the team seemed to quieten down as Barnsley got into the game more. It was a disappointment when the ball was crossed into the penalty area in front of the Kop, only for poor O'Connor to score an own goal to bring Barnsley level. There was

nothing he could do about it and I felt badly for him. To cap it all they very nearly took the lead when Barnsley shot and I was convinced the ball was going in the net. Someone stood in front of me to get out of our row so I couldn't see the outcome but Peacock-Farrell made a great save to keep it out. There were some boos as the whistle went for half time, but to be honest I couldn't understand why because I thought we hadn't played too badly. We weren't losing either.

I actually got back up into the stand before the players had come out for the second half, but as it seemed a long half time I could have sworn they would already have been out. Within six minutes of the restart we had taken the lead after Roofe rounded their player on the wing and crossed the ball for Alioski to put the ball into the net. Cue relief and celebrations all around. It looked like we couldn't keep a lead again when Barnsley had the ball in our net only a short while after we'd scored, but luckily for us the linesman flagged for offside! Although we started to put more pressure on Barnsley, they weren't giving up without a fight, especially when their player missed an open goal. From the Kop I thought he was stood on the goal line and missed but apparently he was a bit further out than that! They could also have had a penalty but luckily for us the ref chose to book the Barnsley player for diving. Talking of Pennington, he had a really good game on the wing in place of Berardi. In fact a few of the players stood out today, which was a vast improvement. Alioski gets a lot of stick from fans for running around and going down easily, but this was causing Barnsley issues as he was closing them down and tackling them. We had Peacock-Farrell to thank once again for making some class saves. One thing I will reiterate is that we need to build our team around these youngsters, and I did say that to Peacock-Farrell, Pearce and O'Connor later on in the evening. Apparently we have a good striker in the under 23s who would be a good addition to the squad too. My stance is quality over quantity, with players who want to play for the shirt and the fans, including our youngsters, and we won't go far wrong. Saiz wasn't happy with his substitution and looked to be having a tantrum in the dugout. I hadn't actually seen anything until others behind me pointed it out. Jamie Clapham did the after game interview with BBC Radio Leeds and when asked about it he said it was behind him and he didn't see or hear anything. I think

my photos show him standing right in front of Saiz, so I think he was being diplomatic and knew exactly what had gone on. Even the players in the dugout didn't know what to do!

We managed to see the game out to get the three points and keep Barnsley firmly near the bottom of the table and in danger of relegation. Sunderland have also suffered back-to-back relegations after it was confirmed they were relegated today from our division. At least with Wigan being promoted back to the Championship it is a ground with a good allocation of tickets for away fans.

After the game we headed to the White Rose to meet my daughter Michelle and other two granddaughters Laura and Alexis as they were taking Hannah back for me. Danielle and I were going back to the Pavilion for the Leeds United Disabled Organisation's (LUDO) player of the year event. I can honestly say that it was a fantastic night with a carvery and pudding all for the grand total of £25 per person. We got to meet the players (even Saiz as I wondered if he'd turn up after his earlier shenanigans) and had a great sing song along to the DJ's choice of songs. With some great Irish Dancing and a bit of bingo thrown in it was really good. It was commented on that I'd got legs and seeing our stewards there not in uniform and having a night off was good to see. Our longest serving steward remembered me from the seventies too. It was the last year of the event being organised by Stuart (not sure if I've spelt it right) due to ill health and it was an emotional night for him. His services to LUDO were recognised by the club as well as LUDO representatives, so a big well done from me as he deserved the recognition. I'd like to say a big thank you to Nikki, and not forgetting Rita her dog, for inviting me to join her and others at the event. I will certainly look forward to attending this again next year and I would encourage other Leeds fans to do the same. Any extra monies raised go to LUDO so it is a great cause.

Next week sees our penultimate game and the last away game of the season at Norwich. Having already thought the season had finished before today's game I'm looking forward to having a great day out with the rest of our fans. If we can get another three points there I will be more than happy. See you there – LUFC – Marching on Together!

NORWICH CITY (A) – 28 APRIL 2018

It wouldn't be Leeds United without more controversy happening at the club. With a post-season tour to Myanmar, formerly Burma, on the cards, my first instincts were of fear for the fans as I thought the Foreign Office had banned all travel there due to the unrest and atrocities going on in the country. That wasn't the case as it turned out to be, as it is deemed safe where Leeds are going. Although there is no way I can go there due to cost and having no holidays, I'm not sure whether I would have gone if given the opportunity. My niece visited the region last year and I have seen photos from her trip. I can only hope that the people living there get the chance to have some normality. As a group of our most loyal supporters will be going, I wish them all a safe journey.

As I headed to Elland Road for the coach with *The Greatest Showman* once again blaring out in my car, the sun started to come out, making me feel really upbeat and looking forward to our

trip to Norwich. Our coach was already there when I arrived at the ground and we got off on time, heading for our stop at Thetford. After leaving Leeds in sunshine, even though there was a nip in the air it felt a lovely day for football. Unfortunately, it didn't take long for the weather to deteriorate as the rain came down. We had Fiona Hanley, the Leeds United SLO, travelling with us today. She had been given an invitation to travel with us to see first-hand the obstacles and distances our disabled fans had to cope with getting to the coaches after games.

The Nottingham Whites and Worksop Whites were already there when we arrived at the pub and the couple of hours stop passed by in an instant. Our group was reminiscing as usual, which ensured we had a good laugh. A loud bang made us jump out of our skins as we saw a young Leeds lad who had tried balancing his chair on two legs hit the floor with a bang. I thought at first he'd knocked himself out but luckily, or unlucky for him, he'd only hurt his knee. I did ask him if he was okay and he thanked me for asking.

We took the opportunity to get off the coach right outside the ground as we were dropping a couple of our fans off and after our search outside the ground went to the turnstile. When a steward saw me with my bag he asked if I wanted to go through an open door at the side instead of having a battle with the turnstile, which I gratefully accepted. I do have visions of getting stuck in one someday but hopefully it stays a vision and doesn't really happen lol!

I brought my flag with me but thought I wouldn't get a chance to put it on show today, as last year I was only allowed to put it up at the back of the stand but had nothing to attach it to. It was

a pleasant surprise to be able to put it onto the netting over the first few rows, so I put it near to where Paul, Reuben and Dave were sitting. I then headed to my seat which was a few rows from the back of the stand. I fail to understand why Leeds seem to put the away season ticket holders as far away from the pitch as possible? Unfortunately I puffed and panted up the stairs showing how unfit I am. At least we were dry up there, although my friend Sue said she never got warm all game but staying in the stand at half time probably didn't help. I'd taken some photos of the Flintstones and other characters already today as a few fans had dressed up for the occasion with this being the last away game of the season.

The team today were: Peacock-Farrell, Pearce, Cooper, Jansson, Pennington, Alioski, Saiz, Vieira, Phillips, Roofe and Hernandez (just signed a new two year contract). Subs were: Grot for Alioski (70), Forshaw for Vieira (74) and Lasogga for Pearce (83). Leeds lost the game 2-1 after taking the lead with a fantastic volley from Phillips (39). Attendance was 26,869 including approximately 2,131 Leeds fans. I was very disappointed to see that O'Connor had been dropped with the recall of Cooper. Whilst I have nothing against Cooper, we should have stuck with the young ones as we should be building the team around them.

After an initial early chance we found ourselves under attack quite a few times, but then we'd gain possession of the ball and race to the other end. The linesman in front of us was never up with play and missed no end of offside decisions for Norwich, and the first time he eventually put his flag up was on 42 minutes. We hadn't been able to have a real chance of scoring though, and many times we started passing back to the goalie, something we hadn't done so much of when Cooper had been out injured. A change of tactics perhaps, but I will always maintain that the best form of defence is attack. To me Hernandez was showing the signing of a new contract syndrome with really bad passing, but he wasn't the only one. On 36 minutes we took a surprise lead when the ball came back out to Phillips on the edge of the area who volleyed a perfect shot into the bottom of the net. That was a fantastic goal, but as usual we shot ourselves in the foot just before half time. We had a corner but wasted it, only for Norwich to gain the impetus from our failing by attacking us and sadly, despite Peacock-Farrell's great effort, we found the ball in our net after it came off the inside of the post. I initially thought that was a narrow escape, only to see the ball cross the line for them to equalise right on half time. What a bummer! Why can't we actually keep a lead without conceding more or less straight away? It was a bitter blow and the timing was crucial too, giving Norwich hope.

At half time I went downstairs and saw lots of fans for photos. A big thank you once again for those who say they love reading my blog. As always the comments are greatly appreciated. After watching some of our younger fans have a good time singing Leeds songs, I went back up for the second half, not realising we had already kicked off. After stopping to chat to someone I knew on the way back up to my seat, I stayed there for a while, but as we kept encroaching on the stairway and being asked to get back into the row of seats I thought I'd better return to my seat.

To be honest the second half was dire in comparison to the first as I had high hopes we could win today. Peacock-Farrell got my man of the match having made some vital saves once again. Sadly, we stood off Norwich instead of closing them down, which was the worst thing we could do. The next thing they had a powerful shot that beat Peacock-Farrell to put them into the lead. It didn't feel like we could get anything from the game then, although we should have had a penalty for a blatant handball which even I saw! There were wide-open spaces down the far side of the pitch as Norwich attacked the stand to our left. I was very disappointed to hear Heckingbottom blaming Pearce for leaving lots of space down the wing which encouraged Norwich to attack. He is in defence so where was our midfield protecting him? When Grot was brought on for Alioski there were chants of 'you don't know what you're doing.' Alioski had been chasing the ball and putting some tackles in, so personally I wouldn't have subbed him plus, with his height, I thought why is Grot on the wing anyway? We had a couple more chances late in the game but nothing good enough sadly. Unfortunately, the gallows humour from the Leeds fans came back to haunt us all. To be honest when some of our fans sang 'how sh*t must you be we're winning away', I thought it was much too early to be singing it, which proved to be the case.

It was very disappointing to see the team, despite clapping the fans, not come anywhere near us. The only one who did was Alioski and fair play to him. He gave his bench coat to a young Leeds lass, who had written a sign, in Macedonian I presume. He also gave his tracky top away so well done Alioski for showing the others what they should have been doing. I went to get my flag from the front of the stand and found it absolutely saturated, showing how much it had rained.

Fiona Hanley got first-hand experience of what our disabled fans have to put up with. Just as we were pulling away from the coach park, I pointed out Ian from the Griffin branch being assisted by a couple of police back to his coach. It was far too long a distance for the lad on our coach too. For the sake of using one of the police vans, surely they could be taken back to their coaches in relative comfort rather than having to struggle? We had a short stop on the way back but we actually came a shorter route back so were at Elland Road by 9.30pm. Luckily for me I slept most of the way back too, plus whilst trying to write this blog! I couldn't believe it when I got on the M621 to come home only to find I had to come off at the next junction for road works. Detours, detours the story of Leeds fans' lives!

There was lots of summing things up at the end of the game and not very complimentary from some fans. We look to be heading for our 'normal' end of season place of 15th at this moment in time. Whatever happens in our last game at home next week against QPR, the stats for our performances, or should I say none performances, make dismal reading since Boxing Day. We can thank Thomas Christiansen for at least getting us enough points from our early run because without that we'd be down and out again from this division but in the wrong direction.

We have a big summer ahead of us and we really need to change things but how? I don't really know anymore. See you next week – LUFC – Marching on Together!

CHAPTER 11 – MAY 2018

QUEENS PARK RANGERS (H) – 6 MAY 2018

How quickly the last game of the season seems to have come round. I didn't attend the player of the year awards on Friday but it was nice to see Peter Lorimer looking so well when given a Lifetime Award after overcoming his recent battle with ill health.

As we headed to Elland Road for our last game of the season, I cast my mind back 46 years to the day I was at Wembley to see Leeds United win the FA Cup for the only time in our history in the centenary year. I'm privileged to have experienced us winning the trophy and the memories will stay with me forever. That takes me back to our present day where, sadly, after a very hopeful start we petered out once again into a disappointing end. From the high hopes at the start of the season the finish we wanted never materialized and turned to the despair on the pitch. After getting off to our great start where we saw some fantastic football played, giving us great hope, we changed what we were trying to do. Sadly, we will never know if persevering with the way we started would have worked, but we never recovered after that, as it looked to me like we didn't know what we were trying to do from then on.

Firstly, I want to thank all my followers on social media for taking the time to read and share my blogs over the season. I especially want to thank all our fantastic fans who have once again followed our club everywhere in huge numbers, showing fantastic loyalty despite the ups and downs. Home games have also had big attendances with over 30,000 fans attending many of the games. Lots of our overseas fans were making regular journeys and in some cases attending every game, which shows our fans are the best in the world in my eyes. I do my blogs as a fan for the fans as I enjoy taking photos which show the fan experience at games. Those fans who regularly want to be part of this experience by asking for their photos

taken show what a great camaraderie there is amongst our fans and it is something I treasure. Watch out as it looks like I will be putting this season's blog into another book for those who have been asking if their photo will be in it! I will include as many photos as possible as with all my books so fans can feel part of following Leeds United, whether they can get to games or not.

I took a photo from a Harrogate White who attended the Fairs Cup play-off on 22nd September 1971 against Barcelona at the Nou Camp. I think I can just work out my friends Margaret and Carole on one of the photos for that game, which was played just as I started to go to all the home games. I'd been asked to take photos of the youngsters waving the flags as the players came out today as they had a relative taking part. Unfortunately, as I didn't know who I was looking for, there are a lot of photos.

The team today were: Peacock-Farrell, Ayling returning from injury, Pearce, Jansson, Alioski, Cooper, Roofe, Ekuban, Phillips, Vieira and Forshaw. Subs were: Pennington for Jansson (46), Ryan Edmondson at age 16 making his debut for Roofe (73) and O'Kane for Forshaw (86). Leeds won the game 2-0 with Roofe (30) and Phillips (47) scoring for Leeds. Attendance was 30,004 including approximately 800 QPR fans.

Just before the end of season applause for Leeds fans who have died over the season, it was sad to hear of the death of Lady Harewood, our honorary club president since December 2017. The whole stadium joined in to pay our respects to everyone. As the game kicked off there were white shirts everywhere as the glorious weather meant no coats and no tops on in some instances. There was a typical end of season atmosphere as fans soaked up the sun and, although I couldn't see from the Kop, we had a crowd surfer in the South Stand. Early on in the game it was surprising to see a steward suddenly taking one of the beach balls that must have come over the wall next to

the pitch from the South Stand. He proceeded to carry it away to the West Stand corner to a round of boos, with the South Stand singing they wanted their ball back. Why I've no idea, as they weren't doing anything untoward and it was a bit of a carnival atmosphere with fans enjoying themselves. When the same steward proceeded to do that again with another ball I thought he'd lost the plot!

On the pitch after a bit of initial pressure from QPR, I thought we settled into the game well. Whilst it wasn't overly exciting, we started to go forward and attack them. It was good to see Ayling return to the side and he showed what we have been missing many a time when he got stuck in. We upped the pressure on QPR and were very unlucky not to take the lead with a massive goalmouth scramble in front of the South Stand. Just a few minutes later we did take the lead with a goal from Roofe after a corner was headed on by Phillips. With another chance just before half time, I felt we ended the half on a positive note.

Jansson didn't return to the field at the start of the second half and Pennington came on to replace him. Within a couple of minutes we got a second goal as Phillips reacted well when a poor clearance gave him the chance to score a great goal. As we were firmly in the driving seat I didn't want us to let QPR have anything as Peacock-Farrell deserved to have a clean sheet. On the whole we limited QPR to very few goal scoring chances, despite the fact they were bearing down on our goal a few times. The ref was trying to make a name for himself by blowing up for a foul numerous times when we tackled their players but not

giving us the same courtesy. Football is not a non-contact sport and you should be able to battle for a ball and win it. As it was we managed to see the game out and get the win and three points to at least give us a good end to the season in that respect.

We waited behind for the players to come around the pitch with their children and applaud the fans for their tremendous support this season. There were actually more fans waiting behind than I thought there would be considering. It was also nice to bump into some of our Northern Ireland fans after the game, including Wesley Boyle who played for us in 1997.

Tomorrow sees a number of our fans flying out to Myanmar for the post-season tour, and I would assume the team too. Who will travel as part of the official party, I am waiting to see, but I wish everyone a safe and enjoyable trip and I look forward to seeing some of the blogs from fans I know who are going out there.

What happens next over the close season will define where we are heading as a club. I always knew it was going to take time but had my hopes built up with our great start to the season before normality resumed on the pitch. Having had so many long-term injuries as a team this season, that has been a great worry for me, but along with suspensions these have both had a great impact on the players available to play. This season has been a big learning curve for Radrizzani in running a football club, especially with the badge gate saga. As much as I love doing the salute, I don't want it as our club badge and this was a unanimous vote amongst our fans. The refurbishment of Bremner Square will also be starting shortly and I am looking forward to seeing the end product, especially my Bremner Stone. Lewie Coyle, who has been on a season-long loan at Fleetwood, should be returning to us after having a great season with them, winning the player's player of the year, so well done to him. We have a spine of youngsters to build on with some old heads, once we have got rid of players who shouldn't be here. I have no thoughts about specific players and will wait and see who stays and who goes before making any judgements. A few additional quality players and with another season before our centenary year, aiming for automatic promotion is a must and isn't too much to ask, is it? See you next season – LUFC – Marching on Together!

FIXTURES FOR THE SEASON 2017-18

DATE	OPPOSITION	VENUE	COMPETITION	SCORE	ATTENDANCE	SCORERS
8.7.17	Guiseley	Nethermoor Park	Pre-season friendly	5-1	4,000 sellout crowd	Dallas 2 Antonsson Irwin 2
29.7.17	Oxford United	Elland Road	Pre-season friendly	2-0	13,295 314 Oxford fans	Roofe 36 Dallas 83
6.8.17	Bolton Wanderers	Macron Stadium	Championship	3-2	19,857 with 4,832 Leeds fans	Phillips 7, 42 Wood 30
9.8.17	Port Vale	Elland Road	Carabao Cup first round	4-1	15,431 801 Port Vale fans	Saiz 12, 60, 62 Ekuban 83
12.8.17	Preston North End	Elland Road	Championship	0-0	32,880 671 Preston fans	
15.8.17	Fulham	Elland Road	Championship	0-0	28,918 576 Fulham fans	
19.8.17	Sunderland	Stadium of Light	Championship	0-2	31,237 approx.3,000 Leeds fans	Saiz 21 Dallas 76
22.8.17	Newport County	Elland Road	Carabao Cup second round	5-1	17,098 631 Newport fans	Roofe 44, 49, 65 Saiz 78 Vieira 89
26.8.17	Nottingham Forest	City Ground	Championship	0-2	25,682 approx.2,000 Leeds fans	Roofe 24 Alioski 87
9.9.17	Burton Albion	Elland Road	Championship	5-0	33,404 372 Burton fans	Lasogga 20, 59 Phillips 35 Hernandez (pen) 44 Roofe 54
12.9.17	Birmingham City	Elland Road	Championship	2-0	31,507 614 Birmingham fans	Saiz 17 Dallas 90 + 2
16.9.17	Millwall	The Den	Championship	1-0	16,447 approx. 2,000 Leeds fans	

19.9.17	Burnley	Turf Moor	Carabao Cup third round	2-2 Leeds win 5-3 on penalties	11,799 2,194 Leeds fans	Sacko 80, Hernandez 90+4 Penalties: Lasogga scored (Leeds pen 1) Wood scored (Burnley pen 1) Barnes scored (Burnley pen 2) Hernandez scored (Leeds pen 2) Klich scored (Leeds pen 3) Brady scored (Burnley pen 3) Tarkowski missed (Burnley pen 4) Alioski scored (Leeds pen 4) Dallas scored (Leeds pen 5)
23.9.17	Ipswich Town	Elland Road	Championship	3-2	34,002 693 Ipswich fans	Lasogga 13 Phillips 32 Bialkowski OG 67
26.9.17	Cardiff City	Cardiff City Stadium	Championship	3-1	27,160 2,674 Leeds fans	Roofe 67
1.10.17	Sheffield Wednesday	Hillsborough	Championship	3-0	27,972 4,600 Leeds fans	
14.10.17	Reading	Elland Road	Championship	0-1	33,900 434 Reading Fans	
21.10.17	Bristol City	Ashton Gate	Championship	0-3	24,435 3,717 Leeds fans	Saiz 4,14 Lasogga 67
24.10.17	Leicester City	King Power Stadium	Carabao Cup Fourth Round	3-1	31,516 3,300 Leeds fans	Hernandez 26
27.10.17	Sheffield United	Elland Road	Championship	1-2	34,504 2,533 Sheffield United fans	Phillips 34
31.10.17	Derby County	Elland Road	Championship	1-2	28,565 852 Derby fans	Lasogga 7
4.11.17	Brentford	Griffin Park	Championship	3-1	11,068 1,647 Leeds fans	Alioski 67
19.11.17	Middlesbrough	Elland Road	Championship	2-1	33,771 2,535 Middlesbrough fans	Hernandez 24 Alioski 54

22.11.17	Wolverhampton Wanderers	Molineux	Championship	4-1	28,914 2,300 Leeds fans	Alioski 48
25.11.17	Barnsley	Oakwell	Championship	0-2	16,399 4,513 Leeds fans	Saiz 23 Alioski 45+ 3
1.12.17	Aston Villa	Elland Road	Championship	1-1	30,547 2,443 Villa fans	Jansson 19
9.12.17	Queens Park Rangers	Loftus Road	Championship	1-3	15,506 3,149 Leeds fans	Roofe 63,68, 90+4
16.12.17	Norwich City	Elland Road	Championship	1-0	30,590 997 Norwich fans	Jansson 41
23.12.17	Hull City	Elland Road	Championship	1-0	35,156 1,794 Hull fans	Hernandez 29
26.12.17	Burton Albion	Pirelli Stadium	Championship	1-2	5,612 1,730 Leeds fans	Hernandez 61 Roofe 64
30.12.17	Birmingham City	St Andrews	Championship	1-0	21,673 2,484 Leeds fans	
1.1.18	Nottingham Forest	Elland Road	Championship	0-0	32,426 917 Forest fans	
7.1.18	Newport County	Rodney Parade	Emirates FA Cup third round	2-1	6,887 1,040 Leeds fans	Berardi 10
13.1.18	Ipswich Town	Portman Road	Championship	1-0	18,638 3,537 Leeds fans	
20.1.18	Millwall	Elland Road	Championship	3-4	33,564 1,285 Millwall fans	Lasogga 46, 62 Roofe 55
30.1.18	Hull City	KCOM Stadium	Championship	0-0	17,237 2,097 Leeds fans	
3.2.18	Cardiff City	Elland Road	Championship	1-4	30,534 624 Cardiff fans	Bamba own goal 54
10.2.18	Sheffield Utd	Bramall Lane	Championship	2-1	27,553 2,236 Leeds fans	Lasogga 47
18.2.18	Bristol City	Elland Road	Championship	2-2	28,004 536 Bristol fans	Lasogga 72 Roofe 80
21.2.18	Derby County	Pride Park	Championship	2-2	27,944 3,152 Leeds fans	Lasogga 34 Alioski 79
24.2.18	Brentford	Elland Road	Championship	1-0	28,428 539 Brentford fans	Cooper 31
2.3.18	Middlesbrough	Riverside Stadium	Championship	3-0	27,621 2,987 Leeds fans	

7.3.18	Wolverhampton Wanderers	Elland Road	Championship	0-3	26,434 approx. 1,250 Wolves fans	
10.3.18	Reading	Madejski Stadium	Championship	2-2	19,770 3,967 Leeds fans	Jansson 43 Hernandez 56
17.3.18	Sheffield Wednesday	Elland Road	Championship	1-2	31,638 2,039 Sheffield Wednesday fans	Grot 86
30.3.18	Bolton Wanderers	Elland Road	Championship	2-1	35,377 2,480 Bolton fans	Ekuban 4 Hernandez 50
3.4.18	Fulham	Craven Cottage	Championship	2-0	21,538 4,003 Leeds fans plus 2,000 'neutrals'	
7.4.18	Sunderland	Elland Road	Championship	1-1	30,461 2,200 approx. Sunderland fans	Hernandez 72
10.4.18	Preston North End	Deepdale	Championship	3-1	14,188 3,550 Leeds fans	Roofe 13
13.4.18	Aston Villa	Villa Park	Championship	1-0	33,374 2,400 Leeds fans	
21.4.18	Barnsley	Elland Road	Championship	2-1	30,451 1,663 Barnsley fans	Pearce 17 Alioski 50
28.4.18	Norwich City	Carrow Road	Championship	2-1	26,869 with approx. 2,131 Leeds fans	Phillips 39
6.5.18	Queens Park Rangers	Elland Road	Championship	2-0	30,004 with approx. 800 QPR fans	Roofe 30 Phillips 47

CHAMPIONSHIP TABLE 2017-18

	P	W	D	L	F	A	GD	PTS
Wolverhampton Wanderers	46	30	9	7	82	39	43	99
Cardiff City	46	27	9	10	69	39	30	90
Fulham	46	25	13	8	79	46	33	88
Aston Villa	46	24	11	11	72	42	30	83
Middlesbrough	46	22	10	14	67	45	22	76
Derby County	46	20	15	11	70	48	22	75
Preston North End	46	19	16	11	57	46	11	73
Millwall	46	19	15	12	56	45	11	72
Brentford	46	18	15	13	62	52	10	69
Sheffield United	46	20	9	17	62	55	7	69
Bristol City	46	17	16	13	67	58	9	67
Ipswich Town	46	17	9	20	57	60	-3	60
LEEDS UNITED	**46**	**17**	**9**	**20**	**59**	**64**	**-5**	**60**
Norwich City	46	15	15	16	49	60	-11	60
Sheffield Wednesday	46	14	15	17	59	60	-1	57
Queens Park Rangers	46	15	11	20	58	70	-12	56
Nottingham Forest	46	15	8	23	51	65	-14	53
Hull City	46	11	16	19	70	70	0	49
Birmingham City	46	13	7	26	38	68	-30	46
Reading	46	10	14	22	48	70	-22	44
Bolton Wanderers	46	10	13	23	39	74	-35	43
Barnsley (R)	46	9	14	23	48	72	-24	41
Burton Albion (R)	46	10	11	25	38	81	-43	41
Sunderland (R)	46	7	16	23	52	80	-28	37

CHAPTER 12

LOOKING FORWARD – WHAT HAPPENS NEXT

Once the season ended and with fans on social media showing a real displeasure that Heckingbottom wasn't the man to take us forward and calling for him to be sacked, it came as no surprise when he was. We are now waiting for our new manager to arrive, although when Bielsa was announced as the one we were looking at, I'll admit I'd never heard of him. My football these days is made up of going to games that involve Leeds United and I don't watch anybody else. I gave up Sky TV a long time ago as I would rather have my season ticket and watch the game in person so it wasn't surprising really. My first Google search revealed all the problems Bielsa had at Lille when he was sacked, so my first instincts about him weren't good. After doing what I normally do and taking a step backwards and looking at the whole picture, I can honestly say that this appointment has stirred my inner emotions. There is something about all the videos he watches of teams that reminds me of Don Revie and his dossiers on other clubs prior to playing them. The more I read of him, the more I like the sound of him coming to Leeds. All I want to see are Leeds players having pride in playing for the shirt and showing they want the success that the fans do, along with a manager who feels the same way. A successful Leeds United will be just reward for the loyal fans who have supported them through thick and thin.

Radrizzani has just shown his ambitions for next season with this appointment of Bielsa, which has seen social media go into overdrive. The ambition is to get promoted to the Premiership which is something I have always wanted to see since our downfall. We will shortly find out who is staying and who will be going because one thing I like the sound of with Bielsa is that the players will be getting fit for the start of the season. As a lack of fitness has stood out for me with the current squad, that is good to hear. With many other clubs starting to have financial difficulties, that is something I don't ever want to get into again so it will be nice to pass these clubs on our way back up to where we belong.

For those fans who were asking about the CD recording of the old songs, please note that we have hit a technical difficulty which has impacted on the release of this. We have been trying hard to rectify this but getting mutually convenient times for a group of us to get together has proved difficult as everyone has very busy lives. We will get there but as usual it will take time so please bear with us.

Just as I have finished writing this book, I was saddened to hear that two of the Fullerton Park members who travelled to away games with us had died. RIP Paul Turner and Keith Horner, you will be missed by everyone in the branch.

With the pre-season tour now taking place in the UK, I am looking forward to a couple of new grounds at Forest Green Rovers and Oxford before the start of the season and our first game at home to newly relegated Stoke on Sunday 5th August. As the centenary of Leeds United being formed will be at the start of the 2019-20 season, it would be a fitting tribute for next season to show us challenging for promotion and the automatic places. Aiming for the play-offs is a non-starter as far as I'm concerned so we have to go for it. With the club finally showing ambition with the appointment of Bielsa, it's time to hang on to your hats Leeds fans (or beret in my case); say goodbye to the downs as the roller coaster is going up with a light at the end of the tunnel. Come and join the best fans in the world to witness our revival and fingers crossed we won't be disappointed!

See you all next season – LUFC – Marching on Together!

ND - #0256 - 270225 - C0 - 234/156/20 - PB - 9781780915784 - Gloss Lamination